TEN DAYS THAT SHOOK CELTIC

Tom Campbell (editor)

TEN DAYS THAT SHOOK CELTIC

Tom Campbell (editor)

FORT PUBLISHING LTD

First published in 2005 by Fort Publishing Ltd, Old Belmont House, 12 Robsland Avenue, Ayr, KA7 2RW

Cover photographs: Clockwise from top: Mo Johnston (left) with his wife and Celtic manager Billy McNeill on 12 May 1989, just weeks before he signed for Rangers (courtesy of Empics); John Thomson; Kenny Dalglish (front right) signing for Liverpool in August 1977, watched by Liverpool manager Bob Paisley, who is jacket-less (courtesy of Mirrorpix); a disconsolate Celtic fan after the last match of season 2004/05 (courtesy of Newsquest).

Graphic design by Mark Blackadder

Printed by Bell and Bain Ltd, Glasgow

ISBN 0-9547431-5-6

For Pauline

CONTENTS

ACKNOWLEDGEMENTS

I have acknowledgements to make: first of all to James McCarroll at Fort Publishing for his enterprise and imagination in coming up with such a project and for his patience and forbearance throughout the travails in completing it.

To Ronnie Esplin, my counterpart in *Ten Days That Shook Rangers*, with whom I have enjoyed an excellent relationship, nattering about football in general, the parsimony of publishers, the parentage of contributors who fail to deliver on time, or at all.

To the contributors who submitted their work for my approval with unfailing good grace and humour, as well as expertise.

And lastly to Senga Fairgrieve who has carried out her responsibilities as typesetter with her customary unfailing patience and efficiency.

Tom Campbell (editor), 2005

INTRODUCTION

Among the editor's multifarious tasks are to encourage, advise and assist his authors, and to that end I thought that a familiar quotation by the curmudgeonly Dr Johnson might well have helped with the chapter on the defection of Kenny Dalglish. So, I looked it up: 'The noblest prospect which a Scotchman ever sees is the high road that leads him to England!' I had always thought that particularly apt with regard to the transfer southwards of many other Scots as well as Dalglish; but in the end we decided not to use the quotation.

I was intrigued by the collected wit of the famed Englishman, and read further. Another quotation illustrating the same theme and equally insulting to the Celtic nations quickly followed: 'For who would leave – unbribed – Hibernia's Land./Or change the rocks of Scotland for the Strand?' In similar arrogant vein was his infamous definition of 'Oats' in his *Dictionary of the English Language*, published in 1755: 'A grain, which in England is generally given to horses, but in Scotland supports the people.'

When I studied eighteenth-century literature at university, I remember thinking that Dr Johnson – lexicographer, critic, celebrated wit and famed tea-drinker – was a man full of himself, more than a shade pompous and pedantic. Admittedly, I had been reacting in part to his frequent put-downs of the Scots but this time, decades later, I was able to recognise some aspects of the man's 'humour' until I came across his description of an editor as 'A harmless drudge'.

That was enough for me! He had gone too far! He was wrong, so blatantly wrong, and not for the first time! It is no easy task to be an editor in nominal charge of a group of highly skilled, proudly independent, and utterly professional, experts. At times, it was so daunting that I had to admit to feeling like a lion in a den of Daniels.

'A harmless drudge!' That's so untrue. Think about it for a moment or two. What sort of man would have the nerve to get an envelope from Bob Crampsey containing his article, and prepare to edit it armed only with a cup of coffee, a red pencil and a shaking hand? It takes steely resolve – as well a brass neck – to pore over an essay from Crampsey looking for mistakes. Frankly, it's a waste of time; the man is almost infallible.

A harmless drudge is not the sort of man who could accept Professor Patrick Reilly's chapter and presume to scan it for grammatical errors: split infinitives, misplaced modifiers or dangling participles. These simply do not exist in the prose of Patrick Reilly.

The other contributors – librarians, teachers, journalists, oil executives, fanzine publishers, website operators – posed different but equally nerve-wracking challenges. Some, the younger ones, wrote in a cavalier, swashbuckling manner – apparently intent on invoking the law of the land particularly those dealing with libel and slander. In such cases the chameleon-like editor has to switch to paternalistic mode exercising a cautious and restraining hand, all the while 'agreeing' with the opinions of the contributors and soothing ruffled feathers. An editor has to be a part-time counsellor as well as administrator.

And what on earth does the harried editor do with the apocryphal story, beloved of football followers in the pubs and virtually written on stone tablets through endless repetition? Especially when exactly the same story is attributed to Jimmy Quinn in 1906, to Jimmy McGrory in 1929 and to Henrik Larsson in 1997. The suspicion is that it never took place at all, but it is a myth that has gained a life of its own. Why spoil a good story with the facts? The decision to print or not then becomes a judgement call from the editor, fearless and bold as ever.

And how does one deal with the contributor who submits an article – highly readable, clearly intelligent, superbly organised – but a mere 6,000 words over the agreed limit? It would test all the powers of a natural diplomat or an autocrat.

Decisions! Decisions! Decisions! This is how the editor justifies his existence – and salary, pitiful as it may be.

The first task, an arm-twisting exercise, was to persuade ten men to agree each to write an article some 5,000 words in length – and for an almost derisory financial reward – at a time when most were occupied with other projects. This required the persuasive powers of a Casanova, and the conscience of a politician. 'Harmless drudge' – indeed!

After signing up the contributors, I thought I could relax. Things at first went splendidly: the authors selected their topics, and set to work with laptops, personal computers, typewriters and quill pens. With pleasing regularity the articles arrived one by one, and I settled down to read and enjoy them, trying not to interfere too much with the authors' prose or argument.

I was pleased and complacent; I should have known better. After all, this was a book about Celtic – and some followers of a paranoid bent are all too aware of what tends to happen in the tabloids just before an important match.

Two of the proposed contributions had been less than forth-coming, and my anxiety was rising daily as deadlines drew nearer and nearer. Sure enough, the situation began to escalate into a full-blown crisis, for me at any rate. I started to identify with a football manager unable to field his strongest side for an important fixture. A predicament.

One of the men was ill and finally realised that he would be unable to complete his chosen assignment on time, or to his own high standards. Reluctantly, he had to call off, like a star player failing a late fitness test, but a replacement had to be found at short notice. Fortunately, one of the best writers on Celtic's history was still available and he stepped into the breach, and submitted his article on time, with little need for editing, and with his customary flair, perception and wit. I admit to feeling a sense of relief that I had kept myself available for just such an emergency.

The other drop-out was a different case entirely, choosing very late in the day to renege on his promise, like a temperamental Maria Callas reluctant to appear at a provincial opera house, or perhaps a bit like Mark Viduka in the Celtic dressing room at half time in the

Inverness Caledonian Thistle cup-tie. Given the lateness of the hour, it posed a major problem for the whole project, but serendipity struck! Serendipity? That's when you go into an expensive restaurant with absolutely no money – and no credit cards – order oysters as a starter and find a pearl in one of them! Tentatively, but spurred on by desperation, I approached a writer for whom I had the greatest respect and admiration and, although – because of the deadline I imposed on him – he must have suspected that he was being recruited in an emergency, he was 'pleased' to accept the invitation. His chapter is included with the others, indistinguishable from them in thoroughness, literary flair and polish.

At the same time yet another of the contributors was experiencing problems with his computer and this was creating havoc with my deadlines. The situation was complicated and I'm not too sure even yet about the ins-and-outs of it: he had no printer and my computer had no means of downloading attachments . . . using an ancient laptop, he was reluctant to send the long article as e-mail and, of course, he had no means of printing it out and relaying it to me as hard copy. Eventually, at the same time as I was working on my chapter and scurrying around for somebody to take on the other article, the matter was resolved; I have the vague feeling that carrier pigeons were involved in getting the material to me.

'A harmless drudge?' What other position involves coping with such simultaneous crises? It reminds me of an airline pilot's description of his day-to-day job: 'Six or seven hours of tedium or boredom, but every now and then ten seconds of sheer terror.'

The original problem had been relatively simple: 'What do we write about?' A lot, apparently, if you were to take the tabloids as gospel. Almost every week's news contains details of a couple of crises at Celtic Park, fan fury, Parkhead bust-ups, player dissatisfaction, boardroom wrangling. So much so that the wonder is that Celtic are able to fulfil their fixture list every season. The fact, of course, is that most of the gossip masquerading as 'news' is highly sensationalised and treated with tabloid hyperbole, and never to be trusted. So, some events have a short-lived interest, intense at the time but largely insignificant in the overall history of Celtic.

However, during Celtic's history – and for many involved in

Scottish sport it is the most interesting, if not fascinating, in the country – there have been moments which could be described accurately as 'crises'. After consulting the publisher, I prepared a list of possible topics in order to give the proposed authors some flexibility and freedom of choice. It was a bit risky because there could have been a similarity of topics and mood and I certainly did not want that. But as the choices became finalised, it became clear – and to my considerable relief – that there would be the variety essential for the publication.

For interest's sake, I will list some of the topics proposed but considered and declined by the contributors themselves: the debates in the 1890s about the direction the new club (Celtic) was heading, Jimmy Quinn's three goals in a comeback triumph over Rangers in the Scottish Cup final of 1904, the Hampden Park riot of 1909 (and 1980), the relegation battle at Dens Park in Celtic's last league fixture in April 1948, the struggle against an apparently vengeful SFA in the matter of the Eire tricolour in 1952, the emergence of Scottish-Canadian businessman Fergus McCann as the club's saviour in 1994, the Jorge Cadete transfer fiasco, the Old Firm match refereed by Hugh Dallas at Celtic Park in May 1999 . . . and this list does not include the inevitably many defeats on the pitch which in the tabloid-speak of the times constituted 'Disaster!' or 'Shame!' or 'Crisis!'

But, to the choices eventually made.

Bob Crampsey, the doyen of sports writers in Scotland, starts us off with Celtic's shock defeat by Arthurlie in the Scottish Cup of 1897, a result that endures as probably the greatest upset in the tournament's storied history, outranking even the heroics of Berwick Rangers in 1967 and Inverness Caledonian Thistle in 1999. But it was an event that led to an historic change in the direction of the club.

John Cairney, typically of a distinguished actor, relates in dramatic form the truly tragic events of 5 September 1931 when Celtic's brilliant – and there is simply no other word – goalkeeper John Thomson lost his life after an accidental collision at Ibrox Park in the league fixture against Rangers. In 'a family club' such as Celtic the loss is still keenly felt so many decades on.

Patrick Reilly takes up a recurring pattern in Celtic's history: the failure to build on success, to strengthen the side when on the crest. In 1938, after the triumph in the Empire Exhibition Trophy, Celtic could claim with a fair amount of justification to be the best club side in Britain, and perhaps even in the world. Taking a scholarly and far-reaching approach Professor Reilly shows how that moment of greatness flickered, and was lost – for almost two decades.

Tom Campbell – the author of many books on the history of the club, including *Celtic's Paranoia . . . All in the Mind?* – relates the almost farcical situation played out in the replay of the Victory Cup semi-final against Rangers at Hampden Park in June 1946. Two Celtic players were carried off and two others ordered off by a referee acting impulsively and hardly in control of his own actions; three players were later suspended, and for lengthy periods, by an SFA committee allegedly 'acting in due deliberation'. Celtic's post-war distrust of the SFA stems largely, but not exclusively, from that notorious match.

Tony Griffin, co-author of *A Season in the Sun* (about 1966/67), captures the mood of the times as Celtic's former captain Jock Stein returned to Celtic Park to take over as manager in January 1965. After outlining the previous 'seven lean years', the author depicts the sea change for Celtic in every sense: from failure to success, from despair to elation, from football mediocrity to global prominence.

David Potter, that most prolific of Celtic authors, remembers the feelings aroused by the departure of Kenny Dalglish to Liverpool in August 1977. It is almost impossible to exaggerate the sense of loss felt by every Celtic follower at the departure of such a talent, and the bitterness caused by the realisation that a small-minded Celtic were at the mercy of other clubs with more financial clout and ambition.

Gerry Dunbar, the founder and long-time editor of the Celtic fanzine *Not the View*, traces the events of the tragi-comical relationship between Celtic and Mo Johnston especially the on-off courtship that ended with Celtic being 'dumped' for a better (or richer) suitor. Rejection at any time is hard to bear, but this was especially bitter.

Craig McAughtrie, the man behind the Celtic website *Keep the Faith*, links the ups-and-downs of Celtic's capture of the league championship under Wim Jansen in 1997/98, an unforgettable emotional roller-coaster in which the hopes of an unlikely success kept conflicting with the dread of failure – which would have meant Rangers surpassing one of Celtic's proudest records.

Tom Shields, distinguished diarist and newspaper columnist, recounts the night Inverness Caledonian Thistle eliminated Celtic from the Scottish Cup at Celtic Park, condemning the club to another trophy-less season, but offering the opportunity to rise phoenix-like from the bitter ashes of that defeat.

Pat Woods, that most assiduous of authors and researchers, recalls the despair that enveloped the entire Celtic support – directors, players and supporters – in the aftermath of the last league fixture of the 2004/05 season: a shock defeat at Fir Park to an undisting-uished Motherwell side that cost the club the championship.

'Harmless drudge?' I ask you: could 'a harmless drudge' gather such a galaxy of stars, persuade them to take on this project and complete it on time? Could 'a harmless drudge' cope with the crises described above without resorting to drugs or drink? I remind you of who came up with the original definition: a depressive, compulsive, misanthropic Englishman, with a pathological dislike of Scots. The same man who defined a 'net' as follows: 'Anything reticulated or decussated at equal distances, with interstices between the inter-sections.' I would have trouble compiling a dictionary, but I know that Dr Johnson – on the evidence of the above definition alone – could not have written or edited a book about football.

Why were these topics finally chosen? The answer, of course, lies in the ten chapters that comprise this book, but a word or two in advance might be in order.

The Scottish Cup defeats by Arthurlie in 1897 and by Inverness Caledonian Thistle in 2000 were shocking in themselves but it was the consequences of those upsets that truly affected Celtic. Within hours of those two defeats the club had taken steps to remedy the situation. In 1895 Willie Maley, after acting as Celtic's 'manager' for some seasons, was able to persuade his committees that the best way ahead for Celtic was to drop its dependence on expensive imports and instead to rely on a pool of home-grown talent. It was a policy that the club would retain, more or less, for almost a hundred years. In 2000 in the wake of Celtic's defeat at home to Caley the club looked for scapegoats and they were not too hard to find: John Barnes was sacked as coach as was his assistant Eric Black; Kenny Dalglish, the director of football, was recalled to take over day-to-day running of the team but his days were numbered; even Allan MacDonald, the club's chief executive, could trace his eventual leaving of Celtic Park to this on-field debacle. To replace the hapless Barnes-Black-Dalglish coalition Celtic would bring in Martin O'Neill and his cohorts. Similarly, the devastating loss to Motherwell at Fir Park in 2005 indicated the real need for a change of direction from everyone at Celtic Park in the wake of Martin O'Neill's departure and the break-up of a previously invincible side.

Celtic stood on the threshold of greatness in 1938 after winning the Empire Exhibition Trophy but it was a shaky and short-lived entrance to the highest levels of British football. Like the Empire itself, which was crumbling from within under its colonial mentality and resentment from 'lesser breeds', Celtic had already started to stagnate: a board of directors more interested in preserving the past and safeguarding their dividends; an aged and ill manager poorly equipped to deal with dissent from a pool of players rightly unhappy with their financial rewards. The situation was critical but largely unseen at the time.

In 1946, after being in the football doldrums throughout the wartime seasons, Celtic started to show some green shoots of recovery but had to deal with two major obstacles: the domination of Scottish football on the field of play by a highly competent Rangers side; and the machinations of supine SFA committees manipulated by a secretariat clearly motivated to harm the club in the council chambers. This scenario was to be a recurring motif in Scottish football for decades.

At last in January 1965 Celtic became a modern football club by appointing a manager in touch with the realities of the modern game, a man with the vision to plan for the future and the drive to realise his vision. It marked the first significant, and lasting, change in Celtic's direction for decades: a change from mediocrity to dominance, from the humdrum to the glorious, from failure to success, and it was accomplished under the guidance of the club's first non-Catholic manager.

Too often the history of Celtic has been marred by the transfer out of genuine talent when a greater effort could have been made to alter the course of events. In fact, Celtic at times have appeared only too eager to cash in on the sale of star players: the attempt to sell Jimmy McGrory in 1928 presumably to pay for the new grandstand; the transfer of Willie Buchan for an astonishing £10,000 days after he had scored the winning goal in the Scottish Cup final of 1937; the break-up of a strong Celtic side with the sale of Bobby Collins and Willie Fernie in 1958 almost certainly to cover the cost of the floodlights at Celtic Park. The list is almost endless but all paled into insignificance compared to the loss of Kenny Dalglish (at a profit of £440,000) to Liverpool in 1977.

Celtic have always been described as 'a family club' and perhaps this is why the departure of certain players arouses such strong feelings of fatalism (Alec Bennett), sadness (Jimmy Delaney), bewilderment (Bobby Evans) – and, in the case of Maurice Johnston, rage and hatred. Nobody should ever want to leave Celtic Park, and certainly nobody could want to leave 'Paradise' for Rangers. 'Betrayal' seemed to be the only word for such an action on the player's part.

Not all incidents that 'shook' Celtic have been unfortunate ones. When Celtic defeated St Johnstone by two goals to nil at Celtic Park on 9 May 1998 before a crowd of 50,032, all of whom appeared on the verge of a nervous breakdown, it marked the end of Rangers' domination. It was a breakthrough – perhaps short-lived – but a turning point nevertheless. With the new stadium built, with a new philosophy in place and with a support becoming acclimatised to success there could never be a return to the days of long-term inferiority.

In short, that is why the events selected emerged as the choices and I cannot but agree that the decisions by the contributors were the right ones.

1

'AN IGNOMINIOUS DISCHARGE'

Bob Crampsey

'A crushing disaster, the worst probably in the history of the Celtic Club.' (Glasgow Observer, 16 January 1897)

As they prepared for their Scottish Cup tie in January 1897 at Arthurlie's Dunterlie Park in Barrhead, Celtic's task was to win the match, and later on to pick up the trophy itself. Founded only ten years previously, Celtic's impact on the game had been nothing short of revolutionary. Unashamedly professional in practice, Celtic had already established a reputation as innovators in terms of playing personnel, facilities for spectators and income generation. Some commentators even took the view that the team from the East End of Glasgow had revitalised Scottish football by attracting thousands who had never given the game a second thought. Indeed, it is far from fanciful to suggest that Celtic were not only Scotland's, but also Britain's, leading club both on and off the pitch. The main reason for their success was that they were able to draw on the needs of the growing Irish community in Glasgow and the west of Scotland, and so build up the biggest and most fanatical following in football.

Celtic's drawing power was amply illustrated in 1892 when they reached the final of the Scottish Cup, after beating Rangers

5–3 in the last four. The final was to be staged at Ibrox and Celtic would face Queen's Park, who had won the trophy on nine previous occasions. The crowds poured out by road and rail to the south of the city and 40,000 paying customers managed to gain legitimate entry to the stadium, then a record for a domestic fixture. The gates were shut at three o'clock with kick-off still an hour away. Such was the crush inside Ibrox, that the first pitch invasion was timed at two, a whole two hours before the game started. There was also a crowd estimated at 20,000 milling around outside the ground, a situation that many of them found intolerable; about a quarter of the dispossessed simply leapt over the barricades while others climbed trees or onto the roofs of houses to gain a vantage point. Following another crowd invasion, and taking into account the heavy snow that had begun to fall, the referee and the two captains decided that the match would be completed as a friendly but there would be a replay to decide the winners of the Cup (Celtic won both matches – the 'official' final in a 5–1 rout and so recorded their first win in the competition).

This popularity at the turnstiles was matched by the business acumen in the boardroom, where men like the autocratic John H. McLaughlin, a wealthy publican, proved both enterprising and visionary. In 1892 the club had completed the construction of a splendid new stadium in Janefield Street, with a capacity of 50,000. When representatives of the Football League in England visited Glasgow shortly after its completion they had no hesitation in hailing it as 'far and way superior to any field in Great Britain'. And it was not just a football venue, being ideal for both cycling and athletics. Celtic took full advantage of the new facility and it played host to a number of international matches, including the games against England in 1894 and 1896. The revenue earned from these fixtures was considerable and was further enhanced by the large crowds that flocked to the annual Celtic Sports to watch world-class athletics.

The net effect of such entrepreneurial flair was a balance sheet that was the envy of the football world. In season 1895/96 Celtic's turnover was £10,142, a figure higher than any club in Britain had ever recorded. And it would have been even more but for the team's defeat in the first round of the Scottish Cup by Queen's Park. Celtic again broke the record in season 1897/98 when its revenues exceeded

£16,000, an enormous sum at the time. But Celtic was by then a limited company – it adopted this new, more businesslike model in March 1897 – and it was noticeable that no money was allocated for the poor of Glasgow at the end of the financial year, which was of course the reason for the club being formed in the first place. Some supporters – mindful of the club's traditions – were also concerned that the directors awarded themselves a healthy dividend.

The company structure and internal politics notwithstanding, these riches had enabled Celtic to build up a formidable squad of players. Most of them were highly paid following the legalisation of professionalism by the SFA in 1893, a decision taken largely at the behest of Celtic. In a veritable galaxy of stars there was keeper Dan McArthur, described by one leading Celtic historian as 'agile and fearless'; full back Dan Doyle, a fearsome competitor and the idol of the fans; James Kelly, a commanding centre half with uncanny anticipation; Sandy McMahon, a quick, free-scoring forward who was nicknamed the 'Prince of Dribblers' but was also deadly in the air. With such talents at their disposal it was no surprise that Celtic had proved to be the most successful outfit in the country, and by some distance. Silverware was lifted in every season from 1890/91 to 1895/96, and it was a roll of honour that made the club the envy of Scottish football. In just six seasons the team won three league titles, one Scottish Cup, four Glasgow Cups and five Glasgow Charity Cups.

Faced with such formidable opponents, Arthurlie's objective was rather different: to do well in the cup-tie and win the desperate fight that would bring league football to the little Renfrewshire town. The Barrhead men were about to test the maxim that 'one crowded hour of glorious life is worth an age without a name'. If it could be done, it would be a Brigadoonish kind of triumph. Readers will be familiar with the scenario whereby a mythical Highland village of that name emerges from the mists for one day every century and for that day villagers must make up their minds to stay where they are or to join the retreat into the timeless past.

The major clubs apart there was little money about anywhere in the country and the grounds on which clubs like Arthurlie played were spartan in the extreme. They were marked off by corrugated-iron sheets with, in luck, a ramshackle shed that was dignified by the name of 'pavilion'. Through the open window of this hut players and spectators held conversations. They were not welcomed by editorial scrutiny, which described such spectators as 'loafers and sneakers'. Facilities for the press were often non-existent; at Dunterlie Park reporters covering big games were often forced to watch from the windows of a house behind the pavilion goal and even then 'they were behind friends of the family making their view almost non-existent' as one contemporary journalist complained.

If the reader wants to know what these grounds were like, he could not do better than recall the appointments of a pavilion such as Arthurlie had. They are set forth as they appeared to John McCartney in his *Story of the Scottish Football League*:

> It is instructive to contemplate the little wooden shanties holding to suffocation twenty-two players plus an unlimited number of 'Kommittee' men, plus several 'rabids' – frenzied rabids, hollering in at the doors and windows for sometimes there are more than one of each. These rabids would kindly tell you 'what had to be done' and 'who had to be watched'. The rear of these cabins generally had a construction disclosing the hallmark of ancient architecture for the display of a few tin basins containing rancid or stagnant water. With only one piece of soap and perhaps a couple of towels players were expected to purify themselves. A shower bath could be obtained simply by tipping overhead a basin (if you were fortunate enough to obtain one) of equal parts mud and water.

In addition, very often the playing pitch itself had been hewn from the side of a bing or hacked from the side of a muddy hill.

The organisation of the game in Scotland was also haphazard, a sharp contrast to the high standards set by top clubs like Celtic and Rangers. There had been league fixtures only since 1890, and before that all other matches for the great majority of clubs were friendlies (or 'ordinaries' as they were more generally known). Without a doubt there was a clamant need for certainty of fixture. And even the cup competition – known as the Scottish Cup – was an uneasy hotchpotch of ideas that had scarcely been thought through. By 1897 its future was about to be decided. The FA Cup was considered the pinnacle of football achievement and Scottish clubs such as Queen's Park and Rangers had competed in it – and done well. The SFA had acted to protect the interests of its own competition but could their ban on Scottish clubs competing for the FA Cup be sustained? Would the Scottish clubs be forced to compete only in their native land? Or would the more powerful FA have the authority (or desire) to conscript every Scottish club for total participation for its own tournament?

Until the early days of the twentieth century there was no seeding in the cup and the result was a totally free draw. 'Good!' said the Romantics. 'Everyone should take his chance.' 'Not so good,' said the Pragmatics, who could then produce a draw that showed that the two great clubs, Queen's Park and Celtic, would be due to meet each other by the last weekend in August and, therefore, one of them would be out of the running before September was upon them.

An additional and quite unnecessary hazard was the decision to play the final of the Scottish Cup in mid-February when the weather in Scotland is as bad as it ever gets. So, many a year, the match was played in appalling conditions with the crowds being told only after they had dispersed that the match they had been watching was not a Scottish Cup final but a 'friendly' that the captains had agreed to play. This had become an alarmingly frequent occurrence and at times seemed close to fraud and to bringing the game into disrepute. The clubs, however, who had profited by an extra game turned a blind eye to the practice, as did the SFA.

None of this seemed to affect Celtic's inexorable progress and the team was set fair for yet more triumphs. But, in the mid 1890s, a deadly combination of greed and arrogance had begun to eat away at the very fabric of the club. In a money-driven atmosphere signs of employee dissatisfaction began to surface. The senior players requested – or perhaps it was in the form of a demand – that there should be a meeting to discuss the financial state of affairs for them. Training – and trains – began to be missed or skimped; last-minute call-offs increased in frequency.

These problems would pale into insignificance by contrast with an incident that was the catalyst for the disappointment to follow. It is not an overstatement to say that it changed Celtic forever. Trouble came swiftly, seriously and inevitably. Three of the senior players

(Divers, Battles and Meechan [1]) took particular offence at a trenchant but perfectly fair criticism of their efforts in a newspaper article and they refused to take the field against Hibernian at Celtic Park on 28 November 1896 unless the reporter was expelled from the press box. By the timing of the next demand – ten minutes before kick-off – the players showed that they were not interested in a negotiated settlement. The match was an important one in the schedule [2] and from somewhere a side was cobbled together. Willie Maley – now the match secretary – had hardly thought to wear football boots ever again but he was pressed into service; Tom Dunbar, playing with the reserves at Hampden, got a telegram telling him to get to Parkhead at full speed and he appeared on the pitch midway through the first half. Despite all efforts, eleven players could not be found at the start of the game but ten were and a creditable 1–1 draw was secured.

The three 'strikers' had big names and reputations, but that did not save them and they were advised to buy a theatrical magazine to see what real criticism was. The three men were first fined, suspended by the club and effectively sacked at the end of the season. Before all that, there was a Scottish Cup tie to be played in January. It would not be true to say that there was any real anxiety for Celtic to play, even with a weakened side. Arthurlie were not giant-killers; they quite simply did not do giant-killing.

It was very different in England where scarcely a year passes without a genuine shock occurring. The mind goes back to Walsall beating Arsenal in the 1930s, of Hereford beating Newcastle United a couple of generations later and the splendid performances of amateur Pegasus in the 1950s. In England there was a pyramid structure which made these upsets distinctly possible; in England every sudden-death competition brought the demise of important clubs.

---

[1] Also known as Meehan. Reporting of names, especially Irish ones, was not an exact science in 1897.

[2] Celtic and Hibernian were in a close race for the league flag. After the match – which had a Hibs equaliser coming in eighty-seven minutes – the Edinburgh side led Celtic by four points, but Celtic still had two matches in hand. Celtic, however, without their suspended players went on to lose three of their remaining five fixtures and finished a disappointing fourth, their worst-ever position until that time.

Nevertheless, the very remote prospects of a cup upset at Barrhead encouraged Celtic to take a hard line against the players. Defeat was unthinkable for a team that was not only Scottish champions but also joint league leaders in the current campaign. There were clubs in Scotland – like Arthurlie – that emerged from obscurity once a year, formed a side from a job lot of players, lost a hatful of goals and retired from public life until the following year. Such was the fate of clubs like Breadalbane for whom league football was not easily obtainable. The SFA had recognized the problem early and attempted to eliminate the more grotesque outfits by instituting the Qualifying Cup in 1897.

Nor did the travelling Celtic support expect anything less than a convincing victory as they made their way to Barrhead in their trains and brakes. Saturday morning came and went, and the first green scarves came into view. One or two of the supporters wandered over the quaint playing-surface, which briefly and almost vertically rose inside one of the halves, attacking from which would be like Pickett's charge at Gettysburg. It is hardly surprising that the Dunterlie pitch had been given the colloquial, yet highly descriptive, nickname of the 'Humph'.

John Byrne, the chronicler of the history of Arthurlie Football Club, casts a gimlet eye on proceedings. Drawing on *The Annals of Barrhead* by Robert Murray, JP, he wrote: 'Celtic was then, as now, one of the giants of the game and Arthurlie was, at that time, not regarded as likely to do more than just stave off a farcical defeat. To this day in football circles this remains almost the only memorable event associated with the local club.'

The forthcoming cup-tie offered the local tradesmen the prospect of some clever and not too costly advertising. A kenspeckle figure in the town of Barrhead, Andrew Cairnduff, promised that, should Arthurlie prevail, he would give every member of the side a new hat. There seemed little chance that he would be called upon to honour his obligations but, when the unlooked-for result came through, he paid up like a gentleman. So that the provenance of the hats would not be ignored, inside each hat he had recorded the date and the result of the match.

Barrhead was a douce place at the best of times and, since the day after the match was a Sunday, any celebrations would be curtailed quite dramatically. It would have been a good guess, however, that the town's ministers on the Sunday morning may well have felt that they were not getting the undivided attention of the congregation. For Celtic – soon to be recognised as the greatest cup fighters of all – had been defeated, and the match belonged to Arthurlie on a convincing 4–2 margin! Later, according to the local paper, the contest was described as having been physical and bucolic but neither rough nor unfriendly.

But let us begin with the teams originally selected by the two clubs:

Arthurlie: Airston, Hirst, Smith, Miller, Tennant, Bodys, Hannigan, Tait, Ovens, McGregor, Spiers.

Celtic: Cullen, Doyle, Orr, Russell, Kelly, Farrell, Morrison, Gilhooley, Blessington, King, Ferguson.

In 1897 Celtic had not yet switched to their famous hooped shirts, their stripes being vertical and probably their shorts were bluish in tint. Arthurlie wore their traditional red-and-white hooped jerseys (similar to Hamilton Academical) and the weather was apposite for an upset: a cold day with a snell wind, and a fine drizzle soaking everybody, players and spectators alike.

In some disarray from the start, Celtic failed to master either the windy conditions or the sloping pitch. According to clearly partisan Celtic accounts, the Glasgow side had to start the match two or three players short; if so, it was an indication of internal confusion and strife, rather than over-confidence. The list of those missing was a talking point for both supporters and commentators. The three 'strikers' – Meechan, Battles and Divers – were of course *persona non grata*. Dan Doyle cried off at the last minute, no doubt embittered by a dispute over his wages. Another star player, Russell, missed his train. While the biggest blow was the injuries to three key men who were, in consequence, not even available for selection: McEleny, goalkeeper McArthur and the peerless McMahon. The latter was sorely missed; as the *Glasgow Observer* noted it was 'a paralysing blow because Sandy could almost win matches single-handed'.

It had all gone wrong for the favourites with the first-half failure, all the more so in that Celtic had won the toss, or in the vivid phraseology of *Scottish Sport* 'guessed the copper'. A significant feature of the match was the surprising score of 4–2. Giant-killing usually comes in at a clogged 1–0, but Arthurlie set about Celtic from the start and were leading by two goals to one at half time, despite playing up the 'Humph'. In the second period, playing down the slope, Arthurlie went for the jugular and raced into a 4–1 lead. Despite a late flurry from Celtic in which they pulled a goal back, the home side was able to withstand their opponents' late attempts to save the tie. Particular praise was reserved for Barrhead's veteran custodian, Airston, who defied the Celtic forwards with a string of heroically improbable saves. Celtic's goals were scored by Ferguson and, according to *Scottish Sport*, 'McIlvany', although no one of that name appears on either team list.[3]

At this time – and for many years afterwards – it was perfectly in order for the small side drawn at home to sell their ground rights and, indeed, for the Arthurlie–Celtic match negotiations had been opened but a fee could not be agreed upon. In fact match secretary Willie Maley wrote to Arthurlie the day after the draw and asked the Barrhead side to name its price for transferring the tie to the East End of Glasgow. As *Scottish Sport*, the sportsman's bible of the time, reported: 'Arthurlie offered to accede for £70. The price however was deemed too high.' Faced now with an away tie, on a ground that was unfamiliar to most of their players, Celtic did not take heed of the old military dictum: 'Time spent in reconnaissance is never wasted.' Dunterlie Park was extremely narrow, to say nothing of the Spion Kop model in the middle of one of the halves. Both clubs suffered by this decision: Celtic felt the pitch's lack of width which deprived them of perhaps their biggest advantage, their extra pace . . . while, as the gate receipts were returned at £46, Arthurlie were none too

---

[3] It was asserted later by 'Ching' Morrison, who played that day, that Celtic actually started the cup tie with only seven men on the field. Other Celtic accounts suggest the team started the match short-handed but this might well have been an attempt to put the blame on established players thus preparing the way for newer blood.

successful in the financial sphere. At one shilling admission, the 'gate' would have been in the region of only eight hundred.

Later, some of the Celtic team seem to have found their way to the Good Templars' Hall and solace was found and victory confirmed in the toasts and sentiments which followed. Sentiments were very popular with Victorian sportsmen and, although they seem excessively sententious to us, they were very popular in their time, a great favourite being 'May the pleasures of the evening bear the reflections of the morning.' There would be very few such gatherings in the future. As Queen's Park had accurately predicted, the post-match functions died almost immediately with the adoption of professionalism and, if confirmation were needed of the connection of these things, let him look at the path which professionalism in rugby has taken recently.

The effect on Celtic

The verdict on the game from journalists, historians and those one might describe as 'Celtic-minded' was unanimous. It was a disaster for the men in green. And more to the point the team had, for the first time in seven years, failed to lift any silverware. The stalwarts of the brake clubs were in high dudgeon; the members of one group let off steam by tearing up their banner and dancing on the remnants. The twice-weekly *Scottish Sport* could hardly believe what had transpired. In its later review of the Arthurlie–Celtic tie it wrote, under the headline, 'The Barrhead Sensation':

> The Celtic's ignominious discharge was a real blue-blooded [sic] sensation and will in all likelihood be included hereafter in the select list of sensations associated with the game. We make no apologies for saying that Hannigan with three goals was the chief weapon of destruction against the Celtic. The home supporters showed their appreciation by giving him a 'shoulder-high' at the finish.

Scottish Sport was in no doubt about where to apportion blame for the 'sensation'. It argued the rot had started with the three players withdrawing their labour for the league match against Hibernian. That 'now historic revolt of November last' was crucial as it threw 'the whole team out of gear' and led inexorably to a display that was 'nothing less than astonishing in its utter feebleness'. Willie Maley, who had never sat easily with defeat, was furious. Even some forty years on – in 1937 – he would sit silent and glowering in his manager's office rather than congratulate the recently appointed manager of Kilmarnock (Celtic legend Jimmy McGrory) on his win against Celtic as protocol dictated he should do. He was equally bitter about the Arthurlie debacle and in his book on the history of the club – *The Story of the Celtic*, published in 1939 – wrote: 'It is no exaggeration to say this was probably the greatest sensation ever known in Scottish football.' Maley also wryly noted the interest the result created in the years ahead among those who followed Scottish football: 'The date and result of this tie has been asked and answered in the "Answers to Correspondents" columns of the press some thousands of times since the event.'

There were immediate consequences for the men who had let Celtic down. Dan Doyle, the crowd's favourite, was fined £5 for failing to appear at Dunterlie after having been selected for the tie. Those who did turn out but performed indifferently were also punished: Madden's wages were reduced to £2 and Morrison's to thirty shillings; King and McIlvenny were paid off. Then, within a few weeks, 'Ching' Morrison was transferred to Burnley for £20 and Meechan to Everton for £100.

In the longer term, there were two things that could have been done in the wake of the Dunterlie Disaster.

The first thing was to dismiss it as a mere blip in the club's progress; the other was to continue the minor war against the players, and escalate it. The coming to power of Willie Maley made it inevitable that this would be the path taken. Maley, an ambitious man from his youth, had been in a difficult position within Celtic Park; still only twenty-nine years of age, he had been employed as player-secretary by the committee in recognition of his administrative talents and he had watched in some frustration the antics of the senior players in recent seasons. Maley, although a competent player, was not a star and he was in some difficulties with players older than himself who were more skilful. He suggested to his friends on the committee that the time had come for a sea change in the club's outlook and he appealed to their sense of thrift by proposing that Celtic should call a halt to buying star players at expensive wages and that eventually the same results could be achieved by signing and developing their own players, culled from a pool of young men desperate to play for 'the Celtic'. His proposals were accepted, and the first step was to appoint Willie Maley as secretary-manager on 3 April 1897, a mere eighty-four days after the defeat by Arthurlie.

The result was a form of governance at Celtic Park that could be best described as a harsh paternalism. No more than any other did it suit everyone who wore the green-and-white and Dan Doyle, who simply neglected to turn up at Dunterlie Park that day, was but the first of a line of 'Wandering Minstrels' whose last representative might well have been George Connelly. Football, which had teetered for several years between being a pastime pure and simple, even for a successful club like Celtic, had at last come down decisively on the side of business. Gone would be the days when J. H. McLaughlin could simultaneously be Celtic secretary and official accompanist to the Rangers Glee Club.

The aftermath was of much more importance in its effect on relations within the industry and the outlook for footballers was dismal indeed. The individual player would not be in a strong position if he attempted to withdraw his labour. His club could refuse him training facilities and the longer he went on without playing the more his transfer value depreciated. A club had certain courses of action against a discontented player. It could immediately drop him to the reserves, thus cutting his income drastically. It could hint that he was a disciplinary problem (although that would assume that the club wanted to keep the player). Other alternatives would be to transfer the player, or pay him more. Some clubs, Celtic in particular, made it a club policy never to keep a discontented player.

From its earliest days Celtic had made a bid to attract large crowds by fielding 'star' players, ostensibly amateur but who could afford to open public houses presumably on savings made from their part-time occupations or apprenticeships elsewhere. But many of these performers – most notably Dan Doyle – were mavericks and could blackmail their clubs into submission. With the larger clubs, where the practice of negotiating individual contracts has always been more prevalent, it is possible to allay the player's discontent by paying him more than his colleagues but this course has obvious difficulties. It is hard to keep such an arrangement secret for long and, in any case, the end of the player's militancy may become very marked.

The men who ran Celtic decided that the star system was over, and turned to Willie Maley – a steady hand – to produce sides of home-grown talent who wanted to play for Celtic more than anything else and who would be prepared to accept low wages to achieve their hearts' desire. There was an immediate dividend; Celtic won the league championship convincingly in 1897/98, the year after Dunterlie. They also faced Arthurlie again in the Scottish Cup that same season, and took the opportunity to administer a thrashing to the upstarts, running out winners by seven goals to nil. Fortunately for Celtic, it was a policy that also worked well in the long term and was the basis of Celtic's first truly great side; a side that won the league championship six times in a row early in the twentieth century. The idea of a home-grown squad of players – cheap to employ, and possibly profitable to sell on later – become a recurring motif in Celtic's history.

The consequences for Arthurlie

There were a few optimistic articles declaring that reaching division one was not beyond Arthurlie and that they might aspire to top-flight football but it never seemed possible nor was it. Arthurlie, in a good season, were one of nature's second-division sides. They eventually joined the league in the early years of the century; in 1901 to be precise.

They sought and obtained membership and pursued a quiet and unambitious career until, on the outbreak of war in 1914, the second division closed down and did not resume operations until 1919. Even then, it resumed without Arthurlie who stayed out of it, apparently of their own volition, until 1923 with the result that their application would now be for the newly created third division.

This was a Machiavellian organisation created by the Scottish League who knew perfectly well that such a scheme was unviable but would prove very well suited for getting rid of unwanted small senior clubs. There was no possibility of a league that pitted Lockerbie against Helensburgh being successful in the long, or even medium, run.

The new division was doomed to failure but by then, having won it in its first season, Arthurlie had escaped to division two as champions. Four reasonably competent seasons followed but the financial pressures were too great and, with six matches of the 1928/29 season to go, they resigned their membership.

There still remained the basic question of the club's future. There were several small leagues around Glasgow – leagues of a sort – where the side could play. Such were the Scottish Combination and the Scottish Alliance. A nearby Ayrshire town, Beith, opted for the Alliance as did its neighbours, Galston. This would have meant another speedy change of scene as the short-lived Alliance collapsed in 1938.

By that time Arthurlie had given up trying to maintain senior football in Barrhead and took the decision to drop down to the junior grade. Happily, they won the Scottish Junior Cup within their first seven years (1937) although three subsequent appearances in the final have all proved unsuccessful.

We have noted that Arthurlie is a Barrhead club and that its football history is not all that distinguished. Perhaps it was awareness of that which led Willie Maley to declare: 'This is the greatest come-down in footballing history.' Apart from the events of 1897, Arthurlie's football history may not be too distinguished but Barrhead – if it no longer provides league sides – was home to two of the best Scottish players of the inter-war years, different in physique and playing style but united in genius. They were inside forwards: the dour and serious Bob McPhail of Rangers (and Airdrie) and the ebullient Tommy McInally of Celtic (and Third Lanark). McPhail was affectionately known as 'Greetin' Boab' and certainly he was not inclined to make a bad pass to him into a good one; McInally, on the other hand, marred his great natural ability with a some-what light and airy approach to his duties and perhaps he proved too exotic a plant for the more puritanical Maley.

The immediate furore over the Barrhead result quickly died away. It was dismissed as a freak, a sport of nature.

The more perceptive were confirmed in what they had been told: that Celtic still remained a paramount power in Scottish football but work for that had to be both sustained and taxing. They may well have learned a painful lesson.

Back in Barrhead, ten young men and a grizzled goalkeeper were removing their hats at every opportunity and drawing attention to the inscription therein.

And that might very well have been that, just the first of a com-paratively small number of genuine shock results, something to be wondered about over a weekend and then quickly forgotten by most people with the exception of the fanatics.

Comments

Surprises and upsets are part and parcel of football and a good bit of its attraction as a spectator sport. The big surprise is that Celtic were such a formidable team as early as 1897 to cause such a shock at Dunterlie.

John Cairney

Arthurlie? That was probably the biggest shock in the history of Scottish Cup football, ranking up there alongside Rangers' defeat at Berwick in 1967 and Celtic's loss to Inverness Caledonian Thistle at Parkhead in 2000. A real shocker – and much more than 'a nine-day wonder'. I'm never too confident about any cup-tie, and those extraordinary results remind me why.

Tom Campbell

I believe that Arthurlie – after beating Celtic – went on to become the biggest club in Barrhead.

Gerry Dunbar

This didn't really happen, did it?

Tony Griffin

It certainly was a major shock, probably the first for Celtic – and clearly self-inflicted. Was this our very first shot in the foot?

Craig McAughtrie

An eerie foreshadowing of what happened to us against Inverness Caley Thistle in 2000 – a mere 103 years later: player discontent at Celtic Park, a shock result, a change in direction for the club as a consequence with the removal of Barnes, Dalglish and MacDonald – and the arrival of Martin O'Neill. Both my father and grandfather always shuddered to recall that far-off day; when Arthurlie, by then a junior club, came to play Forfar East End in the Scottish Junior Cup, they were particularly anxious that the home side win.

David Potter

It had to be the biggest shock in Scottish Cup history until Rangers lost at Berwick in 1967. I understand that Willie Maley used to become infuriated when reminded of this result by those brave enough to tease him about it – even decades later.

Pat Woods

2

DEATH OF A PRINCE

John Cairney

'Quem Di diligunt Adolescens moritur' said Plautus in a Roman play a long, long time ago and Lord Byron translated it in 1818 as 'those whom the Gods love die young'. Since that time, a whole procession of the Gods' favourites have died with their greatest work, like Schubert's, still unfinished. Franz Schubert, however, died at thirty-one.

The darling of the Gods being discussed here passed to his particular Parnassus in his twenty-third year, and he was clearly favoured by the Olympians. Not only in looks, temperament, character and personality, but in the extraordinary skill he brought to the job he did for a living, which was keeping goal for the Glasgow Celtic Football and Athletic Club from 1 November 1926 until 5 September 1931. In those short five years, nevertheless, he rose to become a Celtic legend and Scotland's number one goalkeeper. He was hailed as a genius in his own time and a fantastic future was predicted for him in the game.

That is, until a windless September Saturday afternoon in 1931 . . .

More than 80,000 enthusiastic spectators had gathered on the slopes of Ibrox stadium in the south-west of Glasgow to witness a vital Old Firm encounter between Celtic and Rangers. Just as the

Scottish Cup seemed to have become the sole property of this new, young Celtic side, so the Scottish league championship appeared to be the right of Bill Struth's ironclad Glasgow Rangers. The Ibrox men's incentive for this particular season, however, was that if they won it again, they would equal Celtic's famous run of six titles in a row from more than twenty years before, and this was something that Willie Maley's side was anxious to prevent. They were playing, not only for a prize, (the championship) but also for a prized tradition. They were in with a chance for the title themselves at this early stage of the season, but even if they didn't win it, it was important to them that Rangers didn't either.

The match kicked off at 3.15 p.m. and saw the following players run out of the tunnel, Rangers first as, in those days, teams didn't run out together. Celtic fielded their triumphant USA touring team with John Thomson in goal, Cook and McGonagle at back, Wilson, McStay (captain) and Geatons across the middle and the forward line featured the other two Thomsons, Bertie and Alec, Jimmy McGrory, with Scarff and Napier making up the left wing. Rangers played Jerry Dawson in goal for his debut game, Gray and McAuley at full back, Meiklejohn (captain), Simpson and Brown at half back and their forwards were Jimmy Fleming, 'Doc' Marshall, Sam English, Bob McPhail and Alan Morton.

With so much depending on it, the players on both sides were less concerned about being clever and more about trying not to make a mistake. As a consequence, the game was over-cautious and it seemed as if the match were heading for a dull, scoreless draw. At the interval, only the statisticians were satisfied by a point apiece but then, five minutes after the restart, something occurred that took the event out of the match reports and into the history books.

John Thomson had made a long clearance to Bertie Thomson on Celtic's right wing but the move broke down and Davie Meiklejohn, the Rangers right half and captain, came out with the ball and passed it on to Jimmy Fleming on his right. Fleming beat off a tackle by Geatons before releasing it quickly inside to the young centre forward, Sam English, who had evaded Jimmy McStay well upfield and was advancing to the right-hand corner of the Celtic penalty box. Thomson, in the Celtic goal at the Copland Road end, made to come out but hesitated for a moment on the six-yard line as English pushed the ball ahead of him.

Then, as he saw the centre forward prepare to shoot, he dived full length, knee-high from the ground. There was a crack of bone as his head collided with knee as English followed through with his shot and the ball went harmlessly past Thomson's left goalpost. He had made the save but seemed to know little about it. As he lay on the ground, English stumbled over him and also fell holding his knee. Thomson still lay as he had fallen, one hand outstretched, and the other on his cloth cap which had been pushed to the back of his head. His hand fell to the ground as blood spurted from his right temple on to the grass.

His brother Jim, sitting in the stand, remembered: 'I knew at once it was serious from the way his hand fell slowly.' One St Andrew's ambulance man watching was heard to mutter quietly to a colleague: 'That's the end of him' as they prepared their stretcher. Sam English, meantime, was being helped to his feet by colleagues but Thomson lay ominously still.

The Celtic players were round their young teammate immediately and Willie McStay signalled frantically to the stand, but Will Quinn, the Celtic trainer, was already running on to the park. It was 4.15 p.m., exactly an hour since kick-off.

'Doc' Marshall, the Rangers inside right, was a medical student at the time and he saw at once the seriousness of the injury. He suggested to his colleagues that they stand respectfully apart but one of them made a crude remark and was immediately rebuked by Alan Morton. The Celtic players were in a daze although Willie Maley was already with them trying to hold them together.

The Rangers supporters behind the goal – who couldn't see how grave the situation was – began to grow impatient at the long delay and started to jeer and catcall, suspecting that Thomson was feigning injury to waste time. Davie Meiklejohn immediately went to the running track in front of them and raised both hands, like a priest making an incantation. As he held his hands high the noise gradually faded and Meiklejohn returned to the field, his head bowed. The Rangers end immediately became quiet, sensing something unusual was happening. Their silence spread round the ground until, by the time the ambulance men were carrying the unconscious Thomson past the main stand, his head swathed in bandages, but already red with his blood, a complete hush, far deeper than any formal or token two-minute observance, had come down on 80,000 people. It was eerie. All that could be heard was the hard breathing of the hurrying stretcher party. Suddenly the silence was broken by a woman's scream, which rang out from the stand as Thomson was hurried into the tunnel and out of sight. It took a while for W. G. Holburn of Govanhill, the referee, to get the game restarted. Both managers were now on the field, Willie Maley still trying to organise his depleted team.

Peter McGonagle was the normal substitute, but Maley needed him more in defence; so Charlie Geatons pulled on the goalkeeper's orange jersey, which was brought out. One assumes it wasn't Thomson's. Eventually Mr Holburn blew to continue the match. Oddly enough, it started with a Celtic goal kick. Yet, since Thomson had diverted the ball past his post, it should have been a corner to Rangers but nobody was at all interested. Spectators at the Celtic end were already streaming away from the ground and the players didn't seem to have the heart for it. The atmosphere was quite unnatural and a game of football was the last thing on everyone's mind. The echoes of that scream seemed to hang in the air and it was dispelled only when the referee blew to end the game and the players walked sadly towards the tunnel.

The first act of a tragedy had just been played out.

In the dressing room, the Celtic doctor, W. F. Kivlichan, who had played outside right for both Rangers and Celtic before the first world war, was attending the injured player and did not seem at all hopeful. The Celtic players sat around in the dressing room not even bothering to change. Jimmy McGrory asked Dr Kivlichan how John was. 'Bad enough,' was the terse reply. Davie Meiklejohn came in to ask about John. His team didn't know what to do either. Sam English had been sent home with a friend, also a goalkeeper, Tommy Hamilton. Arrangements were made immediately by Kivlichan and Dr Gillespie, the Rangers doctor, for an ambulance to take Thomson to the Victoria Infirmary, although the Southern General Infirmary was much nearer. Bill Struth, the Rangers manager, immediately attended to the matter and also arranged for a private car to fetch the Thomson parents from Fife. Meanwhile, Jim Thomson, John's brother, had come down from the stand, and saw his brother put into the 1928 Austin ambulance in front of the main door. Mr Struth brought a young girl to the door of the dressing room and said that she was asking to see John. She had been sitting with Jim Thomson in the stand and followed him down but had gone to the Rangers dressing room by mistake. It was Margaret Finlay, a 19-year-old Uddingston girl and John's girlfriend. It was she who had screamed.

It was pandemonium at the Victoria Infirmary. Thomson had been admitted to Ward A amid scenes of confusion both outside and indoors. Word had spread about the incident and people were clamouring for the latest news. Jim accompanied John all the way and gave the hospital the patient's full name – John Murie Galloway McCallum Thomson – and his home address as 23 Balgreggie Park, Cardenden, Fife. Oddly, he didn't give John's Glasgow address, where he was living at the time, which was in digs at 481 Victoria Rd, only minutes away. After an initial examination – which diagnosed a depressed fracture of the skull – an operation was immediately carried out to relieve the pressure on the brain, but at 5 p.m. he suffered a convulsion and the doctors (Messrs Davidson, Daly and Gillespie) recognised that the odds on any kind of recovery were shortening all the time. He was moved to Ward Five and certain visitors were allowed to sit in the ward waiting-room. These were Jim Thomson and Margaret Finlay, Willie Maley, director Tom Colgan, Jimmy McStay and Peter Wilson, who was close to John, and Jim Maguire, a young Celtic player with whom John shared his digs in Queen's Park. He and John had just bought a half-share each in a car and were both in the process of learning to drive. Jimmy must have learned fast, for it was he who drove John's parents back to Fife later that night. John and Jean Thomson, with their other son Bill, had arrived at the bedside at twenty past nine. John Thomson junior died five minutes later. It was as if he'd been waiting for them.

The switchboard at the hospital jammed and all six Glasgow newspapers were being flooded with enquiries – but it was the kind of news that needed no wires. Soon the whole city knew and the shock numbed everyone. All of Scotland seemed to be affected, at least the lower half of it. In the Gothenburg cinema in Cardenden, the film was interrupted and a scrawled message gave the news on the screen. The audience immediately rose and, without a word, filed out of the cinema. Bob McPhail of Rangers learned the news from the front window of the *Sunday Mail* office in Hope Street on his way home from a dinner at Rombach's Restaurant. He had played in the game and knew John Thomson well from their international appearances. He couldn't take it in and burst into tears on the pavement.

The Dunfermline Journal of 12 September 1931 reported: 'During the boxing contests at The Ring, Glasgow, the death of Thomson was announced. As a mark of respect, the MC requested the boxing patrons to be upstanding and observe a two-minute silence. It was a touching tribute.' It was a remarkable tribute too; the denizens at the boxing, late on a Saturday night, high on adrenalin and probably alcohol, are not always responsive to the decencies of life.

Jimmy McGrory remembers that awful night, too:

> I was living in Ayr at the time and motored home. I can hardly remember driving I was in such a daze and when I got home I just didn't know where I was as I waited for news. I was just married . . . and I sat with my wife all evening wondering if the phone would ever ring. Then I decided to phone the Victoria Infirmary itself but the switchboard was jammed with calls . . . Jimmy McStay phoned me about ten o'clock to tell me, broken-voiced, that John was dead – 'He died half an hour ago.' That's all he said and put the phone down, obviously too choked to say any more. I was dazed. I could have died myself. Never in a hundred years did I think he would die – only 22. I went through to the living room and said to my wife, 'He's dead'. 'God rest his soul' she said. I remember we sat there in disbelief. That was the only night in my career that I ever wanted to quit football. I was sickened. I was never afraid of physical contact or taking a knock but to experience a teammate dying playing a game of football was just too much. I never slept at all that night.

A crowd, estimated at a thousand strong, had gathered outside The Bank restaurant, owned by Willie Maley, anxiously waiting for news from the hospital and they remained for some time afterwards in stunned silence:

> Mr Maley and all the Celtic directors were there. They were constantly in touch with the Infirmary. Mr Maley, whose interest in his young players is that of a father, was deeply moved. Phone calls at the Infirmary were at the rate of 150 per hour. These came from all classes of people: Celtic supporters, club managers and officials throughout the country, and personal friends. (*The Dunfermline Journal*)

Few could remember anyone ever dying of a game of football yet three Scottish players had already done so on the football field. Full back James Main of Hibernian died at Firhill in 1909, as did goalkeeper Josiah Wilkinson of Dunfermline FC, also at Ibrox, in 1921, and big Bob Mercer, a centre half, who had a fatal heart attack while playing for a Hearts XI at Selkirk in 1926. Countless players have been seriously injured, and there are those who succumb to sudden illness at the very height of their careers and in the prime of their athleticism. One such was John Thomson's teammate, Peter Scarff, who coughed up blood after one game against Leith Athletic in December 1931, only months after John's death, and exactly two years later he was dead from tuberculosis at twenty-five years of age. When he was buried at Kilbarchan, Willie Maley threw in Scarff's Celtic jersey as the coffin was lowered into the grave. Jimmy Delaney, a young Celt then, but destined to attain legendary status with the club, was there and said to another player beside him: 'I hope they do that for me.'

However, on Wednesday, 9 September, there was no such gesture as John Thomson was laid to rest at Bowhill cemetery, near Cardenden. All that fell on his body were flowers. A railway wagon, packed with floral tributes, waited at a siding, the staff not knowing what to do with them all. Wellesley FC, John Thomson's junior club, at a weekend meeting decided to send a letter of condolence to the parents and also a wreath with the club colours, green and white. Fife Junior Association also sent a wreath in blue and white, the Fife County colours.

On the day before, a funeral service had been quickly arranged at the Trinity Congregational Church in West Claremont Street, near Charing Cross. The minister, the Reverend H. S. McClelland, had actually been at the game himself and, knowing the player to have been a God-fearing young man, he thought a memorial service in Glasgow would be appropriate. The press announced that the service would be at three in the afternoon on the Tuesday with Mr McClelland officiating, and Davie Meiklejohn and Peter Wilson reading from Scripture. The doors were closed with hundreds still standing outside in the street. One who was inadvertently locked out was Peter Wilson, who was supposed to read Revelations, chapter 21, verses 1–7: 'And I saw a new heaven and a new earth.' Reverend McClelland had to read it himself.

Both teams were present with their managers and directors as well as officials from the SFA and Glasgow City Council. It was an all-Glasgow occasion. No one from Fife was there. At the end, the minister took the chance to attack the mindless section of the Rangers support that had bayed obscenities as John Thomson lay on the ground; did they realise that might have been the last sound this brave young man heard? It was also brave of the minister to end his eulogy on such a note, especially as he went on to say that if Jerry Dawson had been similarly injured there was a section of the Celtic support that would have behaved just as badly. He hoped that both sections of supporters would learn something from the tragedy – so that John's death would then have achieved something. Sad to say, this was a fond hope. The service ended with a minute's silence, then Mr McClelland beckoned a tearful Sam English and led him to the vestry and gently closed the door.

As a mark of respect, the league fixture between Airdrie and Celtic, due to be played that day, was postponed; the Glasgow Cup tie between Rangers and Third Lanark, scheduled for the previous night, had already been postponed. Working men took the Wednesday off work to pay tribute, twenty thousand men swamping Queen Street station and its surrounds in Glasgow to see his coffin entrained for Fife. Two special trains were added to take supporters to the funeral. The long road from Parkhead to Bowhill, covering, as it does, the broad Lowland waistband of Scotland, was a veritable rosary of salute. Knots of people stood at every crossing watching those ordinary men in cloth caps, just like a goalkeeper's, some still in working boots, walking all the way from Glasgow; ordinary men, who risked the sack from their jobs through taking time off to walk more than sixty miles to see their fallen hero interred in a wall-side tomb in a village graveyard.

Tents were pitched on the crags above the cemetery to accommodate the thousands who poured into the village all that day. An aeroplane, not a common sight in 1931, landed in the Daisy Field bringing newspaper reporters, who had to cover all that would happen on that sad occasion. From all parts of Scotland mourners came anxious to pay homage to the Prince of Goalkeepers, a future king, who had not yet properly begun his reign.

Scottish football had found its first martyr.

It is estimated that thirty thousand people lined the route across the country. It was a gigantic display of grief on a national scale at a time when the Coalition Government, led by Labour's Ramsay MacDonald, was undergoing a crisis. MacDonald was the only prime minister John Thomson ever shook hands with; but nobody, in the West of Scotland at any rate, appeared to be concerned with anything other than the burial of a football player.

Among those in the crowd that day were the great and the good of the sporting world, like Alec James of Arsenal and Tommy Milligan, the Scottish boxing champion. The only celebrity missing, apart from King George V himself, was the same Ramsay MacDonald, as the Bowhill Pipe and Brass bands led the family and the coffin through the crowds.

Carrying the coffin were Jimmy McGrory, Jimmy McStay, Alec Thomson, Willie Cook, Peter Wilson and Charlie Napier, with every other Celtic player walking either side of it as escort. Many were near to tears, as they watched their club-mate being let down gently into the earth. Only a few days before, he had run out on to the field beside them, full of the same youth. It must have been hard to accept.

It still is.

The Thomson family belonged to the Church of Christ, where there are no ordained ministers, the congregation taking turns to speak at their services. The private service in the house was led by a David Adamson, an elder of the church and a family friend. The graveside service was conducted by an ordinary miner, John Howie, another elder. What a time for Mr Howie's turn! Cap in hand, he spoke simply and plainly, more telling perhaps than any pious rhetoric. John's father, who had borne up well till then, was overcome at the graveside and had to be supported by his other sons, William and James. A family friend, Archie Watters, read from Scripture. As he was speaking, a party of Rangers players – led by Davie Meiklejohn and including Alan Morton, Jimmy Simpson and Sandy Archibald – were seen to arrive. They had been delayed by the immense crowd clogging the approaches to Bowhill. With them was the distraught figure of Sam English, who was later led away weeping.

Tom White, the chairman of Celtic, thanked the vast crowd on behalf of the family and the club, and gradually everyone dispersed as the light faded and evening fell. Typically for a Scottish, and more particularly, a Glasgow occasion, police had arrested the passengers in a Morris Oxford car that had been stolen in Glasgow so that that the 'gentlemen' involved might get to Fife. They were allowed to pay their respects before being taken into custody. Then, eventually, as the sun started to go down in the late afternoon, when all things had been done, and everything said, a huge multitude turned about and dispersed through the little village in silence . . .

It had seemed so little time since John Thomson had signed for Celtic as a 17-year-old on the lid of a roadside fuse box in Galton after a persuasive tram ride with the Celtic scout, Steve Callaghan, during the miners' strike of November 1926. Yet, by the time of his death, he was already Scotland's goalkeeper. He had come from Wellesley Juniors in 1925 after learning his goalkeeping trade with Bowhill Rovers. After a spell on loan to Ayr United, he made his debut for Celtic against Dundee in February 1927 and was an automatic choice in goal thereafter. During his outstanding, if brief, career, he had suffered a double fracture of the collarbone, a broken jaw, concussion and the loss of two front teeth.

He seemed to make a habit of getting hurt, but it never deterred him for a moment from throwing himself into the heat of the action around his goalmouth. His position was made all the more vulnerable through Celtic's reluctance at that time to utilise their centre half and captain (Jimmy McStay) as a third back, which was the growing fashion of the time. Celtic still held to the traditional game with the centre half further forward; in the centre, in fact. This meant that, while they were always an attacking threat in every game, they often left a yawning gap in their own penalty area. Time and time again only Thomson's superlative goalkeeping saved the day but it was an unfortunate and, some might say, fatal tactic, in the way football was being played at that time. This is in no way to blame the club or his teammates for the fatality which followed, but Thomson's job might have been made easier had it relied on some defensive cover rather than on his own daring instincts.

A press picture of the time shows young John, his big, goalie's cap set against the sun, jumping to fist away a high ball. The jump is so high, the punch so defiant! It is an action so typical of his physical zest; yet within minutes of that picture, showing him leaping like Nijinsky high into the air, he was lying inert on the turf, his cap askew, and his head spurting blood. Another photograph shows him, a bandage round his head instead of a cap, being helped on to a stretcher. It was hardly a matter of minutes among these pictures but it was the difference between life and death.

The former Celtic full back, Hugh Hilley, was at the game and insisted that, if John hadn't hesitated for a split second about coming out, he wouldn't have needed to dive for the ball. It was an act of daring born out of sheer instinct, and the result was tragically accidental, also the verdict reached later officially. As required by law, a fatal accident inquiry into the death was held on Thursday, 15 October 1931 at the Justiciary Buildings in Glasgow. This was presided over by Sheriff George Wilton, KC, and after the questioning of witnesses, including Willie Maley and Bill Struth, the respective managers, he instructed the jury to deliver the following verdict:

> That the deceased, John Thomson, while engaged in his employment as a professional footballer with Celtic Football Club, and acting as a goalkeeper in a football match with Rangers at Ibrox Park, Glasgow, in the course of the match sustained injuries to his head by coming into contact with the body of Samuel English, playing centre-forward for Rangers, in attempting to save a goal by diving towards the said Sam English while in the act of kicking

the ball, received a fracture of the skull from which he died [that same day] in the Victoria Infirmary by accidental injury per verdict of Jury.

The prosaic objectivity of that long official sentence does little to convey the enormity of the event in the public's eye and the effect it had on so many people for so long, including people who could never have seen Thomson play. Journalist Hugh Taylor had the same feeling:

> The thin boy had a veteran's coolness, uncanny anticipation, a sure clutch, and an acrobat's agility . . . to thousands of Celtic supporters who weren't even born when he died he is still the best goalkeeper who ever played. It is true his tragic death made him a hero . . . but we must realise that, when he played, he was hailed as a genius, even though he was so young. He magnetised the fans; he was an idol. John Thomson would have been a great goalkeeper in any age. . . . Today he would probably have been named Batman.

John Rafferty, the noted Scottish sports' journalist, put it more succinctly in a book edited by John Arlott (*Soccer: the Great Ones*): 'A great player, who came to the game as a boy and left it still a boy; he had no predecessor, no successor. He was unique.'

Dr J. E. Handley (Brother Clare) summed him up eloquently in his *The Celtic Story*:

> A man who has not read Homer, wrote Bagehot, is like a man who has not seen the ocean. There is a great object of which he has no idea. In like manner, a generation which did not see John Thomson has missed a touch of greatness in sport, for he was a brilliant virtuoso, as Gigli was and Menuhin is. One artist employed the voice as his instrument, the other employs the violin. . . . For Thomson it was a handful of leather . . .

And in that employment he lost his life. A split-second's action on the field, and it has given him immortality. Was it worth it? A goal saved but at what a cost! A career exchanged for a legend! It was an accident, a sad accident, and it belongs as much to the chancy game of life as to a game of football. We must let it pass.

Johnny Thomson, as the supporters called him, had brightened grim days by his grace and thrilled plain people by his courage. His modesty and good looks endeared him to countless thousands who had never met him. This slim custodian armed only with a pair of gloves and a cap against marauding forwards in heavy boots, and all fighting for a leather ball that grew heavier in the mud and rain, became a hero in spite of himself. He was required to be one on a regular basis.

A few days after the events of 5 September, a Glasgow reporter had tried to interview Margaret Finlay at her home in Uddingston but her younger sister refused to let him over the door. He printed a story afterwards as if he had interviewed her, but the mystery of John Thomson's girlfriend remained. Margaret Armour Finlay, the woman who screamed at Ibrox, had known Thomson since she was a 16-year-old when he first came to Celtic, but had recently become more involved with him. She had been too distressed to go to the funeral, but later visited his grave with Jim Thomson. Soon afterwards, aged twenty, she left for London and embarked on a successful career in the Inland Revenue. A young colleague there was James Callaghan, a future British prime minister, and a close friend was the sister of Cecil B. de Mille, the great Hollywood film director. When war was declared in 1939, Margaret was seconded to the Treasury and served in Cairo under Lord Moynes. While there, she met and married an English army officer, Charles Patrick Straker, and in 1946, after service in the Balkans, travelled with him as an army wife, retiring in 1966 to Oakville, Ontario, where she died in 1980 of a stroke. It was in Canada that she told her only child, a daughter, Sybolla, quite casually when John Thomson's name was mentioned on a radio programme: 'You know, I was once engaged to him.' It was the only time she had ever spoken of him in all the years. They were not engaged – officially. She was not his fiancée, there was no ring, but there was no mistaking the pride he had in her, and she in him all those years ago. In the Glasgow phrase, they were 'going together' and generally that meant they were going in the same direction; towards the altar.

It was thought by friends that they might name the day when he got back from the 1931 American tour. When he did return, it was to work in the close season with Piercy and Lawson, highly reputable men's tailors, with shops in Renfield and Gordon streets. He had ideas of setting up on his own when he retired from football. Mr Maley, who knew that trade well, was already advising him. At the same time, the manager had reminded him, half in fun but more in earnest, that football was his job for the moment and he must give all his mind and attention to that. Young John could only agree, but gave most of his attention to Margaret.

Theirs was definitely a football 'match'. It began when her father had taken her to Celtic Park from their home in Uddingston, when he was invited to sit in the directors' box. She saw John Thomson's first game at Parkhead against Kilmarnock when he made his wondrous save against 'Peerie' Cunningham, whose pivot shot swerving on the volley was lethal, but Johnny somehow saw its deflection and, twisting in mid-air, with the tips of his fingers turned the shot round the post. The Celtic players agreed it was the greatest save they had ever seen.

This then was the extraordinary athlete Margaret saw that first Saturday. She was introduced to him afterwards, and saw him on every occasion she could after that. She even attended the 1931 Cup Final celebrations at the Bank Restaurant in Queen Street, and remembered the shy way in which John Thomson took every chance to introduce her to everyone there as his 'girlfriend'. They had to leave early because John had to catch a train just up the street for Cardenden in Fife. He liked to get back as often as he could. That night he had to force his way through the jubilant crowd still standing outside the restaurant. Had he but known, these same Celtic supporters would have carried him to Fife on their shoulders.

A week after the funeral, Mrs Thomson wrote inviting Sam English and his wife, Sadie, to come through to Cardenden. The young Ulsterman did so, and afterwards, the Thomson family extended their practical Christian charity by inserting a notice in the local paper:

The parents of John Thomson have made a request to us to publicly announce that they entirely exonerate the Rangers centre forward,

Sam English, of any responsibility for the accident which resulted in their son's death. They realise it was an accident, pure and simple. The family also wish to express their gratitude for the uniform sympathy that has been extended to them from people all over the land.

Despite this generous statement, and the similar reaction of almost everyone in football, Sam English's troubles were only beginning. He was mercilessly abused at every game he played for the next two seasons with Rangers, by the same loutish element who followed him around, yelling 'murderer' or 'killer' every time he touched the ball. It became so bad that he had to get out of Scotland. He transferred to Liverpool, but he couldn't command a first-team place on Merseyside. He returned to Scotland in 1935 to play for Queen of the South but it was no better there and his trauma continued. Something had gone from his game, and the will to play wasn't there any longer. He tried again at Hartlepool United in 1937 but it was no better. His reputation was beginning to follow him around. Finally, it was all too much and he quit the game. He was just twenty-eight.

He visited the Thomsons again many years later, when he retired to Scotland. He died in the Vale of Leven hospital, Alexandria on 12 April 1967 of motor neurone disease, but really his end had come much earlier. He, too, was a victim of the accident that had happened in Ibrox Stadium at 4.15 p.m. on that windless, September Saturday afternoon.

On each anniversary of that terrible day, Celtic supporters from all over the world gather before his wall-side grave in the little cemetery in Bowhill, Fife to lay green-and-white scarves and caps, and place flowers on the marble plinth together with messages written on scraps of paper and cards all giving the same message – that they love him yet, and are remembering him still.

Out of one heroic moment an immortal was born; and that is why John Thomson still lives today. On his tombstone, which was paid for by subscriptions from all over the world, it reads:

In Memoriam
John Thomson
Scotland's International Goalkeeper
who died on 5th September 1931
aged 22 years

'They never die who live in the hearts they leave behind'.

Note: The author is indebted to Tom Greig and his book, *My Search for Celtic's John* (Ogilvie Writings, 2003) for the detailed information on John Thomson used in the preparation of this article.

Comments

Strange how that event afffects you! I wasn't even born then but still the accounts of the funeral move me close to tears. I know I'm not alone in that regard.

Tom Campbell

An incident like that elevates the person involved, both in the short and long run. By all eyewitness accounts, though, John Thomson was a very graceful keeper, an artist. It was a very poignant time, made all the more so by the fact that the game was played in brilliant sunshine. Nobody should die on such a day. But it might have been an accident waiting to happen; he had a history of previous injuries in similar circumstances.

Bob Crampsey

I remember my Uncle Pat used to sing 'The John Thomson Song' as his party piece at family gatherings. Invariably, the song was treated in total silence almost with reverence – and this was at least forty years after the event.

Gerry Dunbar

My Uncle John was at Ibrox that day and must have been fifteen or sixteen at the time. He never spoke very much about it – only an occasional word in passing – but he used to shake his head sadly at those moments. His wife – a girl in Shotts at the time – remembered that it was a lovely day. That day she remembers seeing an old miner (Willie Kennedy) who was believed to have once played for Celtic; he kept birds in cages, and one of them was a lark.

Tony Griffin

Even to this day – seventy years and more later – John Thomson's memory is revered in Fife in the traditional mining communities. Fifers honour their heroes and Thomson is a particular case – as is Willie Fernie, born and raised only two miles away from Thomson in Kinglassie.

Craig McAughtrie

A tragic and thoroughly accidental affair.

David Potter

I was born a few months after that game but I can remember my brothers talking about it years later. In particular, they spoke about Davie Meiklejohn moving towards the supporters behind the goal and telling them to quieten down as the player was seriously injured. To their credit, the Rangers supporters did stop the noise and it was a ray of hope – an act of common decency – within the context of a bitter rivalry.

Patrick Reilly

The legend of John Thomson lives on in Celtic history even though he can only be a fading memory for those present at Ibrox Park that fateful day in September 1931. A painful, and sometimes, bitter memory too.

I can recall returning from an away match in the 1960s on a football special and listening to an elderly fan recounting his version of the fatality and being struck by his savage denunciation of Sam English: 'Murder, so it was!' he repeated, thumping the table to give added vehemence to his conviction.

It was nonsense, of course, as scrutiny of the incident shows that English was entirely innocent but such has been the martyrology surrounding the tragedy over successive decades that I would not be surprised if that old man's contention was not still held by many surviving members of his generation. The potency of myth is strong – and timeless.

Pat Woods

3

THE ROT WITHIN

Patrick Reilly

No interested or informed observer could fail to note the persisting ironical position occupied from the outset by Glasgow Celtic within Scottish society, but there are special moments when this becomes particularly prominent. The mass exodus of some eighty thousand Celtic supporters from all around the globe to Seville in 2003 provoked a debate at the time as to why this astonishing phenomenon should have occurred and even, in some quarters, as to whether it should be deplored rather than admired. Two other such moments from the more distant past were the victories in the Coronation Cup of 1953 and, more remarkably still, in the Empire Exhibition Trophy of 1938.

The *leitmotif* of this essay – its underlying, governing theme – will be the manifestation of this irony before, during and after the celebration of Empire in Glasgow in 1938. I employ the term 'irony' in its later, modified sense involving not an irony of *words* but of *events* – a discrepancy, a disparity, a contradiction not between words and meaning but between actions and their consequences, between what is anticipated or envisaged and what actually happens. Things turn out completely different from – even completely opposite to – what we expected, almost as if there were some force greater than ourselves, mocking and subverting us; in the words of the old adage, 'Man proposes; God disposes'.

It is this type of irony that I want to examine. My belief is that the whole episode of the Empire Exhibition (the years before, the tournament itself and its aftermath) was informed and shot through with this type of irony. I believe too that, in exploring it, we shall open windows upon certain significant aspects of Scottish life, society and culture.

In a parody composed to commemorate Celtic's triumph in the Coronation Cup competition of 1953, 'Lizzie' (Queen Elizabeth II) is lamenting the miscarriage of her scheme to confer a trophy upon her loyal, beloved Rangers in her 'crowning year'. Instead, the prize has gone, crazily and distressingly, to the team least deserving of all, the supposedly unruly, disloyal 'Irishmen' and their hordes of rebellious, tricolour-festooned followers. In the dialogue the Queen's partner, her consort Prince Philip, advises her as to what must be done to prevent the future recurrence of any similar mishap:

To beat Glasgow Celtic you'll have to deport
All the thousands of Fenians who give them support.

In 1953, more than a century after the arrival of the wandering, famishing Irish on Scotland's shores, such a draconian solution to the problems of a divided society had become no more than a joke. The so-called 'Irish' had been domiciled in Scotland for generations. The crowds at Celtic Park had long since ceased singing the old, traditional anthems such as 'The Dear Little Shamrock' and 'Hail Glorious St. Patrick'. The invocation to the 'dear saint of our isle' had become almost irrelevant to a people now removed from Ireland by three, four or even five generations. 'Our isle' was no longer an accurate, geographical description, but was at most a nostalgic, sentimental effusion. The Boyne, after all, does not flow through Banffshire, nor are Derry's Walls hewn out of Grampian granite, but no one would dream of describing those who weekly sing their praises at football grounds as 'Irish'. The same is surely true of the mass of Celtic supporters today, and it was no different in 1953 when the fictional Philip of the song counselled his wife to repatriate these unwelcome, troublesome, cup-winning intruders back to their country of origin.

The idea of the Queen being distressed by Celtic's triumph in the Coronation Cup is every bit as risible as the canard about sore hearts in the Vatican after a setback for Celtic; the song is simply a joke, a wind-up, a piece of good-humoured mockery aimed at those who raucously bellow that they are the people, all the while draping themselves in Union Jacks to prove it.

Nevertheless, there is a certain irony in the winning by Celtic of a competition designed to celebrate the coronation of a Protestant monarch who must swear – as a condition of accession to the throne – to defend the Reformed faith against the menace of Catholicism. In 1953 the sign 'No Catholics Need Apply' might as well have been securely fixed over the gates of Buckingham Palace and Ibrox stadium alike – but it has been in recent times silently and unobtrusively removed from the latter. However, when the Coronation Cup was being contested, the shared, acknowledged aim and *raison d'etre* of both institutions was to keep Catholics in their decidedly inferior place. This explains why, along the Shankill and Copland roads, the loyal fans could feel a modicum of justification that there is indeed a certain affinity between the team they support and the monarch to whom they so bellicosely proclaim their allegiance. It was this sentiment that the author of the coronation parody song was exposing and deriding – but neither he nor anyone else in his senses seriously believed that the Queen had arranged the competition so that Rangers should win it, far less that she and the Duke of Edinburgh were actually discussing the repatriation of Celtic supporters to Ireland because their team had upset her expectations. It was a joke, a bit of light-hearted fun, no more and no less.

But what was simply badinage and banter in 1953 was deadly serious only twenty years earlier. In the 1930s there were genuine, widespread fears within the Presbyterian community that, unless Irish (that is, Catholic) immigration into Scotland was halted or reversed, a racial-religious civil war would erupt – much as Enoch Powell would warn us many years later in his notorious 'rivers-of-blood' speech about the dangers of allowing too many immigrants from Asia, Africa and the West Indies into the country.

That the anxieties of the Thirties were not simply the product of populist hysteria or the rantings of demagogic extremists is shown by the holding of a top-level meeting in London in 1928 between high-ranking government ministers and senior members of the

Presbyterian church, with the latter demanding an immediate halt to the entry of all Irish Catholics into the country, the immediate deportation of all natives of the Irish Free State in receipt of state benefits or guilty of any kind of legal offence and a vigorous propaganda campaign to persuade or coerce as many citizens of Irish Catholic descent as possible to depart our shores. There were at that time 600,000 Catholics in Scotland, most of Irish origin, and their enemies deplored their presence in the land as a prime cause of eugenic and cultural disaster.

The decades between the two world wars, from 1918 to 1939, witnessed a sharp increase in sectarian tensions within Scotland. An Orange candidate, Hugh Ferguson, had been elected MP for Motherwell in 1923 and had called ominously for 'Cromwellian' measures in a still unsettled Ireland, predictably evoking ancestral memories of massacre and persecution. (Imagine, if you can, the sense of outrage that would possess the nation today if even one British National Party candidate were to be successfully returned to either Westminster or Holyrood.) The Scottish Protestant League had been founded by Alexander Ratcliffe in Edinburgh in 1920 and was soon attracting large audiences at rallies throughout the country. A key element in its manifesto was the compulsory abolition of Catholic schools and, in local elections in Glasgow in 1933, its candidates secured 67,000 votes or 23 per cent of the electorate. John Cormack's Protestant Action, another violently anti-Catholic party, also polled very well locally. Both of these groups did much better at the polls in the 1930s than the more flamboyant, headline-grabbing Blackshirts of Sir Oswald Mosley. Yet today Mosley remains a historical name, indispensable in any discussion of British Fascism, while Ratcliffe and Cormack are remembered, if at all, only by specialists or octogenarians.

The links were, nevertheless, there. The International League for the Defence and Furtherance of Protestantism, based in Berlin, provided a forum where German and Scottish Protestants could meet to debate individual but interlinked problems and to frame a common policy for dealing with them. In consequence, it was then argued at the Scottish General Assembly that the Church of Scotland should refrain from condemning anti-Semitism in Nazi Germany through a sympathetic intuition that the *Judenfrage* (the Jewish question) in Germany had strong parallels with the *Irischenfrage* (the Irish question) in Scotland. Just exactly how should one deal with a large, alien, unwelcome minority who had regrettably been allowed, through negligence or worse, to infiltrate one's country? One way was shown when, in July 1935, the first-ever Eucharistic Congress to be held in Scotland met in Edinburgh. Admittedly, what happened pales into insignificance when set against the infamous *Kristallnacht* outrages in Nazi Germany when Jewish businesses, shops and homes were attacked by mobs of ruffians. It was, nevertheless, shameful enough. Coaches carrying women and children to the event were stoned; ten thousand 'No Popery' protesters turned up at the final celebration, and the police were forced to baton-charge the rabble on numerous occasions. They were the worst anti-Catholic riots to occur in twentieth-century Scotland – and only four years before the outbreak of the second world war. For many weeks afterwards Scottish Catholics continued to suffer abuse and intimidation at work and on the streets of their towns and cities.

The Thirties also witnessed an increase in discrimination in employment in Scotland's heavy industry (shipyards, steel mills, engineering works) and this bias had hardened and been extended into many other areas of work, such as printing. Not surprisingly, these deteriorating relations manifested themselves in football matches between Celtic and Rangers. Things had got much worse at the end of the first world war with the influx of many Northern Ireland Protestants to work on Clydeside. They brought with them the baggage of Shankhill Orangeism and, inevitably, the opposition between Unionism and Republicanism, Union Jack and tricolour, Protestantism and Catholicism became more entrenched and bitter. The 'No-Catholic' policy long followed at Ibrox hardened into a dogma under the stewardship of William Struth, the Rangers manager from the late 1920s to the end of the second world war. It was unavoidable that these animosities should spill over into the football sector, since each of the two great Glasgow clubs was now regarded, not just as a sporting institution but as the religious and ethnic standard-bearer of its respective community. No longer was it simply a matter of winning or losing a football match; the pride, indeed the very self-respect of opposed religious and racial communities, was now at stake and the result could be only one of two things: ecstatic rejoicing or abject humiliation.

Unsurprisingly, crowd trouble worsened at Old Firm matches in the inter-war years to the extent that Percy Sillitoe, appointed chief constable of Glasgow in 1933, threatened to ban the fixture altogether as an infallible sponsor of violence. Celtic's origins and Rangers' policies were together guaranteed to produce religious hostility, especially in an environment of poverty and mass unemployment. In Tom Devine's authoritative view [1] Scotland between 1920 and 1939 was manifestly a deeply divided society, a view that should give some pause to those who argue optimistically that the relatively easy absorption of the Catholic Irish and their descendants represents one of the great self-congratulatory triumphs of Scottish history. Yet Devine confesses to an initial puzzlement as to why things should have become so much worse in this inter-war period. Nothing like this had occurred on such a scale in the nineteenth century when sectarianism was confined to job discrimination, Orange walks and minor sporadic disturbances. When the Catholic hierarchy [2] was restored in England in 1850, the response, from top to bottom of English society, was ferocious. When a parallel restoration took place in Scotland in 1878, the reaction was far less antagonistic. The first world war may have played some part in attenuating ancient antagonisms. Scottish Catholics, most of them of Irish origin, had made a significant contribution to the war effort.

Six of them were recipients of the Victoria Cross. The Archbishops of Glasgow and Edinburgh had blessed those serving in the armed forces. Many thousands of Catholic volunteers flocked to the colours long before compulsory conscription was introduced. Why, then, did the old hatreds revive in such virulent form after the Armistice? Why were these years (1920–1939) so disfigured by a return to bigotry and discrimination?

---

[1] T. M. Devine, as expressed in *The Scottish Nation 1700-2000*.

[2] In 1878, for the first time since the Scottish Protestant Reformation of 1559–60, the territorial bishoprics of the Catholic Church were re-established within Scotland. Six new dioceses were instituted: St Andrews and Edinburgh, Aberdeen, Argyle and the Isles, Dunkeld, Glasgow and Galloway.

Economics played a major role, undoubtedly. The end of the war brought, predictably, an economic slowdown that inexorably deepened into bleak depression throughout the western world. A loss of national confidence accompanied this economic catastrophe, particularly in Italy, Germany and Britain, with Scotland especially affected. Coal production fell by 40 per cent, shipbuilding by 50 per cent. By January 1933 over 30 per cent of the Scottish workforce was unemployed. Between 1919 and 1926, 300,000 Scots left the country for America and the Antipodes. The former, seemingly unshakeable world of economic success and world empire was rocked to its foundations and, in the ensuing crisis of confidence, an explanation – better still a scapegoat – had to be found. It was fertile ground for the recrudescence of religious and racial hatreds and, like the Jews in Germany, the Catholic Scoto-Irish were conveniently to hand to serve as an alibi, a whipping-boy, for national decline. Here is the root cause of the revival of anti-Catholic sentiment in Scotland throughout the dole-dominated Thirties.

There were striking jeremiads pronounced by prominent prophets of doom. George Malcolm Thomson keened over national degeneration. In his despairing vision, the Scots had no future; they were a dying race, supplanted and elbowed aside in their own land by an alien people with an abhorrent creed. It was a charge repeated by the eminent John Buchan [3] and, in even more vitriolic terms, by Andrew Dewar Gibb, professor of law at the University of Glasgow. For him the intruding Irish, compared with the native Scots, were 'immeasurably inferior in every way, but cohesive and solid, refusing obstinately, at the behest of obscurantist magic-men, to mingle with the people whose land they are usurping'.

Although concentrated in the most menial labouring occupations, the Scottish Catholic community was tailor-made to play the role of scapegoat for national decline. This unenviable prominence was accentuated by two further factors. The first was the 1918 Education (Scotland) Act, guaranteeing the existence of separate Catholic schools.

---

[3] John Buchan, the novelist (*Prester John*, *Greenmantle* and *The Thirty-Nine Steps*), was also appointed governor-general of Canada, and carried out his duties in the Dominion with more than appropriate pomp and dignity.

Despite the economic discrimination practised against them, the Catholics of Scotland stood rock-fast in their support for their separate schools. It was this resolve to preserve the faith that provoked Dewar Gibb to condemn them for their 'obstinacy' in refusing to be docilely absorbed into Presbyterian Scotland. An unceasing outcry against 'Rome on the Rates' filled the Thirties; demands for the abolition of the 1918 Act were the key items of every Scottish, anti-Catholic organisation throughout the inter-war period.

The second major factor that fuelled the antipathy of their enemies was the striking and continuing success on the football field of the so-called Irish Catholic team, Glasgow Celtic. In 1938, only three years after the disgraceful attacks upon the Eucharistic Congress and in a Scotland painfully emerging from the pit of economic depression, Celtic were celebrating their golden jubilee. Their impact upon the game had been prodigious and this not simply in the narrow sense of excellence upon the playing field. They were the great innovators – the first Scottish team to extend their ground for the hosting of international matches, to provide telegraphic facilities for the press, to build a double-decker stand for the greater convenience and comfort of spectators, to visit Europe as a club team, to instal a world-famous cycling track, to convene popular two-day sports meetings where international athletes, including participants from America, were allowed an arena to demonstrate their skills.

These pioneering activities were matched by a glittering array of achievements within the sport of football itself. In the half-century since their foundation they had won eighteen league championships, fifteen Scottish Cups, seventeen Glasgow Cups and twenty-two Charity Cups. Six championships had been won in a row, as had been seven Charity Cups, each of these sequences establishing an unparalleled record. In the season preceding their jubilee (1936/37) they had taken their fifteenth Scottish Cup, defeating Aberdeen at Hampden Park before a crowd of 146,433; a record for a club game in Europe and one that in these days of smaller grounds and crowds must surely prove impossible to surpass. Amazingly, at this non-ticket final an estimated thirty thousand would-be spectators were locked out. In their golden jubilee year, despite the retirement in the previous season of their king of goal scorers, Jimmy McGrory, they had claimed yet another league championship and had defeated Rangers 2–0 in the Charity Cup final.

Only two weeks after this double triumph they would be lining up against Sunderland at Ibrox in the opening game of a competition as part of the Empire Exhibition celebrations taking part in Glasgow. Four teams from Scotland and four from England had been invited to participate, the Scottish contingent being composed of Celtic, Rangers, Hearts and Aberdeen while from south of the border came Sunderland, Chelsea, Brentford and Everton. The teams had been selected on merit; Celtic, for example, were the current Scottish champions and Everton, the most formidable of the English contingent, would go on to win the English championship the following season.

The football tournament was only one part of a huge exhibition celebrating the achievements of the British Empire which was officially opened by the recently crowned monarchs, George VI and Queen Elizabeth, on 3 May 1938. It was staged at a time when Scotland was just beginning to emerge from the depths of the Great Depression, and it was held in Glasgow exactly fifty years after the International Exhibition of 1888 had taken place in the same city. In an Empire that covered one quarter of the earth's surface Glasgow was still designated officially as 'the Second City' although that title was already starting to slip from its grasp. But it was also a city that had recently acquired an especially bad image: a city of slums, unemployment, poverty and violence, the city of Johnny Stark, the psychopathic razor-king in the sensational novel *No Mean City*, the city of Billy Fulton, the real-life leader of the Bridgeton Billy Boys, who waged his sectarian campaign against Catholic gangs such as the Norman Conks (whose bastion was Norman Street in Bridgeton). This was the city that Percy Sillitoe came to try to pacify in 1933. Edwin Morgan's poem 'King Billy' [4] catches exactly the mood and atmosphere of the times:

the Conks ambush
the Billy Boys, the Billy Boys the Conks till
Sillitoe scuffs the razors down the stank.

---

[4] From 'King Billy' by Edwin Morgan in *Penguin Modern Poets 15*, published in 1969.

In such an atmosphere Glasgow also had a well-deserved reputation throughout Britain as a city obsessed with football.

The Scottish Development Council was anxious to showcase Scottish industry and enterprise in an attempt to encourage new businesses to come to Scotland as a makeweight for the decline in shipbuilding and heavy engineering on the Clyde. To this end it put up £1 million of the £11 million invested in the Exhibition. It lasted from 3 May until 29 October and was situated in 175 acres of Bellahouston Park, three miles south-west of the city centre and the only site big enough to host it. A whole city of pavilions and palaces was built in the new art deco style with services to accommodate a population of 500,000 people. There were pavilions dedicated to the dominions (Canada, Australia, New Zealand, South Africa and – interestingly – Eire) as well as to the colonies. Two great palaces, one devoted to Engineering and one to Industry, were erected with smaller structures (to Art, Peace and, ominously, the Armed Forces) adding to the attractions. The first Indian restaurant ever to operate in Scotland initially plied its trade there.

An outstanding feature was the Exhibition Tower, built by the architect Thomas S. Tait. It scaled 300 feet and stood on the summit of Bellahouston Hill, itself 170 feet high, dominating the whole landscape and visible from 100 miles away. It was intended to be a permanent landmark but – here is the first of the ironies – its very excellence was its undoing because, when war broke out less than a year after the Exhibition closed, it had to be demolished as it would have served as an infallible guide for German bombers. The Exhibition lasted for six months and, despite appalling weather throughout, it attracted thirteen million visitors. On 29 October 1938, 364,000 people bade it a last farewell. The Empire Exhibition was over; few of the thirteen million who visited (or of the many more millions who didn't) had any inkling that the same would soon be true of the Empire it had celebrated.

A celebration of Empire, but exactly what was being celebrated, and what exactly did 'Empire' in this particular instance mean? I shall produce only one witness but his testimony is so singular, so striking, so arresting in the context in which it is given that it makes, in my view, any additional argument superfluous.

There is a remarkable passage in John Henry Newman [5] where he defends the old, well-established system of education at the University of Oxford – the system in which he himself had been nurtured – against the criticisms of utilitarian modernisers. Newman is very far from asserting that the old system is perfect. What he does declare unequivocally is its superiority to the proposed alternative as a means of moulding character and of promoting a bond of fellowship and union among its beneficiaries.

Education, he protests, is much more than a passive reception of facts, a cramming together of scraps and details in order to pass an examination after which these can be disgorged in disgust or simply forgotten. Education aims at producing a shared experience of life and thought among the young men brought together in a community to be shaped by it; and, judged by that single, paramount criterion, the traditional Oxford system, its defects notwithstanding, must (he argued) be hailed as a great success. True education stays with you throughout life; it is not simply a ladder that you kick away as you rise to higher and better things. Newman concludes that, despite shortcomings, it 'can boast of a succession of heroes and statesmen, of literary men and philosophers, of men conspicuous for great natural virtues, for habits of business, for knowledge of life, for practical judgement, for cultivated tastes, for accomplishments, who have made England what it is – able to subdue the earth, able to domineer over Catholics'.

I still remember the shock I experienced when I first read these concluding words. In my surprise I read them again to make sure that my eyes were not playing some trick on me. But no, this was indeed what Newman had written. My next reaction was to think that it must be satire, the more so since they were addressed to a Catholic audience in Dublin in 1852, when he was about to take up the office of rector in the new Irish Catholic University of Dublin. The people to whom he spoke knew all too well what it meant to be

---

[5] John Henry Newman, English churchman, theologian, Anglican vicar, was a leading member of the Oxford Movement (which tried to defend traditional Anglican orthodoxy against the criticisms of Anglican liberals, and liberals in general). In 1845 he became a Catholic and was made a cardinal in 1879. The quotation is from his work *The Scope and Nature of University Education* (1852).

domineered over by English Protestants. Surely Newman would not have chosen such a venue and such an audience for a straightforward encomium of the great Protestant empire?

Yet, the context compels us to conclude that Newman spoke as he did in absolute seriousness. Far from rebuking Oxford for training-up men able to subdue the earth and subjugate Catholics, he was congratulating her upon her highest achievement. But that Newman of all people should do this – Newman who had been so vilified and who had paid so dearly for his own conversion to the faith which it was his nation's destiny to defeat – this is the remarkable fact to which I wish to draw attention. This is how Newman – not, I repeat, in reproof or condemnation – saw the Empire and it was neither an absurd nor outlandish assessment. It was an anti-Catholic empire and Newman tells us so, not in the tone of one revealing a great discovery but of one casually communicating an obvious, every-day truth. It was a competition celebrating the achievements of this Empire that Celtic were about to enter and win.

This is where the element of irony permeating Celtic's Empire Exhibition Trophy triumph first manifests itself. However trivial in the greater scheme of things, it is without question ironical that a com-petition designed and staged to present the visual proofs of England's imperial greatness should be won by the *one* club in the United Kingdom associated with that despised and defeated faith, that reli-gion which it was England's historical mission to vanquish. There is, of course, the much greater irony in the fact that the celebration of this greatness should have been staged at precisely that historical moment when it was about to crumble and disappear forever.

In 1938 few could have foreseen the future in both politics and football alike. The British Empire still seemed secure and enduring, as did Britain's unchallenged superiority in the realm of football. The Empire Exhibition tournament – and in a significant difference from the Coronation Cup of 1953 – was in all but name a world championship for clubs, the winners of which could claim plausibly to be the best team on the planet. [6] Yet, below the surface, the seeds

---

[6] Editor's footnote. The Mitropa Cup, competed for annually between the wars by clubs from Central Europe such as Austria, Hungary, Czechoslovakia and Italy, could claim an equal pre-eminence.

of decline for both empires – politics and football alike – were sown and their days were numbered. When the fall came for each, it was both precipitous and shocking. Here, as in so much else, the second world war was a watershed. In 1948, only ten years after Celtic had lifted the trophy celebrating Empire, the Labour government in London was acknowledging Jawaharlal Nehru as the first prime minister of an independent India; in 1954 England were being humiliated 6–3 by the Hungarians at Wembley, and later by 7–1 in Budapest. The two dominations had been shattered. Within twenty years of the war's end, the British Empire in Africa and Asia had all but disappeared, while the Latin teams of Europe (Spain, Portugal and Italy) were competing with each other for the European club championship; a monopoly that was to last until the epoch-making breakthrough by Celtic in 1967. The Empire Exhibition might so easily have been the first step to an annual British championship. Instead, the Europeans shouldered Britain aside and the consequence is the prestigious European club championship of our own day, the winner of which may with some justification claim to be the best team in the world.

Looking back, we can identify the Empire Exhibition as the last hurrah, the last great display of British imperialism in politics and football alike, before its collapse and disintegration. The sun was setting after all despite the long, proud boast that it would not and could not do so. Nothing of this was anticipated when, on 25 May 1938, Celtic took the field against Sunderland (the 'Bank of England' club) at Ibrox Park before a crowd of 54,000 in the opening game of the Empire Exhibition tournament. All of the ties, incidentally, were played at Ibrox as the ground closest to Bellahouston Park. The result was a no-scoring draw, a creditable performance by Celtic, considering that Delaney and Carruth, the right-wing pairing, were both carried off injured and unable to continue; in those days substitutes were simply not allowed. Twenty-four hours later, restored to their full complement, and with Matt Lynch and Malcolm MacDonald coming in for the injured pair, Celtic overcame Sunderland by 3–1. Johnny Crum, McGrory's successor, scored once and John Divers twice before a much reduced crowd of 20,000, an attendance attributable in some degree to the unseasonably bad weather and frequent showers that day.

The Scottish teams (with the exception of Rangers who fell by 2–0 to the impressive Everton side) were successful, Aberdeen comprehensively trouncing Chelsea by 4–0 and Hearts rather luckily scrambling through against Brentford by 1–0. In the semi-finals Everton defeated Aberdeen 3–2, while Celtic narrowly edged out Hearts 1–0, the goal scored by Crum in the sixty-fifth minute before a crowd of 45,403.

And so the stage was set for a Battle of Britain clash between the original favourites, Celtic, and the new favourites, Everton. On 10 June 1938 the teams met in front of an attendance of 82,000. Everton were a galaxy of international stars, composed of seven English internationalists, two Irish, one Welsh; their one Scottish cap, Torry Gillick, [7] was missing through injury sustained in the semi-final. Leading the line was the great Tommy Lawton, about to become the scourge of Scottish defences for years to come.

The Celtic side, rated by some reputable judges as one of the greatest in the club's history, was made up of a litany of names that still trip off the tongue: Kennaway; Hogg and Morrison; Geatons, Lyon and Paterson; Delaney and MacDonald; Crum; Divers and Murphy. [8] The pundits of the day paid especial tribute to the inventiveness of Celtic's attacking play. Sir Robert Kelly later declared that Celtic (pioneers here, as in so much else) were the first British club – indeed the first club ever – to develop a constantly interchanging forward line in which any one of the five forwards might suddenly appear in the striking centre-forward position. More remarkable still, this was not the product of coaching or pre-match preparation, but resulted from a kind of telepathy, of intuitive understanding and inspired improvisation arising spontaneously from the players themselves. But the defence was organized – marshalled by the captain Willie Lyon and a rare Englishman in Scotland – and formed a very solid group in front of Joe Kennaway, who had replaced the tragic John Thomson.

---

[7] Torry Gillick, a most accomplished inside right, was soon to join Rangers and become a thorn in Celtic's side throughout the wartime seasons and beyond.

[8] Editor's footnote. I am delighted to note that Professor Reilly has listed the team in the traditional 2–3–5 formation, comprising two full backs, three half backs, and five forwards.

Individually, Everton were a match for the Scottish champions but, in terms of teamwork, Celtic held the upper hand. It was a match of much fine football which ended after ninety minutes with no scoring, but in the seventh minute of extra time Johnny Crum scored the only and decisive goal. His ensuing jig of jubilation behind the goal before the ecstatic spectators was unprecedented in those days and called down the puritanical disapproval of the newspaper reporters covering the game. Otherwise, the reaction to Celtic's victory was unstintingly generous, one newspaper proclaiming: 'They're fed up winning cups; now they're winning towers!' – an allusion to the fact that the victorious team received from the Earl of Elgin at the end of the match a replica in silver of the Tower of Empire. Each of the winning players was presented with a silver miniature of the trophy, with the runners-up receiving a plate one. Kenneth Wolstenholme, much later to become a well-known English commentator, graphically described his experience of the final and his 'first taste of Scottish fervour . . . especially the brand turned on by the Celtic fans. They waved their banners, they waved their flags, and they sang their revolutionary songs and their special war-cry of 'The Dear Little Shamrock'.'

Many in Scotland might have objected to the singing of this song as evidence of 'Scottish' fervour. Certainly, it could not have endeared the singers to those powerful forces within Scottish society who had vociferously deplored the presence of these 'aliens' within the land and who had campaigned strenuously for their removal by persuasion if possible, by compulsion if necessary. I have already pointed to the irony of a so-called 'Catholic' team winning a competition designed to showcase the achievements of an Empire whose historical mission was to secure the triumph of Protestantism over the Catholic powers of continental Europe. A more parochial irony was that the so-called 'Irish' team, supported in the main by the descendants of the Famine immigrants, should triumph in a Scotland that had recently been the stage for a vigorous, sometimes virulent, campaign, waged not by lumpenproletariat demagogues but by some of the most distinguished members of the Scottish Establishment to cleanse these intruders from the land.

The final irony has to do with the aftermath of this outstanding football success. The wonderful 'jubilee team', so deservedly praised at the time, was to last no longer than the tower that Thomas Tait built to stand for hundreds of years. Everyone recognises that the outbreak of the war, less than a year after the closing ceremony of the Empire Exhibition, was directly responsible for the levelling of the tower but there is still debate as to how far the war was similarly to blame for the woes that were soon to lay low Celtic. Certainly, from a Celtic perspective, the prospect immediately following the Exhibition triumph seemed auspicious. On 16 June 1938, only six days after that victory, a banquet was held in Glasgow's Grosvenor Restaurant to celebrate the club's golden jubilee. Present were two hundred guests, including representatives of the SFA and of Scottish league clubs, the lord provost and senior council officials, and all Celtic's players, past and present. On display too were the trophies: the league championship, the Exhibition Cup of 1901, the newly acquired Empire Exhibition Trophy, plus the silver shield presented by the SFA to commemorate the six successive championships won between 1904/05 and 1909/10. The now legendary manager, William Maley, whose association with Celtic was co-terminous with the fifty years of their existence, was presented with a cheque for 2,500 guineas, fifty for each year of his service. Congratulatory speeches flowed from all quarters; a glittering future seemed assured.

But below the surface all was not well. The players were unhappy. A bonus, allegedly promised by a director for their exploits in the jubilee year, remained unpaid; the captain, Willie Lyon, approached the manager on behalf of his teammates in order to have the promise made good. The reception he got was brutal; he was told to seek out the director in question and get the money from him personally. (This curiously anticipates the incident in the 1980s when the club chairman laughingly commented that, if the manager wanted to get new players, he should buy them from his own pocket.) It is easy to believe that the disgruntled Celtic players entered season 1938/39 in a state of considerably low morale. Despite a promising start, during which Hearts were crushed 5–1 at Tynecastle and Rangers 6–2 at Celtic Park, the team began to falter. Then, in April 1939, playing against Arbroath, Jimmy Delaney was struck with disaster when he broke his arm in two places, an injury that was to keep him sidelined for twenty-seven months. In a season described by Maley as 'one of the most disappointing, if not the most disappointing, in our fifty-one years of existence', the league and cups were all lost.

Clearly, the disappointment was all the greater because of the huge expectations that everyone had invested in one of the most promisingly great teams in the club's history. To say that the side never achieved its full potential would be to commit the grossest flattery; the truth is that, after 1938, it never achieved anything at all. So much is generally agreed. It is in attempting to uncover the reasons for this surprising, abysmal failure that we not only meet with controversy but unearth the last and most crowning irony of all.

In discussing this decline it is impossible to avoid referring to the outbreak of war. The shadow of major conflict was already hanging over Europe even while Celtic were defeating Everton in the 1938 final. The Exhibition itself was designed to be a microcosm of Empire, an enclave of sanity and order in a Europe visibly lurching towards catastrophe. Among its many pavilions Bellahouston contained two, one dedicated to Peace and another to the Armed Services. Most informed observers, reluctantly sensing that the future lay with the latter pavilion, had resigned themselves pessimistically to the inevitability of war.

In 1939, Maley, in a heartfelt plea to Old Firm supporters not to succumb to the upsurge in violence that was increasingly disfiguring the fixture, begged them 'to keep your muscles and sinews for the greater fight which may be with us all sooner than we expect'. On 3 September 1939 that 'greater fight' erupted and, among its more trivial repercussions, was its significant impact upon football in general and upon Scottish football in particular.

There are sharply divergent views explaining the very different fortunes of Celtic and Rangers following the Empire Exhibition tournament. In 1938, Rangers were in decline after suffering a season of failure; by contrast, Celtic – the league champions – seemed set for a period of sustained success. Instead, Celtic were about to descend into one of the blackest, most barren periods in their history . . . while their great rivals were laying claim to a position of dominance that was to last throughout the war and for many seasons afterwards. No one disputes that the outbreak of war was chronologically crucial as a marker in the fall of one team and the rise in the other. Disagreement arises as to why this should have been so.

Gerry McNee, in what purports to be an official history of Celtic,[9] written presumably with the support and advice of Celtic directors, tells a tale of discrimination and favouritism. On this reading, the great jubilee team broke up because its players were summoned to serve in the armed forces while their counterparts at Ibrox were provided with reserved occupations on the Clyde, remaining at home to establish a football supremacy that was to endure for a generation and more. McNee is nothing if not forthright in presenting his case:

> No team in Scotland had changed less in personnel during the war than the Ibrox men, most of whose players managed to find jobs in the shipyards. Celtic's players had not been so fortunate for the kind of reasons that only the West of Scotland – and Northern Ireland – can produce.

Fortune, clearly, had nothing to do with it. Sir Robert Kelly takes a predictably similar line: 'The Second World War affected Celtic more than many other clubs.' No need to add that among these many other less-affected clubs were the great rivals, Rangers. But Kelly's remark, while undoubtedly true, does not in itself call a halt to further discussion. Are Celtic to be regarded as the completely blameless victims of unfair treatment or, in addition to this, were they at least partly complicit in their own misfortunes?

Certainly, McNee has a strong *prima facie* case to present. I can vouch from personal experience that this was the prevalent view among Celtic supporters on Clydeside at that time. The gifted Willie Thornton of Rangers, decorated for gallantry in the war, was the only high-profile Ibrox player to be called to the colours, whereas in season 1945/46 – right at the war's end – as many as thirteen players were still absent from Parkhead on armed service, including the team skipper, Willie Lyon, now an army captain and recipient of the Military Cross for gallantry. Before the start of season

---

[9] See Gerald McNee, *The Story of Celtic: An Official History 1888–1978.*

1942/43 Willie Corbett – Celtic's best centre-half since Lyon and being groomed as his successor – was called up to the Navy, and only six players from the pre-war side were left at Parkhead. The war (so runs the argument) made it so difficult for Celtic to field a team that they were forced to turn to youngsters who had only weeks before been playing at Boys' Guild level. Jimmy Delaney is on record as saying that he regularly had to be introduced to whichever new youngster had turned up to partner him on the right wing. Extensive changes in personnel and position had to be made from one Saturday to the next, and this at a time when their great rivals had the immense advantage of consistently sending out a settled and experienced team.

Tom Campbell and Pat Woods, in their authoritative history of Celtic (*The Glory and the Dream*), take a significantly different view. For them, the foregoing account smacks too much of special pleading, ignoring as it so conveniently does the maladministration of the Celtic directors in contributing to the catastrophic decline in the club's fortunes. At the Grosvenor dinner in 1938, Tom White, Celtic's chairman, had declared that 'the name of Maley is synonymous with the Celtic club and almost with the name of soccer'. But, in February 1940, Maley was dismissed. There followed the perverse and foolish decision to reject out of hand the advances of would-be 'guest players' during the war years – that is to say, players from English clubs serving in the armed forces who found themselves stationed north of the border and free to play for a team of their choice. In consequence, when the redoubtable Matt Busby of Manchester City turned up at Celtic Park eager to perform in Celtic's colours, he was curtly advised that his services were not required – and this despite the plea of Maley's successor, Jimmy McStay, to grab this piece of good fortune. Busby promptly caught a train to Edinburgh, joined Hibernian, and was largely instrumental in helping to mould them into a team capable of challenging the domination of Rangers. (McNee, to his credit, also calls attention to this blunder.) Even worse, star players such as Crum and Divers – who had scored between them all of Celtic's goals in the Empire Exhibition tournament – were transferred to Morton without the slightest attempt at finding anything resembling equivalent replacements.

Football throughout Britain had shrunk during the war. There were travel restrictions caused by a shortage of petrol. Fear of bombing raids led to a drastic limitation on the size of crowds permitted at football grounds. League competitions were reorganized on a severely restricted regional basis. Some English clubs simply closed down, and stopped playing altogether. Celtic did not go to this extreme, but 'unlike other clubs, notably Rangers, Celtic did not take wartime football too seriously. They made little effort to attract big-time guests and went into a period of lethargy from which it subsequently proved difficult to emerge.' They did not stop playing football but they did, in effect, stop playing competitive football, to the extent that some of their more disgruntled, humiliated supporters asked that they should at least change their name until such time as they were once again prepared to mount a serious challenge for honours. Teams once proud merely to share the same field with these giants were now beginning to feel ashamed when they failed to beat them. The best team on earth in 1938 had within a few short years become a jest and a byword within Scotland.

All of this is doubtless true. The version of events that would have us see Celtic as the wronged innocents, the blameless butts of discrimination and prejudice, is altogether too exculpatory, too blind or forgiving to the very serious faults within the Celtic board in the years following the Exhibition Trophy triumph. The wartime doldrums were not simply ascribable to the myth that the Celtic team went to fight for king and country while the Rangers players stayed at home. This is altogether too simplistic and one-sided; the war should not be used as a screen behind which gross managerial shortcomings are concealed. Nevertheless, even after allowing in full for the sheer ineptitude of what was euphemistically called 'the Celtic management', enough evidence remains to support allegations of selective and uneven-handed treatment. It is not a question of accusing Rangers of any misconduct in their strenuous and successful efforts to keep as many of their players as possible at home in reserved occupations during the course of the conflict; it is simply a matter of recording that this is precisely what they did. That the Rangers players on the whole stayed at home is an indisputable fact; that half of the myth, at least, is certainly true. The Thirties, as has been shown, were a period in which the 'No-Catholic-need-apply' sign was raised, not only over Ibrox stadium but also over many shipyards and foundries throughout Scotland. It is undeniable that Rangers exploited their considerable influence in these industries to secure exemption for their players from service in the armed forces. They succeeded to such an extent that no other Scottish team was so unaffected by the outbreak of war in 1939 as Rangers.

I am convinced that this is what happened, and I have one piece of hard, anecdotal family evidence to back it up. During the war my father and two of my older brothers were employed as insulating engineers on the Clyde. One of these brothers, himself a Junior player of some ability, had assigned to him as a labourer the young and talented Jimmy Duncanson, at that time an inside left with Rangers and who went on to become a regular member of the wartime Scottish international side. At the lunch-time break the workers would have a kick-about in which Duncanson would join in along with the rest.

Did Celtic ever make comparable efforts to obtain exemption for their personnel? I do not know. Had they done so, would they have been as successful as their Ibrox rivals? I very much doubt it, given the atmosphere of discrimination that pervaded Scottish heavy industry throughout the whole inter-war period and especially the dark decade that was the Thirties. All we do know for certain is that the war came – that 'greater fight' that Maley had predicted – that Orange parades and other sectarian demonstrations were suspended 'for the duration', that the vilification of religious foes at home was officially frowned upon while the enemy abroad was still undefeated, and that Celtic and Rangers supporters alike – together with everyone else – went off to fight alongside (instead of against) each other.

We know too that the wonderful Celtic side of 1938 that had promised so much broke up in large measure because of the war, while Rangers, their great rivals, gained a stranglehold upon Scottish football from 1940 to 1946 despite the war.

It is the last, the crowning and consummate irony. The players who were supported by the so-called disloyal and dissident Irish Catholic republicans went off to the war, while the players who were supported by the self-proclaimed, Crown-loving, Union-Jack bedecked loyalists stayed at home.

It was a fitting conclusion to perhaps the most ironical period in modern Scottish history.

Comments

The award for winning the tournament was a silver miniature of the Tait Tower which was the feature of the Empire Exhibition at Bellahouston Park, Glasgow in 1938. Sadly, the original art deco masterpiece was dismantled soon afterwards 'for strategic reasons', they said. Had Celtic the same excuse for dismantling the 'best of the best' before the next season was out?

John Cairney

The decline had already set in, and it is hard to figure out how long that Celtic side might have stayed at the top. Maley was old by then and not really interested in signing new players; he was more concerned about selling them, I think. The second world war served as an escape clause to hide Celtic's subsequent inadequacies – but some were self-inflicted.

Bob Crampsey

It was a wonderful achievement but was it such a great surprise? After all, Celtic were the Scottish champions – and would go on to beat Rangers 6–2 at Celtic Park a couple of months later at the start of the next season.

Tony Griffin

Along with the Lisbon Lions of 1967 and the all-conquering team that won six league championships in a row between 1904 and 1910, this side must have been the greatest in Celtic's history. While 1938 was a marvellous year for Celtic, it would anticipate and mirror the so-called centennial season (1988). The Empire Exhibition Trophy triumph proved that Celtic were the best team in Britain and that was the only thing 'the Faithful' could cherish during the dreadful years to come. During the second world war, Scottish troops in the African desert and Italian campaigns could establish bragging rights over their English colleagues by referring to this triumph.

David Potter

As a young schoolboy I used to make a regular income at family gatherings by reciting the Celtic side that won the Empire Exhibition Trophy. Delighted uncles would press sixpences and shillings on me for this feat of memory. How depressing that the side was allowed to break up so soon afterwards!

This triumph was typically Celtic. When a 'one-off' trophy is up for grabs, nip down to the bookies and put every penny you can muster on The Bhoys coming up trumps. Celtic have had a long love affair with such tournaments. Like the Coronation Cup, the Empire Exhibition came after years of Rangers domination in the Old Firm rivalry. Despite a couple of title wins, Celtic were very much in the shadow of the Ibrox men during the inter-war period and this breakthrough must have seemed like an aberration. How appropriate that the trophy was a miniature of the Exhibition's landmark – Tait's Tower – which, when lit up at night, was a beacon in the encircling gloom. Winning the trophy was for Celtic the metaphorical glimmer of hope for the future, an expectation that would soon be extinguished by the onset of war – and the club's subsequent mismanagement.

Pat Woods

4

THE SAME OLD STORY . . .

Tom Campbell

Old Firm clashes are essentially dramatic and the Victory Cup semi-final in 1946 for Glaswegians – conditioned to twice-weekly visits to the picture houses – was another 'blockbuster' and the list of characters was a familiar one.

Playing a leading role would be the referee – a certain M. C. Dale. He had arrived on the SFA list in 1936 and, accordingly, was not an inexperienced official in over his head. He had had ten years as a senior referee, admittedly most of which were wartime seasons when the standards of refereeing had plummeted. In fact, Mr Dale had contributed notably to the downward spiral with some breathtakingly erratic performances. On 3 December 1938 he had been nominally in charge of the Celtic versus Hibernian league fixture at Celtic Park, won 5–4 by Celtic, and infuriated both sides and the spectators with his inconsistency; at the end, Hibernian had the greater cause for complaint because Celtic's winning goal scored by Frank Murphy only three minutes from time was blatantly offside.

During the 'unofficial' seasons throughout the second world war everybody complained about the standard of refereeing. Well, almost everybody with the exception of Rangers who were the main beneficiaries of refereeing decisions. Ironically, they had little need of help from the officials because the Ibrox men were by far the best – and most settled – team in the country; so much so, that they could afford to have a reserve team participate in the North-Eastern league competing with the likes of Aberdeen and Dundee United. But with a shortage of qualified referees, the SFA was forced to lower its standards and to recruit from a broader base; inevitably, referees known to be partial to Rangers from boyhood were entrusted with the job of refereeing the Ibrox club and the accusations of favouritism were widespread. These accusations did not come just from Celtic; several clubs felt hard-done by in fixtures with the Light Blues.

Things had got so bad that mainstream sports journalists were commenting openly on the situation. W. C. Gallagher of the *Daily Record*, writing under the pseudonym of 'Waverley', was a highly respected and veteran writer on football. After one particularly shambolic performance by Mr Dale in a league match between Rangers and St Mirren at Ibrox on 21 September 1940 his column was headlined: 'We Must Not Have Such Refereeing!'

Among the things that had incensed the reporter was Mr Dale's decision to deny St Mirren a penalty kick:

> When Stead was being attended to, I wrote in my notebook, 'St Mirren awarded a penalty kick seventeen minutes after the interval.' Then I looked up and I could hardly believe my eyes – Referee Dale was signalling for a free kick inches outside the eighteen-yard box. For a moment I thought that either Dale or myself had gone crackers. It was so clear-cut, so obvious, that in my opinion there is absolutely no excuse whatever for the referee.

Later in the match Rangers were awarded a penalty kick, and this was a correct decision but the St Mirren players protested strongly after Alec Venters converted it on the grounds that Gillick had encroached so far into the area that their goalkeeper claimed that he was not sure which Ranger was going to take the kick. In the furore Craven of St Mirren was ordered off for his protests, and the journalist highlighted this incident in his account of the match:

> Two paramount errors in one game! Dale in the closing half hour appeared to have lost control of the game and it was a good thing that the St Mirren players kept their heads. They almost lost them

when Craven was ordered off and nearly all his mates wanted to join him in the march to the pavilion. If officialdom fails to make an inquiry, officialdom is letting down football!

In the 1940s newspapers did not launch campaigns against referees, choosing to believe, perhaps optimistically, that doubtful decisions eventually even themselves out. If anything, the journalists were on the side of the football establishment and considered that criticism should be constructive rather than damning. What was behind this journalist's attack? – and remember that he was one of the most respected in the country. Was he just fed up to the teeth with Dale's incompetence? Or his erratic, inconsistent decision-making? Or was there something else?

M. C. Dale (Glasgow) was of average height, if not exactly on the small side; an ordinary man thrust into a limelight that oddly he seemed to relish. Certainly he was not the tall, square-jawed, laconic sheriff of the Westerns that Glasgow filmgoers lapped up. Nobody would mistake him for a John Wayne, Randolph Scott, Joel McCrae or even a Glenn Ford. Rather than a man exuding quiet authority, he was yet another technocrat promoted beyond competence and, characteristic of the type, he tried to bluster his way through awkward moments. He exhibited the inconsistency of the weak, inevitably overdoing things on occasion and overreacting to circumstances. Common sense was not his forte, nor was fairness apparently. Less of an M. C., he was more a Lord of Misrule.

Ask the St Mirren players at Ibrox Park on 21 September 1940 who were on the brink of walking off the pitch in disgust. Ask the Celtic players at Hampden Park on 5 June 1946 in the replay of the Victory Cup semi-final who similarly came within seconds of marching off.

No, he was a bureaucrat with a whistle, a minor official pumped up with a sense of his own importance, a referee who – even in wartime – was never entrusted with the handling of a major event such as a cup final nor one of the frequent 'unofficial' international matches. Mr Dale – when he was not on the football pitch – had a quietly useful war, working as a plater in the Clydeside shipyards in a reserved occupation. It was a legitimate wartime activity but the shipyards were 'no-go' zones for Catholics, entry being denied by the Ulster-influenced groups who controlled things with an iron grip. This was the same crowd, located mainly in Govan and employed at the Belfast-owned Harland & Wolff, who had predominantly supported Rangers since their migration to Scotland from the 1920s on.

The Celtic players at Hampden Park that June night were also recognisable, made familiar as screen stereotypes. At first glance Jimmy Mallan, Celtic's full back, looked like a matinee idol with his dark, oiled hair and deep tan; and in the 1940s it would have been a natural tan. One noted football critic felt that he resembled Tyrone Power, the dashing Hollywood leading man, and – a boy at the time – he almost suspected that after games Mallan would emerge somewhere in Glasgow as Zorro, 'the Masked Swordsman'. He was that handsome.

And yet there always was a question that lurked in the mind. In a film he would be cast as 'the troubled youth'; the sort who is released from prison on probation and who tries to keep out of trouble despite returning to the old neighbourhood and resuming contact with his old pals. James Dean with muscles. Trouble waiting to happen. His main problem lay in controlling his temper; even his teammates were reluctant to contest a ball with him at training as the session would frequently be abandoned while Mallan and another player – usually a reluctant one – would end up fighting. In fact, earlier that season he had been ordered off at Love Street for striking an opponent and with little or no provocation. The other Celtic players used to complain bitterly about his quick temper. 'He always appeared to be itching for a fight,' one complained. 'You learned to leave him alone. He had a temper and he was handy with his fists – I think he might have been an amateur boxer as well. But we learned to steer clear of him.'

Jimmy Mallan was a regular in Celtic teams but not entirely a fixture, his temperament remaining suspect despite his impressive physique. Insecure, often surly, quick to respond to perceived threats, easy to goad into rashness: Jimmy Mallan needed an authoritative and mature referee to handle him. Instead, he got Mr M. C. Dale (Glasgow).

Matt Lynch was yet another archetypal Celtic player: red-haired and a fierce, relentless competitor; in modern parlance, he would be described as 'a ball-winner' but he could play too either as a right half or as an occasional outside right. He was a man who played for the jersey – as long as it was green and white. Like Mallan, he had been in trouble with the Scottish 'part-time' referees during the wartime seasons; he had been ordered off against Rangers at Ibrox on New Year's Day 1943, an event that contributed to Celtic's humiliating 8–1 defeat.

But, according to most reports, Lynch had turned over a new leaf. As a rare university graduate in Scottish football – and a player nearing the end of his career – he was starting to prepare for life after football and was considering entering teaching. More settled, more experienced, he was enjoying his football but he could not have been pleased about becoming involved in the machinations of Mr M. C. Dale (Glasgow).

George Paterson was another recognisable Scottish type: a clean-living, well-spoken and respectable young man, an officer in the Boys' Brigade and a regular churchgoer. On the field, he had never been in trouble with referees despite his wholehearted approach to the game. Intelligent, hard-working, committed – he had won several caps for Scotland during the war when on leave from his active service in the Royal Navy – George Paterson was a credit to the sport. A natural leader, he had assumed Celtic's captaincy from Bobby Hogg and his influence on younger and less experienced colleagues was generally a calming one . . . but he was a man whose innate sense of fair play and patience would be tested to the limits by the quirkiness and pettiness of Mr M. C. Dale (Glasgow).

* * *

The calendar year 1946 had begun with a decree from Emperor Hirohito of Japan announcing that he was not a god and that his subjects were not divinely destined to rule the world. This may have been a shock to his subjects although it was a scarcely surprising reaction to the dropping of the atomic bombs on Hiroshima and Nagasaki.

In Scotland, however, things were unchanging as Rangers continued to dominate the domestic scene, helped on occasion by dubious refereeing decisions.

The end of the war may have been a relief to millions but it served only to increase the day-to-day misery of ordinary people on a global scale; statesmen and organisations alike started to warn about food shortages and the prospects of famine unless supplies and distribution practices were not improved.

The Empire – and it still was an empire in those days – rallied to help Britain: on 6 January Australia promised to increase shipments of foodstuffs up to one million tons consisting of 1.5 million bushels of apples, one million cases of canned fruit, 275,000 tons of frozen canned meat, 60,000 tons of butter, 12,000 tons of cheese and 380 million eggs; on 17 February enough tea to brew one billion cups arrived from Ceylon; on 2 May four million gallons of rum left Kingston, Jamaica for Britain; on 20 May food shipments from Canada arrived at Liverpool: eleven million shell eggs, 1,530 tons of bacon and sixty-seven tons of dried eggs; on 5 July Canada prepared to ship 4.5 million tons of grain to Britain, the rest of the Empire and Europe to ease fears of starvation.

The threat of starvation and famine on a global scale was real and the more affluent countries – or those least affected internally by the war – moved to help. The United States announced plans to cut down on flour consumption to divert food to other parts of the world; similarly Canada and Australia imposed rationing on basic foodstuffs as part of their contribution.

But Britain still had to tighten belts; on 6 March the Ministry of Food actually issued a recipe for 'squirrel pie', and bread rationing was due to start in mid-July.

Other snippets of information indicative of those grim times were released: on 4 January the government revealed that more than 10,000 evacuated children would not be able to return home because they were now orphans and that they would remain in care; on 7 June the War Office warned holidaymakers and ramblers that 800,000 tons of ammunition and explosives were still lying in fields and country lanes and estimated it would take three years to render the countryside safe again.

On 8 July Margaret Hilda Roberts of Somerville College was elected president of Oxford University Conservatives; and on the following day Australia would announce a new immigration policy because 90,000 Britons had already applied to seek a new life there.

The local newspapers in Scotland on 5 June 1946 – the day of the semi-final replay – gave some indication of the times: in Glasgow the night before housewives had started queuing outside bakers' shops for bread in anticipation of the Victory Day celebrations on the Saturday, and the newspapers featured photographs of them sleeping on the pavements with only the comfort of pillowcases and blankets; Airborne, a 50–1 outsider, won the Derby at Epsom, a fact that encouraged Celtic supporters to anticipate another upset at Hampden Park.

The main source of entertainment, apart from the football, was the cinema and Glaswegians flocked there regularly, usually more than once a week; the dedicated filmgoer could go to his or her 'local' twice a week, the programme changing in midweek. The more dedicated could visit other picture houses across the city in search of entertainment or diversion; within the city centre there were the Bedford, the Coliseum, the Cosmo, Cranston's, Green's Playhouse, La Scala, the New Savoy, the Paramount, the Picture House, the Regal and the Regency. Similarly Glasgow was well served with theatres: the Alhambra, the Empire, the Empress, the King's, the Metropole, the Pavilion, the Princess's, the Royal, the Queen's. That coming weekend Glaswegians had a wide variety of entertainment to chose from: at the Regal cinema in Sauchiehall Street they could watch *Saratoga Trunk*, a melodrama starring Ingrid Bergman as 'a Creole beauty from the wrong side of the tracks, bent on achieving a fortune' and Gary Cooper as 'a rough-edged Texas millionaire'. Green's Playhouse in Renfield Street was showing *The Seventh Veil*, billed as a psychological Gothic romance' starring Ann Todd as 'a beautiful young pianist' and James Mason as 'her tyrannical guardian'. At the King's Theatre near Charing Cross, Harry Gordon – the self-styled 'Laird o' Inversnecky', a mythical village in the north-east of Scotland – was appearing in *The Half-Past Eight Show*, modestly described as 'Glasgow's Brightest Song-and-Dance Show'. You could get 'a night's entertainment' at the Barrowland Ballroom in the Gallowgate, but even cheaper was the open-air dancing from 8 to 10 p.m. in Kelvingrove Park: 1s. 6d. admission or 1s. for servicemen and women in uniform and only 4d. for spectators.

Back to the Victory Cup. It was a competition set up in some haste by the SFA to celebrate the end of the war, 8 June being designated as Victory Day. Both members of the Old Firm had advanced comfortably enough to the semi-final stage. Celtic had disposed of St Johnstone on a 13–2 aggregate, Queen of the South by 3–0 and Raith Rovers by 2–0; Rangers had eliminated Stenhousemuir by an aggregate of 8–2, Airdrie by 4–0 and Falkirk in a replay by 2–0 after a 1–1 draw.[1]

Rangers were naturally the favourites; the strongest side in the country, they had just strengthened their team by signing Bobby Brown (Scotland's wartime goalkeeper) from Queen's Park and Sammy Cox (a hard-hitting full back from Dundee). For the first match on the Saturday, Celtic were in their customary state of turmoil. Alan Breck, writing in the Glasgow *Evening Times*, noted that only half an hour before the kick-off 'the Parkhead people were in a huddle about their side'. Their most pressing problem was a replacement for Jimmy Delaney, recently and surprisingly transferred to Manchester United after a salary dispute. Celtic had depended on Delaney throughout the wartime seasons and had no recognised match-winning forward to replace him. The general feeling among the support – and in Scottish football generally – was that Celtic remained content to muddle through; this feeling was reinforced by the surprise selection of John Conway, an inside forward just returned from the forces but chosen at outside left.

The same journalist in his match report, filed for his evening newspaper on the day of the semi-final, stated that Celtic 'played surprisingly well in the opening stages' and had forced Bobby Brown into a couple of fine saves. However, as the match progressed, Rangers began to exert pressure and Willie Miller – Celtic's goalkeeper, who had passed a late fitness test – produced three brilliant

---

[1] For some reason the first round was a two-legged affair, but thereafter the competition evolved into a straight knock-out affair. Some of the Old Firm's opponents had only recently started to play competitively after the war.

saves before the interval to keep Celtic in some sort of contention. He dived at Willie Thornton's feet following a Corbett mis-kick and dived to foil the same Ranger's twenty-yard drive a few minutes later, diverting the ball at fingertips for a corner; he also frustrated Rangers' powerful winger, Willie Waddell, with 'a swallow dive' to deflect a long-range shot.

Remarkably, for all Rangers' dominance, Celtic missed the best chance of all to open the scoring when Jimmy Sirrel elected to place the ball past Brown rather than blast home from close range; the ball trickled past the post with the goalkeeper helpless.

Rangers continued to boss things in the second half, Miller saving spectacularly from a Duncanson header and Alan Breck summed up the scoreless match: 'Rangers showed the finer touches but never mastered a Celtic defence which played magnificently. Miller was the hero, and the personality of the tie.'

Celtic: Miller; Hogg, Mallan; Lynch, Corbett, McAuley; Rae, Kiernan, Gallagher, Sirrel, Conway.

Rangers: Brown; Cox, Shaw; Watkins, Young, Symon; Waddell, Gillick, Thornton, Duncanson, Caskie.

Rangers – a much-more settled outfit – were unchanged for the replay on the Wednesday night, but Celtic revamped their forward line to read Sirrel, Kiernan, Gallagher, Paterson, Paton.

A crowd estimated at 65,000 had watched the first game played out in brilliant sunshine, but only 45,000 turned up for the replay on the Wednesday. This match was played under blustery conditions, a strong wind whipping up the corner flags and the sky remained overcast. Rain threatened throughout the match, but held off.

Rangers, having won the toss, kicked off with the wind at their backs, and with the heavier leather ball being used in the 1940s that was considered a real advantage. They controlled the early exchanges and scored after ten minutes; Gillick's deft pass searching out Waddell and the winger's fierce cross-shot found the net off the far post. Celtic were struggling and Gillick – always a most dangerous forward – struck the crossbar with Miller well beaten; Duncanson's close-in shot was miraculously saved by the Celtic keeper just before half time.

In the other goal, Bobby Brown had little to do as Celtic's forwards rarely threatened but Jimmy Sirrel, switched to the right wing, was giving 'Tiger' Shaw, Rangers' captain and left back, a difficult evening. A heavy tackle on the 'experimental winger' badly affected his mobility, however, and Sirrel ended the first half limping badly. The referee had been at his irritating worst with a series of dubious decisions; unfortunately, most of them had favoured one side. As one critic opined: 'Mr Dale officiates with all the objectivity of a detached retina.'

The scenes at half time in the tunnel and in the Celtic dressing room at Hampden must have been memorable. George Paterson – Celtic's captain for this match and a senior player – spoke animatedly to the manager Jimmy McGrory. He was incensed after one particular incident when the referee awarded Rangers a free kick on the edge of Celtic's penalty area; Celtic players objected to the award and, as a flustered Mr Dale stooped to place the ball on the exact spot, he momentarily lost his balance. As the nearest Celtic player, Paterson routinely helped the official to his feet and, possibly still annoyed at the controversial decision, asked him if he was feeling all right; Mr Dale immediately cautioned him for dissent – and it was probably the first time in Paterson's eleven-year career with Celtic that he had ever been cautioned. While being booked, Paterson became aware of a possible explanation of some of the referee's strange decision-making in that first half; Mr Dale's breath smelled of spirits.

This awareness posed a major problem for the players and the clubs – or at least one of them – but even more of a difficulty for the tournament's organisers.

Jimmy McGrory, still relatively inexperienced as Celtic's manager and a most diffident man, listened carefully and puffed on his pipe; other players chipped in vehemently with their observations, and the accusations mounted up, several of them insisting they too had smelt alcohol on Dale's breath. The manager decided to inform his directors of this bizarre development and almost certainly approached Bob Kelly, the youngest member of the board.[2] According to the *Glasgow Herald*'s Cyril Horne, a long-time confidante, Kelly immediately sought out SFA secretary George Graham to voice his concerns.

Graham was perturbed and rightly so: if a referee was unfit to continue, obviously he had to be replaced . . . but what reason could be offered to the public and the press in this particular case? And who would take over at such short notice, especially as few linesmen in the 1940s indicated any interest in advancing to become referees? And would an appeal on the public-address system produce another qualified linesman to replace him?

It was a mess – a potentially embarrassing one – and George Graham knew it! The SFA secretary listened to Kelly, nodding seriously: he would look into the matter right away, and 'something would be done' he assured the Celtic director. Kelly assumed reasonably enough that the response would be immediate – if the suspicions of the Celtic players were correct – but Graham might well have meant that action would be taken after the match with the referee being reprimanded, or possibly demoted.

Whatever action the SFA secretary took, if any, Mr M. C. Dale emerged from the tunnel still in charge of the game, and Celtic players, lining up for the restart, must have approached their task with the enthusiasm of patients awaiting root-canal work from a student dentist. Desmond White, as Celtic's secretary, was present at the game and he summed matters up bluntly: 'If the man was not capable of driving a car, how could he possibly be left in charge of a fraught Celtic–Rangers cup-tie?'

Within minutes of the restart, the Celtic players were outraged as the referee continued with his doubtful officiating; the decisions continued to go Rangers' way and frustration on, and off, the pitch was growing. If Jane Russell in *The Outlaw* had been described as

---

[2] Tom White was the club's chairman but he was elderly and in failing health; in fact, he had little more than a year to live. A long-time director and SFA official, White was an establishment figure and not a man likely to cause waves. It was doubtful, in view of his health, if he was even present at the Victory Cup semi-final replay.

'Mean, Moody and Magnificent', then M. C. Dale surely was on the way to earning the description of 'Petulant, Peevish and Pompous'. Rangers still looked the better team but Celtic, playing with that strong wind at their backs, were putting up a fight despite the first-half injury to Jimmy Sirrel who was now merely 'a passenger'.

As Alan Breck reported in the *Evening Times*: 'In the second half a simmering pettiness came to the surface.' The ingredients for trouble were brewing, and in seventy minutes came the flashpoint. Willie Thornton, making for a cross-ball that was slightly deflected, literally dived to make contact with his head; a Celtic defender, going for the same ball, attempted to clear it with his foot; and Mr Dale awarded a penalty kick. [3] Alan Breck, in the more restrained style of football reporters of those days, commented: 'Generally, it was not considered what one might call a clean-cut offence.' This extremely harsh decision was the last straw for most Celtic players. Most of them surrounded the referee in protest, and George Paterson, clutching the ball and reluctant to hand it over till he was heard as the side's captain, stated his case. Promptly, Mr M. C. Dale ordered him off. [4]

Other Celtic players were equally incensed; Jimmy Mallan had moved into the penalty area and was studiously rubbing away at the penalty spot with his boot. Even while the crowd of players

[3] I actually attended the first match, but missed the replay. For many years I had assumed that the reporting in the newspaper accounts that Thornton had 'dived' indicated that the Rangers player – a man noted for his sportsmanship and always highly respected by Celtic followers – had cheated in order to gain the penalty kick. I am indebted to Patrick Reilly, who was present at the replay, for correcting this impression; Patrick is clear in his recollection that Thornton, always a brave header of the ball, had flung himself forward a few feet above the ground in an attempt to contact the ball.

[4] Unsurprisingly, accounts vary as to what George Paterson actually said to Mr Dale to warrant his dismissal: Matt Lynch suggested that, when Paterson eventually handed the ball over, he said: 'Take it then; it's a bag of wind, just like you!' The *Glasgow Observer* was the only newspaper to attribute words to the Celtic player, and it claimed he said: 'You should keep the ball; you deserve it!' It should be pointed out that cautions were rarely given to players in those days, discipline being much better than nowadays. The earlier caution administered to Paterson may have been a factor in his dismissal, but it is more likely that the referee's decision was provoked only by the penalty-kick incident.

surrounding Dale was starting to break up, Mallan remained at work and ignored the beleaguered official. Eventually, Dale approached him, and Mallan, kicking the ball away, informed the referee: 'There's no penalty spot, referee!' He too was ordered off for his observation and for his action.

The situation was approaching farce as Celtic – already a goal down to the favourites, and with one player crocked, and now with two others sent off, and facing a penalty kick against them – were in no mood to continue. It was clear that some among them were actively advocating leaving the pitch in protest.

Matt Lynch and his immediate opponent Jimmy Duncanson, on the periphery of the unfolding drama, watched Mr Dale's struggle to restore order. Jimmy Duncanson was Rangers' inside left and, in the 1940s when the Ibrox club were much superior to Celtic, a most frequent scorer against the Parkhead men. Immediately recognised by his flaming red hair, Duncanson was a hard-working and intelligent inside forward who had won several representative honours for Scotland during the war years. He was a man who had earned respect from opposing players and supporters alike through his honest play and sportsmanship.

Duncanson of Rangers would earn an honourable mention in Celtic's history, and he continued his conversation with Lynch:

> Lynch: 'That was never a penalty, was it?'
> Duncanson: 'Aye, it was a soft one, but he's given it, Matt.'
> Lynch: 'Well, I'm keeping out of this, Jimmy. I've been in trouble before, and it's just not worth it.'
> Duncanson: 'You're quite right. Just don't get involved.'

However, others did get 'involved'. After George Young had duly converted the penalty kick – some six or seven minutes after the award had been made – one spectator broke out from the Celtic end of Hampden Park and attempted to attack the referee: 'Immediately afterwards a man was seen running across the field towards the referee. He aimed a blow at the official with a bottle, but Mr Dale ducked and avoided injury. By this time several other men had rushed on to the field, but were quickly stopped by the police.' (*The Scotsman*: 6 June 1946)

The howls of anguish, and disbelief, from the Greek Chorus of Celtic supporters had translated itself into the potential of violent action against Mr Dale.

Things did not improve for Celtic when Jackie Gallagher was injured also and spent a few minutes hirpling on the left wing before retiring to the pavilion, and Mr Dale continued to referee the contest in his inimitable manner. Content with a two-goal lead against handicapped opponents, Rangers quietly – and sensibly – played out the remaining fifteen minutes of a semi-final described by the *Glasgow Herald* as 'what had previously been a hard and sporting game'.

It is always a let-down to lose an Old Firm match and this had been a disappointment for Celtic. Those feelings can be overcome – eventually – but the sequel to this defeat was even more shocking for Celtic Football Club.

Given the 'village mentality' of Scottish football, the suspicions of the Celtic players about Mr Dale's condition were an open secret, but no newspaper raised the matter nor alluded to it. Some newspapers did suggest that Celtic had a right to feel aggrieved about some decisions but that was as far as it went. On the surface it looked as if Celtic players – facing defeat against a superior team – simply had lost their discipline and paid the price for it. That was the establishment view and that was the perception that prevailed. Armed with the referee's report – and Cyril Horne stated unequivocally that the referee 'had required assistance' to write out that report after the match – the SFA came down hard on the Celtic players mentioned in that document.

Celtic soon found out that the SFA secretary's assurance that 'something will be done' was a statement worthy of a Delphic oracle. George Paterson – who had never once been in trouble with referees in a lengthy career – was suspended for three months presumably for voicing his dissent while acting as the side's captain. Jimmy Mallan, who had an admitted problem with self-discipline, was also suspended for three months presumably for kicking the ball away. Matt Lynch, who had studiously avoided any involvement in the scenes, was suspended for one month allegedly for 'inciting his team-mates to leave the pitch'. Surprisingly, Bobby Hogg, generally recognised as a peacemaker in the fracas, was censured (apparently as a footnote) as he 'had the responsibility of maintaining discipline amongst his players on the field and should have shown them a better example'.

The Celtic directors were enraged, feeling that they had been double-crossed. They had been assured that 'something will be done' – and this was the result! They felt betrayed but helpless. The actions of four or five spectators in invading the field and attempting to attack the referee had fatally weakened their position; only a few years previously Celtic Park had been closed for a month for less reprehensible behaviour by supporters at Ibrox.

If the matter of Mr Dale's alleged condition were raised and pursued by Celtic, the club could be considered to be 'bringing the game into disrepute', and this was something Celtic did not want to happen. 'Totally finessed!' – that was the opinion of one Celtic director at the time, and absolutely helpless, too, apparently! Their only response in public was to comment acidly on the developments in the next season's handbook: 'History will surely record that indiscretions in refereeing and harshness of punishment have imposed an undeserved penalty on club and players alike.' And for those comments in an official publication, Celtic were later fined by the SFA, and ordered to post warning notices about the behaviour of their supporters.

* * *

For Celtic partisans – and many objective commentators – it was clear evidence that the SFA (and its secretariat in particular) was waging a vicious campaign against the club. George Graham had firmly established his position as the czar of Scottish football and he was an anti-Celtic man. Of that there is no doubt and he acted on the accurate assumption that Celtic, once the leading club in Scotland, had gradually slipped in importance and influence after decades of maladministration by a supine board of directors. They were vulnerable, almost criminally so, and the secretary took full advantage of that situation.

Bob Kelly, youngish and energetic, was emerging as Celtic's spokesman, and he was appalled at the developments; in particular, the suspension of Celtic players for offences that did not constitute violent conduct. He resented the inherent injustice of it all and he would remain suspicious of the motives of the SFA secretary for the rest of his life. Celtic's suspicions – termed as 'paranoia' by critics – were enduring and justified.

And what would have been the role of George Graham in a film; a heartless bank manager foreclosing on farms during the Depression, or an oily politician 'fixer' adroitly charting his course through troubled waters?

In later seasons Kelly would find ample justification for his doubts – as Celtic faced a threat to their very existence in 1952 in a campaign organised and orchestrated by Graham. Despite the campaigns against them throughout the 1950s – nominally in response to misbehaviour by Celtic fans – Celtic eventually managed to regain credibility as a force within Scottish football. Bob Kelly, later president of the SFA, had the personal satisfaction of seeing George Graham ousted – or 'retired' – as the organisation's secretary under a cloud of financial irregularities. Revenge (or justice), no matter how belated, is always acceptable.

The players suffered, especially George Paterson.

Bob Kelly waited several years – until the publication of his autobiography in 1971 – before commenting on Paterson's case:

> The most unfair punishment ever meted out by the Referee Committee, however, was to a Celtic player, George Paterson. The cruelty of Paterson's sentence was shattering to both player and club. What horrified all of us at Celtic Park was that Paterson, a man of most temperate language, had never in a career of eleven years been sent off or asked to appear before the Disciplinary Committee. We were forced to the conclusion that he was punished as he was for one of two reasons: (1) he was adjudged to have provoked the misconduct of some of the spectators; (2) he had annoyed someone or other by making allegations against the referee at half time.

Paterson slumped into a form of depression at the punishment and was transferred by a 'concerned' Celtic to Brentford during his suspension 'for his own good'. Considering that he later returned to

Celtic Park as a full-time coach in the early 1950s, Celtic's motivation for having him transferred appears genuine.

Jimmy Mallan had to accept his punishment despite its harshness; three months' suspension for kicking the ball away! It was a wise decision on his part. In the 1940s, when field discipline was better, the general rule was that any player sent off three times in his career faced a *sine die* sentence, an indefinite ruling that effectively ended careers. Ordered off twice within a few months in 1946, Mallan did clean up his act and was rarely in trouble again with referees throughout the rest of his career with Celtic until 1953 and with St Mirren till 1956 when he retired.

Matt Lynch's reaction was different. Initially astonished at his inclusion in the referee's report, he was incensed at the suspension; he had no knowledge that he had even been cautioned during or after the match, and he was aware that he had remained distant from the contretemps at the penalty award.

He decided to seek out Jimmy Duncanson for confirmation and, in the days when telephones were less common than now, he ventured into a Rangers pub in Bridgeton to find Duncanson's address. In the hostelry he was greeted warmly by the habitués and directed to his opponent's house; Lynch recalls that his reception in both places was sympathetic: 'The punters in the pub and Jimmy knew I had not been involved. They assured me of that.' To his eternal credit, Jimmy Duncanson volunteered to write a letter exonerating the Celtic player of any wrongdoing, and this was an action which did not meet with any great approval within Ibrox. Despite that sporting gesture, Lynch's suspension stood, a further appeal being dismissed out of hand.

The actions of the SFA in punishing Celtic for field offences and misconduct by a handful of outraged spectators were vindictive, and fuelled Celtic's growing conviction that they could expect little sympathy from within the echelons of power of Scottish football. It is an attitude that still colours the perception of many Celtic supporters to this day.

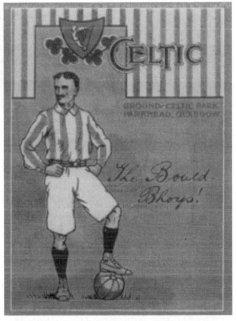

Celtic Park. The revenue generated by such a magnificent stadium (seen in 1900) enabled Celtic to assemble a team of star players, but with mixed results. Celtic's exit at Arthurlie in 1897 soon led to Willie Maley (*above*) being appointed as manager.

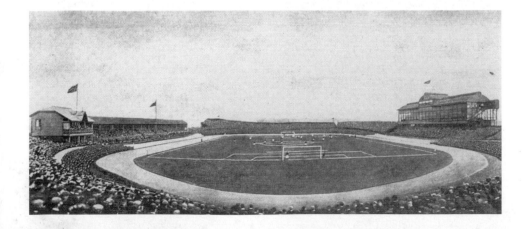

Death of a Prince.

Above: The tragic moment when Celtic goalkeeper John Thomson collided with Rangers forward Sam English on 5 September 1931.

Below: Thomson, on the ground, is surrounded by worried players from both teams.

The bereaved parents of John Thomson,
beneath a photograph of their son.

J. KENNAWAY (CELTIC) J. DELANEY (CELTIC) W. LYON (CELTIC) R. HOGG (CELTIC)

Above: Four stalwarts from the Celtic team that won the Empire Exhibition Cup of 1938. *From left:* Kennaway (the goalkeeper who replaced John Thomson); speedy outside-right Jimmy Delaney; Willie Lyon, centre half and captain; R. Hogg a steady, long-serving right back; will-o'-the-wisp centre forward Johnny Crum, who scored the only goal of the final against Everton in extra time but left to play for Morton during world war two.

Below: Lyon is presented with the trophy by the Earl of Elgin at Ibrox stadium after the match.

OFFICIAL PROGRAMME

VICTORY CUP

SEMI - FINAL
at
HAMPDEN PARK
SATURDAY, 1st JUNE, 1946

RANGERS
versus
CELTIC

3^{d}

The Old Firm meeting in the semi-final of the Victory Cup of 1946 led to controversy, violence and the unwarranted punishment of Celtic players.

Left: the match programme.

Below: the *Daily Record* felt the match and its aftermath warranted coverage on the front page.

Daily Record
and Mail

Presbyterian

EST. 1895—No 15,803   THURSDAY, JUNE 6, 1946   A KEMSLEY NEWSPAPER

GRANITE HOUSE
BUY SELL AND EXCHANGE
NEW & USED FURNITURE
PIANOS
RADIOS, etc.
TRONGATE

5 People Arrested: 2 Celtic Players Sent Off

HAMPDEN BREAK-IN: SPECTATOR ATTACKS REFEREE

By W. G. GALLAGHER

POLICE have begun an investigation into the cause of the fire early yesterday in the luxurious thousand-room La Salle hotel in the "loop" district of Chicago, which cost the lives of at least 59 people and injured 200 others, among whom were 30 firemen.

U.S. "Fireproof" Hotel Blaze: 59 Die

"This was a fireproof modern hotel and it is incredible that the fire should have spread with such speed," the chief of the Chicago Fire Brigade said.

Flames leapt through the hotel after a panic - stricken man rushed from the cocktail lounge. Exclaiming "It's hot in here," he had stood up. When he lifted a cushion from his chair flames spurted high in the air.

The fire flashed round the crowded cocktail lounge as the blazing man ran from the room. Curtains flared and even paper money in the customers' hands burst into flames.

Firemen were hindered in their work by thousands of people who flocked from nearby theatres and night clubs.
The crowd jostled and

TWO CELTIC PLAYERS ORDERED TO THE PAVILION, AN ATTACK ON THE REFEREE BY A SPECTATOR ARMED WITH A BOTTLE, POLICE STRUGGLING WITH OTHER SPECTATORS ON THE FIELD OF PLAY, FIGHTS ON THE TERRACING WHILE HUNDREDS OF SPECTATORS RUSHED FROM THE SLOPES FOR SAFETY.

THESE INCIDENTS MARRED THE REPLAY AT HAMPDEN PARK, GLASGOW, LAST NIGHT, OF THE VICTORY CUP SEMI-FINAL BETWEEN CELTIC AND RANGERS, WATCHED BY A CROWD OF ABOUT 50,000.

POLICE TOOK A HAND

Five arrests were made. The accused will appear at the Southern Police Court this morning. The disgraceful scenes will be the subject of a special inquiry by the Scottish Football Association.

The trouble started twenty minutes from the start of the second half.

The referee, Mr M. C. Dale, Glasgow, awarded Rangers a penalty kick. He was immediately surrounded by most of the Celtic team vigorously protesting. The name of one of the Celtic players was taken by the referee.

Young, Rangers' centre-half, stepped forward to take the kick, but the Celtic players refused to give him freedom to do so, persisting in their protest

Increase For Women In Engineering

The return of Jock Stein to Celtic Park as manager was arguably the most significant day in the club's history. *Above*: Billy McNeill heads the winning goal of the 1965 Scottish Cup final; it was Celtic's first trophy under Stein. *Below*: Stein (far right) awaits the arrival of European opponents. The other Celtic officials are (from left) assistant manager Sean Fallon and directors Jimmy Farrell and Desmond White.

Above left: Fergus McCann, the man who saved Celtic from bankruptcy, a move that enabled the club to stop Rangers from winning ten league titles in a row in 1998.

Above right: Wim Jansen – the manager in that highly successful campaign of 1997/98 – who left after just one season in charge following a personality clash.

Below left: Henrik Larsson and Harald Brattbakk celebrate the latter's goal against St Johnstone on 9 May 1998. It was the strike that clinched the title.

Scott McDonald – an Australian of Scottish extraction and a Celtic fan – fires home the first goal for Motherwell in the last match of the 2004/05 season to deprive his idols of the championship.
(courtesy Empics)

Comments

An allegation of unfair refereeing is always a serious matter, and an emotional one – as we have seen in the recent Hearts–Rangers affair at Tynecastle. I've always thought that some real statistics should be used, rather than selective ones. The argument about the Old Firm being awarded more than their share of penalty kicks is an old one but it has rarely been researched properly. Defenders of the Old Firm always claim that Rangers and Celtic attack more than their opponents, and therefore get more penalties. True enough but an interesting exercise would be the following: shortly after world war two both Hibernian and Hearts enjoyed boom periods, each winning the championship more than once. Why not take those seasons and consider the following for the leading teams: how many goals did they score? How many penalties did they get? What is the ratio of penalties and total goals scored? If there is a basic discrepancy between the Glasgow sides and the Edinburgh ones then there might be a problem.

Bob Crampsey

I don't know very much about this match. Two Celtic players ordered off, and two carried off? And giving away a dodgy penalty? Who were they playing, by the way?

Tony Griffin

Are you sure that Hugh Dallas wasn't the referee?

Craig McAughtrie

That replay in the Victory Cup semi-final surely indicated the poor quality of Scottish referees during the war – and their lack of training or supervision by the authorities, namely the SFA. To be honest it was more a matter of incompetence rather than anything more sinister.

David Potter

I cannot remember too much about the first game as it was the day I was born.

Pat Woods

5

THE ONCE AND FUTURE KING

Tony Griffin

There's a New World somewhere, they call the Promised Land,
And I'll be there someday, if you will hold my hand

Those were the opening lines of the number-one song in the charts on Monday, 8 March 1965. How prophetic these words now seem to Celtic supporters as that was the day Jock Stein returned to Celtic as manager. The move from Hibernian to Celtic had been announced at a Parkhead press conference on 31 January when it was stated that Stein would stay with Hibs 'until a replacement had been found'. By March, Bob Shankly, brother of Liverpool's Bill, had been lured to Easter Road from Dens Park where he had led Dundee to the league championship in 1962.

Ironically, Jock Stein's last game in charge of Hibs was a Scottish Cup quarter-final against Rangers at Easter Road on 6 March. Hibs won 2–1, their third victory over the Ibrox side that season. This was despite the surprise return to the Rangers team of Jim Baxter, playing in his first game for three months following a broken leg sustained in the last minute of Rangers' European Cup second-round victory over Rapid Vienna at the Prater stadium.

Stein inherited a Celtic in total disarray, and that was the reason for his return. The club had failed to win a major domestic trophy since beating Rangers 7–1 in the 1957/58 League Cup final.

How had it all gone so wrong?

Let us start in 1957 and that League Cup final. It is a match that is second only to Lisbon in the Celtic firmament: the majestic 7–1 thrashing of Rangers on 19 October 1957. This joyful explosion of goals, as glorious as it was unexpected, was surely the harbinger of better days for Celtic. Sadly, despite a warm afterglow following the Hampden holocaust, with the team remaining undefeated from the start of the season till late December, reality bit with a vengeance over Christmas and four consecutive games were lost, all at home, between 21 December 1957 and 1 January 1958. The last was the most galling, a loss to Rangers by one goal to nil. A huge letdown after the 7–1 game, and a chance lost to consolidate dominance over their Old Firm rivals.

Celtic also lost 2–0 at home to the eventual winners, Clyde, in the Scottish Cup quarter-final on 1 March, and a string of exhilarating league victories was punctuated by frustrating defeats away at Tynecastle, Dens Park and Palmerston Park. The team ended the season in third place, sixteen points behind runaway champions Hearts, but only three shy of runners-up Rangers. It was to be the last reasonably satisfactory season for some time.

Maladministration

The League Cup triumph was revealed as a last hurrah for an ageing Celtic team: injury, transfers – and Father Time – exacted a toll. Celtic did not have the organisation to cope with the necessary transition and nowhere was this more visible than in the development of the younger players. Billy McNeill recounts in his autobiography, *Hail Cesar*, how at this time:

> There was a dreadful lack of direction at the club. The senior players had taken it upon themselves to offer advice and guidance, to the extent that they issued instructions on how we should play but, with the bulk of them gone, we were forced to provide our own education. To be frank, several careers were ruined because of the apparent apathy and disinterest that pervaded Celtic Park.

Promising youths like Bobby Carroll, John Colrain and Mike McVittie had failed to fulfil their potential while Bobby Lennox had not shown much indication of the lethal finishing skill he possessed in any of his rare first-team opportunities. Others, like John Divers, John Hughes, Steve Chalmers, Jimmy Johnstone and Charlie Gallagher were first-team regulars but lacked direction; Bobby Murdoch and Billy McNeill (the captain of Celtic and Scotland) were the brightest hopes for the future, but appeared destined for obscurity if they stayed with Celtic for much longer.

The answer to some of these on-field woes was already available at Celtic Park. Forced to retire with an ankle injury, Jock Stein was worried about his future until the club offered him a coaching post, which he jumped at, and he worked with the youngsters in the reserve team until leaving to manage Dunfermline Athletic in 1960. Unfortunately, Stein's influence did not extend to the first team in the late 1950s when repeated Old Firm humiliations, and frustrating cup disappointments, were brightened only by two consecutive League Cup triumphs.

Around this time a fresh crop of Celtic youngsters, including new recruits Billy McNeill and Pat Crerand, began working with Jock Stein; he held these promising youngsters in thrall with his endless football talk and infectious enthusiasm. Famously, Stein would insist that the youngsters who travelled by bus from Celtic Park to Lanarkshire would have to wait till his own bus arrived, even if theirs came first. Eventually the club allowed Stein a car and he had a captive audience of passengers. The reserves enjoyed their football, and they enjoyed the big man's novel approach to training. They were not subjected to the mindless slog round the running track that was the lot of the senior players; they actually had the chance to play with the ball. Crerand, McNeill, Duncan MacKay and Stevie Chalmers all made their top-team debuts in the 1958/59 season, MacKay going on to play for Scotland against England at Wembley before the season was out.

But the progress being made by the younger players was not matched in other departments. Celtic were a desperately poorly administered club for the seven years that followed the Hampden humiliation of their greatest rivals and the problem lay with the relationship between the chairman (Bob Kelly) and the nominal manager (Jimmy McGrory). In reality, the chairman acted as manager with complete control over team selection, club discipline and transfer policy. As if aware of the shortcomings of his long-term 'manager', Kelly promoted Sean Fallon, generally considered his protégé and Celtic's next manager, within the club's hierarchy but the chairman remained in charge.

By 1963, club captain Billy McNeill was nearing the end of his tether. In *Hail Cesar* he recalls how anyone who dared to stand up to Bob Kelly 'didn't have a future at Celtic Park', citing the example of his close friend Mike Jackson. For McNeill, enough was very nearly enough. He had been made aware that Tottenham Hotspur were keen to sign him as a replacement for their ageing stopper, Maurice Norman, but heart ruled over head and Billy stayed in Glasgow.

Tommy Gemmell, who was enjoying his first season (1963/64) as first choice left-back, reveals in his autobiography that by this time 'tactics' were decided by Sean Fallon, but heavily influenced by Bob Kelly. According to Gemmell, Fallon insisted that defenders, and especially full backs, should forget any notions of playing the ball out of defence, but rather should thump it sixty and seventy yards upfield to the forwards. It was with this primitive outlook that Celtic came up against MTK in the semi-final of the European Cup Winners' Cup in Budapest and went there with a three-goal lead; Sandor, the veteran winger who had played in the great Magyar team of the 1950s, proceeded to teach the young Tommy Gemmell a football lesson, jinking round him effortlessly and setting up chance after chance for his colleagues. Celtic's hopes of reaching a European final was gone as MTK won by 4–0, and Gemmell, while admitting his own shortcomings, blames the defeat on the lamentable lack of tactical awareness shown by Fallon.

Still Bob Kelly continued to sail the good ship Celtic ever nearer to the rocks of ruination. Something had to give. Behind the scenes, according to Archie Macpherson (and others), Jock Stein, by then manager of Hibernian, had contacted Kelly, ostensibly to ask his advice about an offer he had received to manage Wolverhampton Wanderers in the English first division; Macpherson confirms that

Stein was fishing, and sure enough Kelly took the bait. Eventually he asked Stein if he would be interested in returning to Celtic as assistant manager to Sean Fallon. Stein rejected the offer forthwith, as he did Kelly's next offer of becoming joint manager with Fallon. As Macpherson puts it: 'No three-legged-race for a man who was the supreme individualist.'

Finally, Kelly and the Celtic board came to terms with the inevitable: it was time to change history and offer full control of the playing side of the club to a non-Catholic. It had taken almost seven years for Celtic to change managers, and to bring the club into the way of modern football. Others would argue, with less justification, that it had taken Celtic almost seventy years to appoint a Protestant as manager.* For the Celtic support – many years ahead of their directors in this matter – Jock Stein's religion was of no consequence; in fact, they almost welcomed the idea of a non-Catholic being in control.

Inconsistency

The main consequence of Celtic's maladministration had been an understandable inconsistency on the field. The period, known to some Celtic supporters as 'the seven lean years', was punctuated with distressing setbacks, either on routine occasions but often on potentially glorious days. It would be salutary to recall those times.

Celtic did well enough in their attempt to retain the League Cup in 1958 storming through to the semi-final, and looking a good bet to win the trophy for the third year running, but were beaten 2–1 by Partick Thistle at Ibrox, despite the fact that Thistle lost their goalkeeper, Ledgerwood, to injury only four minutes into the second half. The highlight of that season was a third-round victory over Rangers by 2–1 in the Scottish Cup. However, any hopes that that surprising victory – achieved by a very young, inexperienced side – aroused in the support that the Scottish Cup might return to Celtic Park after an absence of five years were to be cruelly dashed.

---

* This ignores the fact that Willie Maley was in charge of Celtic for almost fifty years, and Jimmy McGrory for twenty-two. Managerial change at Celtic Park was an infrequent occurrence.

St Mirren ran rings round the static Celtic defenders in the semi-final at Hampden, and inflicted a humiliating 4–0 drubbing.

The slump continued into the following season, 1959/60, in which Celtic got off to the worst possible start. The team lost its first three League Cup sectional matches to moderate opposition in shape of Raith Rovers, Partick Thistle and Airdrie, and eventually finished third in the section. The league campaign proved to be nine months in which Celtic and consistency were total strangers. There were encouraging performances including a league double of 3–1 wins over St Mirren, who fielded the same forward line in both games that had decimated Celtic in the Scottish Cup semi-final the previous April.

In fact, Celtic beat St Mirren in the second round of the Scottish Cup, but only after a three-game epic series; a 1–1 draw at Love Street was followed by a 4–4 roller-coaster replay at Parkhead, in which Celtic were 3–1 down at half time, but rallied to draw level through Neil Mochan five minutes from the end. The second replay took place at Celtic Park on 29 February 1960, and this time Celtic dominated from the start. They led 3–0 at half time thanks to a Mochan hat-trick, and he added two more in the second half. It was Celtic's, and particularly Neil Mochan's, night. The next round nearly produced one of the most embarrassing results in Celtic's history: drawn to play Highland League opponents Elgin City away from home, Celtic found themselves 1–0 down at tight little Borough-briggs with only six minutes remaining. Finally, Johnny Divers came to the rescue with an equalizer, and just as Elgin were consoling them-selves with the prospect of a money-making replay in Glasgow, right half Eric Smith struck Celtic's late, face-saving winner with only two minutes left to play.

On 13 March 1960, Jock Stein – at the age of thirty-seven – left his coaching position at Celtic to take over as manager at Dunfermline Athletic, charged with the task of saving the Fifers from relegation, a fate that appeared inevitable. Stein's first match as Dunfermline manager was a home league fixture against, of all teams, Celtic. The Fifers centre forward Charlie Dickson had the honour of scoring the first goal of Jock Stein's managerial career, and he took only fifteen seconds to do it as the Fifers went on to beat Celtic 3–2. Dunfermline took off like a scalded cat under Stein; they promptly won six consecutive league games for the first time in their history, and comfortably avoided relegation.

Celtic, on the other hand, slumped to an embarrassing ninth place in the table by the season's end, and capitulated to Rangers by 4–1 in the Scottish Cup semi-final replay after a 1–1 draw.

The opening League Cup matches of season 1960/61 hinted at a new beginning but it was yet another false dawn. Playing in an all-Glasgow section, Celts beat Third Lanark 2–0 at home, drew 1–1 with Thistle at Firhill, then, thanks to a sensational Old Firm debut by the 17-year-old John Hughes, pulled off a surprise 3–2 victory over Rangers at Ibrox. Victory at Cathkin over Thirds by 3–1 followed; then, after Thirds had done Celtic a massive favour by beating Rangers, Celtic blew it by losing at home 2–1 to Thistle.

They could still qualify by drawing their final game at home to Rangers, and even took the lead through Steve Chalmers in the second minute, but with a sickening inevitability Rangers – calling on experience and tactical nous – powered back to score twice in the second half and end Celtic's interest in the competition for another year.

The return of Willie Fernie from Middlesbrough in October added composure to the performances, and the league position gradually improved. So much so that from twelfth place in December, Celtic found their goalscoring form and rose to finish in fourth place, behind Rangers, Kilmarnock and Third Lanark, who were far and away top scorers. Incidentally, Rangers pipped Kilmarnock to the title by one point and Celtic took three points out of the four from the runners-up, including a late equalizer in the first league game of the season at Rugby Park, and an even later winner on Hogmanay at Parkhead.

The Scottish Cup saw Celtic reach the final and Celtic were installed as odds-on favourites to beat Dunfermline, and Jock Stein, in the final; after all, the Fifers had never even reached the semi-final before. Celtic supporters are all too familiar with what happened next. A blinding display of goalkeeping by Celtic fanatic Eddie Connachan in the Fifers goal in the first game at Hampden, which finished goalless, was followed by another master class between the sticks in the Wednesday-night replay. Celtic battered away at the Fife goal but could not find a breakthrough, and were to be sickened by a smartly taken headed goal by Thomson for Dunfermline with only twenty-three minutes left on the clock.

As Celtic grew more and more frantic, and Connachan more and more inspired, the minutes ticked away until Frank Haffey relieved all the tension for Dunfermline with a ghastly error, letting the ball slip out of his grasp, straight to the feet of Dunfermline's Charlie Dickson only two yards out. The image of Haffey lying prone in the back of the net in abject despair stays in the mind's eye. As the final whistle blew the remnants of the Celtic support trudged away over the top of the Kings Park terraces into the murky night like the stragglers of a defeated army. Meanwhile, a burly figure in a white raincoat ran with his arms raised aloft in triumph onto the Hampden turf to acclaim his team and celebrate his first domestic trophy.

Celtic actually had a reasonably good season in 1961/62, inconsistency being again the major complaint, but they failed to survive the sectional stage of the League Cup, the traditional curtain-raiser to the season. This time, they finished runners-up to the excellent Hearts side of the time. As a footnote – and perhaps another indication of lack of organisation – Celtic's second-top scorer of the previous season, John Divers, turned up for the opening game against Hearts, and found that he had forgotten his boots. He was dropped and replaced by a 19-year-old debutant, Bobby Murdoch, who scored and retained his place. Divers had to wait till September to reclaim a regular spot in the team; it is unlikely that the kindly Jimmy McGrory had decided on such a harsh punishment.

In the league campaign the team settled down and played some entertaining football. The defence picked itself. Haffey, MacKay, Kennedy, Crerand, McNeill and Price played virtually undisturbed from September through to February, when John Clark replaced Billy Price. Even the forward line, so often the chairman's plaything, remained largely constant, along the lines of Chalmers, Carroll, Hughes, Divers and Byrne, with Jackson and Brogan also making regular appearances. The Old Firm league games were drawn, and on both occasions Rangers struggled to score late equalizers.

However, yet again, Celtic did their damnedest to hand Rangers the championship by beating front-runners Dundee, Craig Brown and all, 2–1 at Celtic Park in March, with two goals in the last ten minutes. Fortunately, the Dens men eventually won the title, which they richly deserved.

Once again, Celtic made good progress in the Scottish Cup and reached the semi-final by way of beating Hearts 4–3 at Tynecastle, and Third Lanark 4–0 at Hampden after the teams had shared eight goals at Celtic Park. The semi-final against St Mirren at Ibrox proved to be the low point of the season. Celtic – who had defeated the Saints by 5–0 at Paisley only a week previously – picked this game to produce their worst display in months and St Mirren, running rings round the feckless Hoops, were three up after thirty-five minutes. Their star performer, and scorer of their first goal, was none other than Willie Fernie, who – deemed surplus to requirements at Parkhead – had joined them early in the season. This let down overshadowed what had been a season of reasonable achievement, if any trophy-less season can be termed reasonable by Celtic's standards. They finished third in the table, five points behind Rangers and eight behind champions Dundee.

A year later, in1962/63, Celtic had slumped to fourth place in the final table behind Rangers, Kilmarnock and Partick Thistle (always recognized as the most inconsistent side in the country). Celtic had been capable of scoring four, five, and six goals against decent opposition, and even scored thirteen away from home for the loss of only one on consecutive Saturdays, beating Airdrie 6–1 at Broomfield on 27 October and St Mirren 7–0 at Love Street on 3 November. However, these spectacular successes were followed by a grisly run of form which saw defeats at home to Queen of the South and Partick Thistle, and away to Third Lanark, and every other game till Boxing Day drawn. They reached the Scottish Cup final, however, drawing 1–1 with Rangers, thanks largely to the heroics of Frank Haffey in the Celtic goal. Jimmy Johnstone (called 'Jim' Johnstone by the newspapers) made his cup debut for Celtic in this game, and it was the first time Celtic wore crew-neck jerseys in place of the familiar button-up collars that had been in use since the 1930s.

The replay on 15 May 1963 coincided with the orbital space

flight of Major Gordon Cooper of the United States in his Mercury rocket. Sadly, Celtic were not on the same planet as a Rangers team that was one of the greatest in the history of the Ibrox club. The Light Blues also took full advantage of yet another inexplicable team selection by the Celtic chairman. With the 'Wee Prime Minister' (Ian MacMillan) running the show in midfield, Henderson rampaging down the right and Baxter in imperious form, Rangers totally out-classed Celtic. When Ralph Brand added a third unanswered goal midway through the second half, thirty thousand Celtic supporters turned their backs on the team and headed straight for the exits. It was arguably the single worst event of this period, and made even worse by the chants of 'Easy, Easy' emanating from the Rangers end of Hampden. Jack Harkness of the *Sunday Post* summed up the situation perfectly:

> Different folk have different ways of showing resentment. Some go in for passive resistance. But 30,000 fans at Hampden Park on Wednesday night created history. Thirty thousand fans, almost as if it had been organized, deliberately turned their backs on their team and stole quietly into the night. It was surely Hampden's most distressing sight ever. Celtic in a Scottish Cup final replay . . . half an hour still left for play. Then suddenly this mass exit from the Celtic End of the ground. A demonstration of resentment, pro-claiming to the board that 'the Faithful' had lost faith in their team; a demonstration that cannot be lost on those whose responsibility it is to run Celtic.

If ever there was a time for radical change this was surely it. The club was a shambles from top to bottom; one journalist noted that Celtic had gone into the replay with their 'thirty-ninth forward per-mutation of the season'. And everyone knew who was to blame: Bob Kelly, whose constant interference in selection matters had enervated the team and dispirited the supporters. But Kelly was still unwilling to do what was now a necessity and appoint a strong manager; that development would have to wait. In the meantime, Celtic fans could expect even more pain.

Season 1963/64 saw Celtic again drawn in the same League Cup section as Rangers, and the Ibrox men continued their easy dominance with 3–0 victories both home and away, and duly won the cup. The league campaign began badly, with defeat at Ibrox by 2–1 followed by a remarkable game against Third Lanark at Celtic Park. Celtic were, incredibly, 4–0 up after only fourteen minutes through Divers, Lennox, Turner and Brogan, but Thirds hit back immediately and had pulled it back to 4–3 by half time. Winger Bobby Graham equalized for the Hi-Hi only five minutes into the second half, and the goals then dried up!

Celtic slumped to seventh place in the league. Then, as though a switch had been flicked, Celtic began scoring a torrent of goals; Aberdeen and Dundee United were each beaten 3–0, at Parkhead and Tannadice respectively, then Airdrie were put to the sword by 9–0 at Celtic Park. Hughes and Divers each scored a hat-trick, and goal-keeper Frank Haffey was invited to take a late penalty to make it ten, but his effort was saved by his opposite number, Ulsterman Roddy McKenzie. Consecutive 5–1 romps followed against East Stirling (away) and Partick Thistle (home), and a 1–1 draw at Easter Road was followed by a 5–0 thumping of Kilmarnock at Celtic Park. The goals continued to flow in lesser quantities, but the inevitable defeat at Ibrox on 1 January 1964 (1–0 this time) was followed by a 1–1 draw at Cathkin and a 7–0 home win over Falkirk. Celtic finished the season as top scorers, with eighty-nine goals – four more than treble-winners Rangers managed – and secured third spot, two points behind Willie Waddell's Kilmarnock side and eight behind Rangers.

The club's adventure in the European Cup Winners' Cup, for which they qualified by dint of Rangers winning the cup-and-league double in 1962/3, provided a welcome shaft of light in the enduring depression that came with forever playing third and fourth fiddle behind Rangers, Hearts, and Kilmarnock in these depressing times. But, losing 4–0 in Budapest after routing the Hungarians 3–0 at Celtic Park, only underlined Celtic's fatal inconsistency.

Frustration

The awareness that the club was handicapping itself by maladminis-tration off the field and inconsistency on it was breeding frustration among supporters and players alike.

Only a year after the 7–1 triumph that team was effectively broken up, with Charlie Tully retiring, and Willie Fernie and Bobby Collins being transferred to England (Billy McPhail and Sean Fallon had earlier retired through long-term injury). A year later, in 1959/60, to compound the gloom, fans favourite Bobby Evans was transferred to Chelsea, and the industrious Eric Smith to Leeds United in the close season. The transfers were one-way with very little indication that the board was serious about bolstering a youthful squad. This apparent lack of interest infuriated the support, who increasingly vented their spleen on Bob Kelly as he sat stone-faced in the directors' box at home games.

The 1961/62 season got off to a bad start as Celtic were handicapped by the SFA in a staggering example of draconian 'justice'. Pat Crerand, undoubtedly the club's star player had been sent off in a pre-season five-a-side tournament at Falkirk, and was suspended for a month. This meant that he missed the first five games of the season, including League Cup sectional ties against Hibs at Easter Road, Partick Thistle home and away, and St Johnstone home and away. Celtic lost both games to St Johnstone, finished second to the Perth club and thus found themselves out of the tournament. Crerand also missed the first league game of the season, a 3–2 defeat at Rugby Park. It seems inconceivable that such a savage punishment – effectively a six-game ban – could be meted out for such a relatively trivial offence.

The semi-final of the Scottish Cup against St Mirren at Ibrox on 31 March 1962 ended on a sour note when the huge Celtic support, bitterly disappointed at yet another humiliation, sent a hail of bottles raining onto the front terracing, causing an invasion of the playing surface. The referee stopped the game with Saints 3–1 ahead and only minutes remaining; Bob Kelly – acting as a senior statesman within Scottish football – immediately conceded the tie to St Mirren.

Predictably, there was complete inertia at Celtic Park in the summer of 1962 as far as the transfer market was concerned. The directors, and chairman Kelly, were singularly unwilling to invest in the team, to build on the apparent progress made in 1961/62. Complacency, totally misplaced, shrouded Celtic Park like a blanket of fog.

In 1962/63 the only transfer activity of note at Celtic Park was the move of the club's star player – and Celtic diehard – Pat Crerand, to Manchester United for the huge sum of £56,000. This was largely a disciplinary measure, for Crerand had had a blazing row with coach Sean Fallon at half time at Ibrox during the Ne'erday game, which Rangers won 4–0. The home side led only 1–0 at the interval, but Celtic's discipline and will crumbled after the dispiriting events of the half-time break, and Rangers won as easily as the scoreline suggests, to complete the league double over the Celts yet again.

In 1964/65 it was imperative that Celtic should build on the sound performances in Europe the previous season but, by Christmas, Celtic were in fifth place in the league, fully eight points behind joint leaders Hearts and Kilmarnock. Something was stirring, however.

On 14 January 1965, Bertie Auld, who had left Celtic under a disciplinary cloud, rejoined the club from Birmingham City. Auld was contacted by an intermediary, Dougie Hepburn, and when he asked who wanted him to join Celtic, he was told that it was Jock Stein. Knowing that Stein was at Hibs, Auld quizzed his contact but was told to keep it quiet for the time being, but that an announcement would soon be made.

A run of heavy league defeats was brought to an end with a stunning display against Aberdeen on 30 January 1965 at Celtic Park. The players, perhaps sensing a wind of change, scorched to an 8–0 victory, with John 'Yogi' Hughes, revelling in the icy conditions in his rubber-soled boots, scoring five. Murdoch, Auld and Lennox completed the rout. Twenty-four hours later came the bombshell news of Jock Stein's imminent arrival, and six weeks later, Bob Kelly, the Celtic chairman, greeted his returning protégé with a firm handshake and the words, 'It's all yours now.'

It was an end to seven years of maladministration by the directors, inconsistency by the players and frustration for the supporters. Since the 7–1 victory at Hampden Park in 1957, 2,661 days had passed, and these were the days that shook Celtic more than those surrounding Jock Stein's appointment.

The news of Stein's forthcoming arrival had an immediate, galvanising effect upon the players. They followed up the blitzing of Aberdeen with a convincing 3–0 win over St Mirren at Love Street in the Scottish Cup first round and repeated the treatment in the league the following week by 5–1. Then, after scraping through nervously by a Lennox goal against Queen's Park in the Scottish Cup second round at Hampden, they dealt successive league and cup defeats at Celtic Park to the champions-elect, Kilmarnock, by 2–0 and 3–2 respectively.

Jock Stein's first game in charge was against Airdrie at Broomfield on Wednesday, 10 March, and Bertie Auld took the opportunity to impress his new boss, scoring five goals in Celtic's 6–0 win. John Hughes got the other goal. The bubble burst with a 1–0 defeat by St Johnstone the following Saturday, after which the story of season 1964/65 was one of stuttering league form and smooth progress in the cup. Stein clearly got his priorities right and used the league fixtures to evaluate his squad. Motherwell gave Celtic a fright in the semi-final at Hampden, drawing the first game 2–2 before going down 3–0 in a replay.

The Scottish Cup final of 1965, Celtic versus Dunfermline Athletic on 24 April, was the game that, by common consent, marked the beginning of the Stein era at Celtic Park. The notorious 'Hampden Swirl' played a part in an absorbing final. Dunfermline, playing into the blustery wind, took the lead in fifteen minutes when Fallon was tempted too far out of his goal and could only fingertip the ball as far as Dunfermline captain Harry Melrose, who smartly hooked it into the empty net. Celtic equalised in thirty-one minutes. Charlie Gallagher picked up the ball midway inside the Dunfermline half, zigzagged forward, then unleashed a terrific drive that struck the crossbar, soared high into the air and was blown down and back into play by the wind. The alert Bertie Auld had stationed himself underneath the dropping ball and he outjumped the Fife defence to head home. Dunfermline snatched the lead again one minute before half time, McLaughlin scoring with a low, angled drive from Melrose's tapped free kick. Such a blow would have knocked the stuffing out of the pre-Stein Celtic, but not this team.

They set about Dunfermline in the second half, forcing them onto the defensive. Auld and Lennox sliced open the Pars defence with a series of one-two's that culminated in Auld boring deep into the box before carefully driving home Celtic's second equaliser in the fifty-first minute. From then on, wave after wave of green-and-white attacks broke upon the black-and-white defensive wall, until Bobby Lennox forced an historic corner kick on the Celtic left, at the Mount Florida end. It was nine minutes from time. Charlie Gallagher flighted the ball perfectly for Billy McNeill to soar into the box and head Celtic's winner!

It was a moment of destiny for McNeill and for Celtic:

> For perhaps two seconds, Hampden's vast bowl was still, stunned by the sudden shock of decision and then erupted into bedlam. The roar continued, minute after minute and its prevailing note changed: it was not a roar of joy that a cup final produces; rather, it was a tumultuous welcome to the future and the instinctive realization by all Celtic's support that the young men had grown up and that nothing, now or in the years to come, would withstand the collective spirit of their manhood. (Tom Campbell, *Glasgow Celtic 1945-70*)

Jock Stein himself acknowledged the significance of this win years later when he reflected: 'It would not have gone so well for Celtic had they not won this game.' The Celtic team that day was: Fallon; Young and Gemmell; Murdoch, McNeill and Clark; Chalmers and Gallagher; Hughes; Lennox and Auld.

The long wait was over! With Stein's hand at the helm, the frustration had ended for the support, and that same grasp on the day-to-day running of the club would soon end the inconsistency. Common sense, pragmatism and a remarkable awareness of the modern game – allied to hard work – would make the difference.

The summer of 1965 was long, hot and pleasurable for Celtic fans. At last, Rangers had been outgunned in terms of trophy-winning: Kilmarnock pipped Hearts to the title by 0.04 of a goal (in the days of goal average) by winning 2–0 at Tynecastle on the same day that Celtic were winning the Cup at Hampden, and the Gers had to be content with the League Cup.

Stein made only one significant close-season signing for Celtic; on 5 June, he bought Joe McBride from Motherwell for £22,500. Meanwhile, the supporters went off on holiday, anticipating the new season with relish. That summer they watched Peter Thomson of Australia win his fifth and last British Open golf championship at Royal Birkdale, and another Australian, Roy Emerson, triumph for the second year running in the Wimbledon singles, beating his countryman Fred Stolle in the final. Yet another Aussie, the awesome Margaret Smith, took the ladies' title by beating the graceful Brazilian, Maria Bueno. Scotland's Jim Clark won the British Grand Prix in a Lotus-Climax, en route to his second world drivers' championship. Elvis Presley's 'Crying in the Chapel', the Hollies' 'I'm Alive' and 'Mr Tambourine Man' by the Byrds took turns at the number one position in the charts. In the cinema, Peter O'Toole starred in *Lawrence of Arabia* and the Beatles film *Help* was a huge success. The title song naturally shot to the top spot.

Then it was back to football business.

All the high expectations among the support seemed to be justified when English first division side Sunderland (Jim Baxter and all) were dismantled 5–0 on their own Roker Park pitch. A couple of hiccups followed in the League Cup sectional games for 1965/66. Dundee United beat Celtic 2–1 at Tannadice in the first competitive game of the new season; Motherwell were narrowly beaten 1–0 at Parkhead the following Wednesday; then Dundee came to Celtic Park, defended in depth, and left with a 2–0 win, thanks to two breakaway goals.

Celtic refused to panic. Dundee United were crushed 4–0 at Tannadice in the opening league game of the season on Wednesday, 25 August, Joe McBride opening his account; then United were beaten 3–0 at Parkhead in the return League Cup game. Two potentially difficult away hurdles were successfully negotiated in the remaining League Cup sectional games: Motherwell were beaten 3–2 at Fir Park, more comfortably than the scoreline suggests, and Dundee went down 3–1 at Dens.

The acid test of Celtic's progress under Stein came at Ibrox on 18 September but Jim Forrest, so often the scourge of Celtic defences, gave Rangers a 1–0 lead in the seventh minute. Celtic levelled through a Hughes penalty eleven minutes later but George McLean scored Rangers' second and winning goal only two minutes later, also from the spot. Rangers managed to contain Celtic's increasingly frantic attacks and held out to win 2–1.

Thereafter, the Old Firm ran neck and neck in the title race, and both continued their inexorable progress towards a meeting in the League Cup final. Celtic, having disposed of Raith Rovers 12–1 on aggregate in the two-leg quarter-final, survived a scare in the semi-final against Hibs at Ibrox on 4 October, Lennox scoring a last-gasp equaliser after Neil Martin's two goals had overhauled Joe McBride's eighth-minute opener for Celtic. Extra time proved goalless and the replay was set for 18 October, again at Ibrox, to the indignation of both clubs, who justifiably claimed that the winners of the other semi, Rangers or Kilmarnock, would have the advantage of a recent game at Hampden before the final.

When the dust had settled, Hibs were swept aside 4–0; Celtic's goals in a thrilling display came from McBride, Hughes, Lennox and Murdoch. So it was that on Saturday, 23 October 1965, at Hampden, the following teams lined up for the twentieth Scottish League Cup final:

Celtic: Simpson; Young, Gemmell; Murdoch, McNeill, Clark; Johnstone, Gallagher; McBride; Lennox, Hughes.

Rangers: Ritchie; Johansen, Provan; Wood, McKinnon, Greig; Henderson, Willoughby; Forrest; Wilson, Johnston.

The referee, as at the Scottish Cup Final, was Mr Hugh Phillips of Wishaw.

This was the game that would show how far Celtic had come. They set out in determined fashion, tackling like tigers for every ball. Ian Young was lucky to escape with only a caution for a blood-curdling tackle on the always dangerous Willie Johnston after only two minutes. Rangers, however, settled quicker and Forrest was thwarted by Simpson when the opening goal seemed certain. Rangers' international centre-half, Ron McKinnon, gifted Celtic a penalty kick by reaching up and clutching the ball as it passed over his head for what would have been a harmless goal-kick. Hughes converted the award, sending Ritchie the wrong way.

Ten minutes later, Celtic went 2–0 ahead courtesy of another penalty, awarded when Provan hauled Johnstone down on the byline. This time Ritchie got a hand to Hughes's drive as it sped past him into the net. The autumn sun was shining for Celtic, who held out in the face of furious Rangers pressure in the second half, with a composure that the pre-Stein teams seldom managed. So when Ian Young diverted a Greig header past Simpson six minutes from the end, it was, for Rangers, too little too late.

Unfortunately, Celtic's victory celebrations were marred by a pitch invasion by Rangers supporters that disrupted their lap of honour. This incident led to a ban on such celebrations that remained in force throughout Jock Stein's time as Celtic manager. Shamefully, this measure applied even to finals that did not feature both Old Firm sides; so Celtic supporters were denied the pleasure of seeing the team parade their hard-won trophies round Hampden Park during the most successful period in the club's history. One wonders how long the ban would have stayed in place had Rangers been the dominant club!

Celtic sustained their league challenge and a happy Christmas was ensured when Morton were crushed 8–1 at Celtic Park, while Dunfermline beat Rangers 3–2 at Ibrox. Early in the New Year, Rangers were trounced 5–1 on an icy Celtic Park, with Hughes running riot, again showing amazing poise and balance for such a big man in the treacherous underfoot conditions. Chalmers scored a second-half hat-trick and Murdoch and Gallagher rounded off the scoring to eclipse Davy Wilson's second-minute goal for Rangers.

So ended 1965, the year the modern era began for Celtic. Although the Scottish Cup was lost to Rangers by a single goal in a replayed final, and the team lost to Liverpool 2–1 on aggregate in the European Cup Winners' Cup semi-final in controversial circumstances (an apparently legitimate goal by Lennox was disallowed for offside in the last minute), the season finished with a golden afterglow. The championship was won, and even before the title was clinched with a 1–0 victory at Fir Park, a telegram had been received at Celtic Park from Rangers chairman John Wilson, graciously conceding defeat with the words: 'The chase is over.'

The league championship – the true test of consistency – had been won; it would be a long time before Celtic's hold on that trophy would be loosened.

Comments

The Stein song sung by thousands of relieved Celtic fans lifted the terraces higher than all the rebuilding did and finally took the rusty roof off the jungle by sheer fervour. The Messiah had come back to Paradise – and he was a Protestant.

John Cairney

Jock Stein's return to Celtic? We knew – all of us – that things would be different. We just knew.

Tom Campbell

Jock Stein? I used to wonder what would have happened if Jock had gone to Colombia as a player in the late 1940s. He was a respectable-enough performer, and unhappy at Albion Rovers; he was ambitious . . . and other players, admittedly better, went there: Charlie Mitten (Manchester United), Neil Franklin (Stoke City) and Bobby Flavell (Hearts). Remember that Flavell played against Stein frequently for Airdrie against Albion Rovers. Certainly, the history of Scottish football might have been changed forever. I suppose the apprentice-ship – highly successful – at East End Park was a useful testing-site for his later career with bigger clubs.

Bob Crampsey

It has to be a seminal moment in Celtic's history. What a contrast to the previous two decades! If you ever want a definition of 'turning point', then the appointment of Jock Stein would be it!

Gerry Dunbar

In the beginning was Jock Stein . . . I'll always remember Billy McNeill's goal, or the picture of it, with Billy rising above the defenders, even above the crowd at the Celtic end by the look of it, to score the winning goal!

Craig McAughtrie

The news sent confidence racing through the Celtic community like a surge of electricity. William Wordsworth (describing the impact of the French Revolution in 1789) got it just right:

> Bliss was it in that dawn to be alive,
> But to be young was very Heaven.

David Potter

In retrospect, and despite some claims by Celtic chairmen, it seems obvious that Jock Stein's return to Celtic Park was not planned. If anything, Stein himself was the person who originated the idea of his coming back and planted the idea in the chairman's head.

Patrick Reilly

I literally jumped for joy when I heard the news on television. I knew in my bones that Celtic would start winning trophies again.

Pat Woods

6

DEFECTION

David Potter

Celtic supporters just do not like players who, for whatever reason, decide to leave the club.

There are honourable exceptions to this truism, the most notable being Henrik Larsson who left to go to Barcelona in the summer of 2004 after seven glorious years at Parkhead. Of course disappointment was expressed, but there was a lack of bitterness. The same is not true of other transfers. Feelings of betrayal are experienced and hostility directed at those who allow a star to go, and at the player himself for abandoning the greatest privilege of all: that of wearing a green-and-white jersey. Think of Pat Crerand who deserted Celtic in favour of Manchester United at a low point in our history in 1963; think of Charlie Nicholas who decamped for Arsenal in 1983; worst of all, think of Kenny Dalglish in August 1977.

The first half of 1977 had been kind to Celtic. The league and Scottish Cup double had been secured, and there was every sign that the team was on the way following the difficult times of 1975 and 1976. The manager, Jock Stein, was back in harness after his serious car crash in the summer of 1975 and appeared to be in the business of building his third great Celtic side since taking over in 1965.

The Scottish Premier League had been won comfortably. Until the New Year no team had dominated but, starting in January,

Celtic began to play consistently well, upping several gears when required to do so. With four games to spare, the title was secured on 16 April at Easter Road, the occasion being slightly tarnished by the vindictive refusal of Hibernian's board to allow the television cameras to record the event.

The Scottish Cup had been won also, but in a less satisfactory way. The third Old Firm cup final of the decade had seen Celtic triumph 1–0 in the rain through an Andy Lynch penalty, an award hotly disputed by Rangers. It had been the first final to be televised live in twenty years and it was by no means a classic, but Celtic fans were less concerned about entertainment than by the winning of the Scottish Cup for the twenty-fifth time. The viewers were puzzled to see Celtic's captain Kenny Dalglish in tears at the end of the obligatory lap of honour, and being comforted by Jock Stein. He had lost his winner's medal! Apparently, while showing it to some disabled supporters in wheelchairs, he had let the medal fall out of his hand and it disappeared into a spectator's umbrella. It was eventually found and handed to a policeman who returned it to the player.

The success of the 1976/77 season could be attributed to two things. One was Jock Stein's apparent recovery from the horrendous injuries suffered in the car accident, and the other was his sheer genius in judging a player's value in the transfer market. The hitherto unheard-of Joe Craig had proved a fine acquisition for the forward line, and Scottish football had been shocked at the start of the season when Pat Stanton – indelibly associated with Hibernian, but considered to be past his best – had been persuaded to forsake Edinburgh to join Glasgow's green and white. Stanton had a fine season for Celtic as a sweeper, refuting the taunts of those who thought he was now too old and slow for top-flight football.

But the finest manoeuvre in the transfer market came on 1 March when ex-Ranger Alfie Conn joined Celtic from Tottenham Hotspur. This was an excellent piece of business for two reasons. One was that Conn still had a great deal of football left in him, and would do well for the rest of the season; the other was that it dealt a vicious blow to Rangers in an area where it hurt, capturing, without a shadow of doubt, the moral high ground for Celtic.

Conn had played for Rangers before his transfer to Tottenham Hotspur in 1974. Rangers had missed him and had recently made a bid to bring him back to Ibrox where their fans were known to chant his name when things on the field were not going well. When he got wind of Conn's availability, Stein immediately put in a higher bid and, to the utter bewilderment of all those of a Rangers persuasion, Alfie joined Celtic to become one of the very few players (and up to then the only one in the modern era) to turn out for both Celtic and Rangers.

This transfer, apart from being a shrewd piece of football business, proved yet again that Celtic were prepared to sign any player regardless of his background. Rangers were in some turmoil about religion at that time. After their fans rioted in a friendly match at Birmingham the previous autumn, Rangers' general manager, Willie Waddell, had to make an announcement that they would now sign Roman Catholics. This simple statement caused all sorts of problems for them: the 'loyalist' support stayed away in protest, and serious questions were now being asked in public of Rangers. Even bodies like the Church of Scotland and the Labour Party – institutions that had previously turned a blind eye to the apartheid at Ibrox – sat up and took notice. The leader writers of the broadsheets were prominent in this campaign.

Rangers did not help themselves by failing to enlist anyone of the Roman Catholic persuasion, even after making their statement of intent. The announcement, therefore, was regarded rightly as empty rhetoric that had only served to further alienate much of their support. Stein looked upon his rivals' discomfort with glee and, seizing this opportunity, swooped like a hawk to sign Conn, having consulted senior players Kenny Dalglish and Danny McGrain about the advisability of doing so.

The trio of Stein, McGrain and Dalglish were all Protestants, a point noted by the leader writers of *The Scotsman* and the *Glasgow Herald* (as it was then known). However, the Celtic support welcomed Alfie Conn with open arms; in another demonstration of anti-bigotry the denizens of the Jungle sang 'He used to be a Hun, but he's all right now – Alfie, Alfie Conn'. Their joyful attitude was in stark contrast to the dispirited, disorientated and increasingly depleted Ibrox terraces. Jokes circulated in Glasgow to the effect that Rangers indeed had played a Catholic in a closed-doors friendly . . . but he had beaten them 2–1!

With righteousness firmly on his side, Stein could look even more approvingly on his team and in particular the aforementioned McGrain and Dalglish. Both were now automatic selections for Scotland and would play a great part in the national side's success that year. Their play for Celtic was a joy to behold. Danny McGrain was like Alec McNair of old in his tackling, distribution and ability to read the game; whereas Kenny Dalglish on his day was simply the best player in British football. His goal scoring (twenty-five goals that season in Celtic's domestic games) was just one part of his game. He could lead the line in the style of the old-fashioned centre-forward, pass well and pick up a misplaced ball and make the most of it. To sum up: he was an inspiration. Not until Henrik Larsson emerged twenty years later would Celtic Park resound to such genius.

Dalglish had been signed in 1967, a significant year, and had broken into the first team in 1971/72. In the opening match – Dalglish's first participation in an Old Firm encounter – he had been authorised by captain Billy McNeill to take a penalty kick. Calmly tying his bootlace, Dalglish went on coolly to score. From then on, he never looked back. By 1977 he had won four Scottish League medals, four Scottish Cup medals and one Scottish League Cup medal. Crucially, however, he had enjoyed little success in Celtic's European campaigns; a distressing European Cup semi-final against a thuggish Atletico Madrid was a particular disappointment. In some respects Kenny Dalglish suffered from his own brilliance.

Occasionally, in the eyes of supporters, he failed to deliver at Parkhead in the same way that the Tartan Army, as it later became known, did not always see Kenny at his best for Scotland. In such circumstances – and frequently in the wake of a defeat – the crowd would turn on Dalglish simply because they knew he could do better. On most supporters' buses anti-Dalglish factions argued with those who admired him and one recalls a game at Tannadice in September 1976 when Celtic lost 1–0 to a competent Dundee United. Celtic supporters tore into Dalglish in a way that amazed an English visitor, who commented: 'It's unbelievable they could turn on a player who is already a household name in England. Besides, he didn't really have such a bad game!'

Dalglish having a poor day was, of course, more significant because so much depended on him. He was the hub of the wheel and the focus of attention. In addition, he was exactly what every mother would want in her boy. A young man of sober temperament, modest, hard-working, dedicated, seldom in trouble with referees – and never falling out with the irascible and increasingly quirky old Jock – he encapsulated and sometimes transcended the word 'professional'. He seemed to have the knack of avoiding serious injury, and recovering quickly from minor ones. The girls all loved this fresh-faced youngster who was considered, in the idiom of the 1970s, as 'cute' or 'groovy' and they envied his beautiful wife Marina.

It was felt that the best was yet to come. Born on 4 March 1951, he was still only in his mid-twenties and Celtic – with Dalglish on board and Stein back on song with his infallible eye for a player – appeared to have turned the corner. It was thought that the Celtic crowds would now start to reappear. The more optimistic dared to hope that another serious assault on the European Cup might be in the offing.

But 1976/77 was illusory. The snag was that the success was apparent rather than real and, not for the first time, Celtic were suffering from being a Scottish club. Rangers had had a poor season but there had been no sustained challenge from any other quarter. True, Aberdeen had defeated Celtic in the League Cup final in November 1976 but their championship challenge had evaporated soon after the New Year when hints of a bribery scandal – a fictitious suggestion – had sapped their morale. Hibs, Dundee and Dundee United were capable of having a good day every now and then, but they were not up to a sustained challenge. Another potential challenger in Hearts had found themselves relegated. Scottish football was in a poor way. The introduction of the new-style Premier League a couple of seasons earlier had been meant to improve competition and to increase attendances.

Instead, the opposite had happened. The crowd at the 1977 Scottish Cup final was only 54,252, something that could not be explained away by television coverage and vile weather on the day. Celtic's home gates in a successful league campaign had struggled to reach 20,000 on occasion, and those of Rangers were considerably lower. It was impossible to escape the conclusion that Scottish domestic football was in decline.

Before the end of the 1976/77 season mischievous articles started to appear in the *Scottish Daily Express* and the *Daily Record* encouraging Dalglish and others to try their luck down south or elsewhere. Hypocrisy such as 'What a loss Kenny Dalglish would be!' and banal statements like 'Everyone has a right to better himself' could not hide the subversive elements at work. Occasionally, one read things in the *Daily Express* like: 'If, as seems certain, Dalglish leaves Parkhead at the end of the season' or 'the discontented Dalglish'. These articles were written with no evidence to back up the statements made, nor the innuendo suggested. The gentlemen of the press had certainly played a part in the departures of Lou Macari in 1973 and David Hay in 1974; they were back at work in the leave-taking of Kenny Dalglish.

In addition, Kenny's frequent appearances in the Scotland team would have facilitated meetings with Anglo-Scots such as Bruce Rioch of Derby County, Don Masson of Queen's Park Rangers and Lou Macari of Manchester United; no doubt, discussions about salaries would have been a regular feature at the lunch table. Some of those Anglo-Scots were grossly overpaid, as the events in the World Cup in the Argentine would prove later. But talk of an Eldorado south of Hadrian's Wall must have further unsettled a young and impressionable Dalglish.

In fact, he had already disturbed the waters at Celtic Park. The midsummer of 1975 had seen Jock Stein's road accident and Dalglish, noting Stein's likely absence and McNeill's retirement, would have considered that the good times had gone, demanded a pay raise and threatened to ask for a transfer if he did not get what he wanted. Sean Fallon's negotiating skills had managed to smooth out that crisis, and Dalglish was also awarded the captaincy.

Another dynamic could have been at work. Dalglish was a Glasgow boy, born and bred. He had been brought up in a Rangers household, his father still apparently an active Rangers supporter who suffered understandable agonies and crises of loyalty at every Old Firm match. Presumably, Kenny had learned to live with the fact that he was playing successfully and happily enough 'for the other side' – but it could have been that he had had enough of Glasgow with its sectarianism, bigotry and obsessions with the fortunes of its two football teams. Nothing in his performances would have indicated any disloyalty to his employers, his manager, nor to the countless fans whom he professed to love so dearly . . . but he may have sensed it was time for a change.

In the meantime, Liverpool were also enjoying another fine season. They won the title on 14 May 1977 but lost the FA Cup final to Manchester United the following week. More importantly, they won the coveted European Cup a few days later by getting the better of Borussia Moenchengladbach. Much of their success had been due to the excellent Kevin Keegan but he had announced his intention of moving on. He was transferred to SV Hamburg on 3 June; on 4 June, Kenny Dalglish scored at Wembley in Scotland's 2–1 triumph.

It was a fine win for Ally MacLeod's men, marred only by the triumphalism of the Scottish fans, who broke the goalposts and tore up the turf. But the real significance lay in the fact that Liverpool – with half a million pounds in hand – could now see an obvious replacement for Keegan. Celtic fans delighted with the success of Dalglish (and McGrain) in the Wembley game began to fear that a swoop might come for Dalglish, and not only from Liverpool. Would Stein be able to convince the pusillanimous directors to stand firm?

The Celtic directors at this time lacked ambition. Liverpool, on the other hand, had enjoyed recent success and were clearly thirsting for more. They were a bigger club, wealthier and more successful than Celtic. Yet Celtic's fan base remained potentially just as large as that of Liverpool, and there was no real reason – even allowing for the poor fare that was domestic football in Scotland – why Celtic should have seen themselves as a breeding ground for English football. It was an attitude that Celtic supporters would never accept nor forgive in their directors.

In the meantime, Dalglish now took himself off to South America with Scotland for what turned out to be a reasonably successful tour. Scotland beat Chile in a fixture that roused the ire of church congregations, trade unions and human rights groups because the match was played in the same stadium that less than four years previously had been used by the military junta for the wholesale massacre of supporters of Salvador Allende, the democratically elected Marxist president. Dalglish scored in that 4–2 victory; then there was a creditable 1–1 draw with Argentina; and an inevitable but respectable 2–0 loss to Brazil.

Dalglish clearly needed a break after Scotland's return from South America at the end of June. But, at the beginning of July, Celtic were off on their travels to Singapore and Australia where they had been invited to participate in the World of Soccer Cup, a glorified pre-season competition. Celtic won this tournament, beating sides like Arsenal, Red Star Belgrade and the Australian national team. However, they did so without Dalglish who had insisted on staying in Scotland. On this occasion Kenny had won his point, and no-one could really quibble; it had been a long season for Celtic and Scotland, and Dalglish was surely entitled to some holiday time.

There may have been more than meets the eye in the refusal to travel but it did not become a major issue. Yet not even Jock Stein could solve the Dalglish problem. Some time after the Celtic party returned from Australia in early August 1977, Dalglish approached Stein and asked for a transfer. Whether he had made a similar request earlier that summer is not clear but the player had now decided that he had had enough of Celtic and was set on going. Normally, the manager would have smiled politely, listened benignly and waited for the problem to evaporate. His habit had been to ignore approaches from other clubs about his stars. In fact, the player would not even be told! Jimmy Johnstone and John Hughes, for example, had been enquired about and bidden for far more frequently than the press, public or even the players were told

But Kenny Dalglish was different. This young man was determined. Jock tried everything in his 'fatherly-approach-to-a-wayward-son' repertoire. Emotional blackmail, feigned indifference, pleas, threats, even honest assessments: all the cards were played. Stein realised that Kenny was immovable in his determination to leave Glasgow and at last phoned Bob Paisley to tell him that a solution to the problem caused by Keegan's departure was at hand.

The fact that it was Stein who approached Liverpool leaves him open to the charge of being in on a kickback or, in football parlance, 'a bung'. Apparently, Stein had had a long-standing agreement with Liverpool's manager to inform him if Dalglish ever became available, and it was another indication of the friendly relationship between the two clubs. It must be stressed there is no evidence of a bung being either asked for or paid. Nor can any inference be drawn from Stein's apparent anger some four years earlier when Lou Macari opted for Manchester United rather than Liverpool, depriving him, it has been alleged, of a personal share in the transfer fee.

Paisley acted quickly and meetings were arranged on Monday, 8 August as news started to spread among the Scottish press that something was beginning to happen about Dalglish. Liverpool initially offered £200,000 and, incredibly, some Celtic directors were prepared to accept this sum until Stein told them 'not to be daft'. Eventually, on the night of Tuesday, 9 August 1977, the clubs agreed on a transfer fee of £440,000, a record at the time between British clubs. After Dalglish accepted Liverpool's terms, the deal was finalised on Wednesday, 10 August 1977, just three days before the start of the new Scottish season.

The role of the key players in this business remains open to question and interpretation. Certainly, there was a divergence of opinion between the Celtic directors on the one hand, and, on the other, Jock Stein and his assistant manager Sean Fallon. Not for the first, nor the last, time the directors gave the impression of being interested only in the money, whereas Stein would have preferred to retain the player and Fallon would have raised heaven and earth to do so.

According to a biography of Dalglish by Stephen F. Kelly, Sean Fallon remains adamant that Kenny Dalglish would have stayed at Celtic Park if he had been persuaded in the right way. Fallon often claimed to have a direct line to Dalglish in a way that Stein did not. After all, it was Fallon who had signed the boy in 1967 and persuaded him to stay in 1975, and perhaps Jock Stein's tactics in talking *at* Kenny were faulty. Perhaps he relied too much on bullying and emotional blackmail and did not emphasise the great side that Celtic could become if Dalglish stayed. Certainly, we were told, the manager made a famous last-minute plea to Kenny to stay, but it was too late. The die had been cast.

For his part, Dalglish has always denied that money was the

deciding factor. In any case, it is hard to believe that Celtic's wages, even if substantially below those of Liverpool, would have been insufficient. Dalglish later claimed that it was the ambition to win European trophies and to perform on the biggest possible stage that were the determining factors.

Yet, how could he have been so sure that this would not have happened with Celtic? In 1977 no-one would have argued that Celtic were anything like favourites to win the European Cup of 1978, but there seemed little doubt that things were improving and that Celtic, under a fully revived Jock Stein with his inspirational use of the transfer market, were on the way back. After all, it had been only ten years since they won the trophy at Lisbon and, in 1970, had contested another final in Milan, and had reached two other semi-finals. It was not entirely outwith the realm of possibility that at some time in the near future the glory days would return.

For the Celtic legions it was a bitter blow. Celtic fans in particular have difficulty in understanding anyone – in whatever circumstances – who does not want to play for Celtic. That is not a venial sin; it is a mortal one. In truth, it had not been unexpected since his seeking of a transfer two years earlier but the pain was nevertheless intense. Those whose whole existence seems to revolve around Celtic were demoralised. It is a football truism that clubs who transfer players without replacing them immediately will lose out because of the effect on the supporters.

On a personal note, the author can recall the depression of the time. The boy who had ripped the pictures of Pat Crerand off his bedroom wall with a ferocity that amazed and shocked his mother back in 1963 was now a man. The feelings in 1977 were more adult and controlled, but they were no less intense. Crerand had taken the Judas money and gone off to Manchester United fourteen years ago; now Kenny Dalglish was doing much the same. The feelings were akin to seeing the lady of one's life running off with another man. It was profoundly upsetting and the one thing that could not be said with any degree of veracity was: 'I don't care.'

Therefore, the prevailing mood at the first game of the 1977/78 season – as 34,000 gathered at Parkhead to see Celtic and Dundee United – was disorientation. What should have been a celebratory occasion proved a damp squib as the supporters wondered why 'they' had done this and, more importantly, what 'they' were going to do now. Stein himself looked uncomfortable and uneasy as he shuffled towards the dugout, shaking hands with Jim McLean, the manager of Dundee United. Nobody actually booed him but, significantly, in the main stand there was no great encouragement for him either. No cries of 'Go on, Jock!' were raised, as might have been expected at the start of a new season in which the team would defend the double won so convincingly the season before.

Sections of the support made brave efforts to lift the players but as the ballad said of another – and more tragic – occasion 'a famous face was missing from the green-and-white brigade'.* Long periods of the match against Dundee United were played in silence and it was a miserable start to a season as United did what they were notoriously adept at doing; coming to Glasgow to earn a goalless draw. What should have been an occasion, with the league flag being unfurled in the sunshine, was a flop.

At half time in the Jungle the discussions were surprisingly restrained and sober; it was much the same leaving the ground and heading home. Of course, rumours were spread about the 'real' reason for Kenny Dalglish's departure. Everybody seemed to have a brother who knew someone . . . Dalglish's Rangers background and a desire to earn more money for himself were the obvious reasons but unpleasant ones were being aired: conspiracies, kickbacks, bungs, pocket linings, the necessity to clear Jock Stein's massive gambling debts and, most unlikely, a sexual liaison between Stein and one of the player's relatives.

Most of this was rubbish but human beings need to blame misfortune on something. The whole mood was summed up when a supporter from Fife said, 'This means that Celtic dinnae want to win the European Cup ony mair!' It was this point that hit home and hurt. Since the glory days of only ten years earlier Celtic had always considered themselves rightly as potential winners of the European Cup. As recently as 1974, only three years before, they had reached the semi-final. This latest example of asset-stripping –

---

* The ballad refers to the death of John Thomson.

a melancholy Celtic tradition imposed by the directors – indicated that ambition had gone and that mediocrity would now suffice.

There was also a Scottish dimension to the affair. Since the days of Rabbie Burns (who declared 'We're bought and sold for English gold, sic a parcel o' rogues in a nation') there had been no shortage of Scotsmen who would depart southwards for financial gain. It was utterly predictable that Dalglish would do well for Liverpool, winning European Cups and English championships galore. Yet those of us who hurled obscenities at the television screens the following year as he jumped the advertising hoardings at Wembley after scoring the winning goal for Liverpool in the European Cup final could have consoled ourselves with the thought that such success was not unusual for talented Scots. Scotsmen are credited with numerous inventions – television, the telephone, penicillin and goodness knows what else – but very few of them have actually done so in Scotland.

On 13 August 1977, as we trudged along London Road or the Gallowgate, the hope lingered that we were being too pessimistic. Perhaps the £440,000 would be put to good use? It was a British transfer record and, for 1977, a considerable sum of money. Certainly, much football talent was available both in Scotland and England. In 1977 the Scottish international squad was full of genuinely great players. Could Jock Stein not use his imagination and insight to redeem himself and the club? Could there still be hope?

At the time it was scarcely considered relevant but may have been an omen: two Celtic players sustained injuries on 13 August. Both occurred just before half time as Pat Stanton hobbled off and Alfie Conn was carried off; Stanton and Conn were key players and by the Monday the bad news was confirmed that the knee injuries were serious. Conn would be out of action for a considerable part of the season after a cartilage operation and, upon his return, was not the same player; Stanton was given the news that he would never play football again, a shattering blow for him, and for Celtic.

This was too much to bear. On top of the self-inflicted loss of Dalglish we now had been deprived of the services of Celtic's two most experienced players. Now was the time for Stein to move in the transfer market, to act quickly before the damage could spread and before the season was irreparably ruined. It was not as if Celtic were a poor outfit at the time. Danny McGrain, of course, was genuinely world class and did not give the slightest impression of wanting to leave Celtic Park; there were other men like Ronnie Glavin, Johnny Doyle and Johannes Edvaldsson who were good enough for any team; Roy Aitken and Tommy Burns were more than promising youngsters. Certainly, the nucleus was there, but Celtic needed reinforcement, and urgently.

Sadly, this did not happen. At this time Jock Stein gave every impression of suffering from depression or, at least, burnout. There were good reasons for this. He was now in his mid-fifties and had been in this extraordinarily high-profile job for more than twelve years. In addition, he was still recovering from the serious road accident of two years previously; physical injuries can heal within that period but emotional and mental ones can take longer and do not always respond to rational analysis. Burnout was a definite possibility.

The most significant factor in Stein's ability to cope adequately was the departure of Kenny Dalglish. Rightly or wrongly, he seemed to blame himself for this happening. He was aware, more than most, that he had witnessed the departure of a class act. He had aged considerably and was no longer the buoyant showman who could manipulate the media at will. He was abrupt, moody and, occasionally, downright nasty. At times, he seemed to suffer from catatonic inertia and to lack the will to rehabilitate Celtic. 'Where can I replace a player like Kenny Dalglish?' he would growl repeatedly to journalists.

He had performed miracles before, spectacularly in 1965 when he had taken Celtic from a middle-of-the-league side going nowhere to the capture of the Scottish Cup, and to European glory in 1967. Less spectacular, but highly praiseworthy nevertheless, was his feat in bringing Celtic back from a potentially catastrophic defeat in the 1970 European Cup final to successive league and Scottish Cup doubles in 1971 and 1972.

Could he do it yet again?

Very soon the answer came. By the middle of September, Celtic had lost four league fixtures and the challenge for the title was over, almost before it had begun. In those games Celtic neither got too many breaks from Lady Luck nor from refereeing decisions, but these were no excuses. The faithful supporters began to think that the gods had turned against them. At Ayr, Johnny Doyle was sent off by a stunned referee (literally) who, after treatment from the trainers and partially recovering, decided that Doyle had deliberately kicked the ball against his head! Against Motherwell, ex-Celt Vic Davidson was the main cause of the defeat and his celebrations – excessive and almost provocative – made the point to Stein that he should been kept at Celtic Park and not sacrificed for his contemporary, Dalglish, who had since abandoned the club. At Ibrox, Celtic were two goals up at half time but opted for containment in the second half, and lost 3–2; at Pittodrie, Celtic took the lead in forty-nine minutes but could not hold on for a victory. The final blow came when Celtic played well to beat Hibernian 3–1 but Danny McGrain suffered an ankle injury so stubborn that he was lost to Celtic for almost eighteen months.

Meanwhile, Dalglish seemed to be scoring every week for Liverpool and the BBC were forever showing us that familiar face in an unfamiliar and now hated red strip, arms aloft, celebrating yet another goal as the Kop sang 'Kenny's from Heaven'. It was as if the whole world had turned on Stein and Celtic in a particularly unpleasant, nasty and gloating way. The only crumb of comfort was when Scotland, with Dalglish on board, qualified for the World Cup in Argentina in 1978; the key game against Wales was played at – of all places – Anfield, now Kenny's home ground.

Faced with all this, it was no surprise that Stein withdrew further into his shell. Prickly and insecure when he emerged, he was no longer the reassuring figure of the past. His limp, caused by an ankle injury in 1955, seemed all the more pronounced; other questions were being asked about his health. For the first time since his return to Celtic Park in 1965 a whispering 'Stein must go' campaign was heard among the supporters. Only a year earlier this would have been considered the most dreadful of blasphemies. Now it was being couched in terms that it was all for the benefit of his health.

In fact, Jock Stein did make a few forays into the marketplace but more, it appeared, from a desire to appease supporters rather than from any conviction that he had landed the right man. Noticeably, the buys were all cheap and only one of them, Tom McAdam, was of any lasting success, and that was some seasons later and in a different position under a different manager. Some of his other buys were embarrassing to say the least: John Dowie, Joe Filippi and Frank Munro. A Celtic-daft man from Dundee, Munro was now over thirty and looked upon as a kiss of death wherever he went; but he was signed on trial, immediately made captain and scored an own goal on his debut!

These purchases were in stark contrast to the manner in which Stein had enriched his squads over the past twelve years. Joe McBride, Willie Wallace, Tommy Callaghan, Harry Hood and Dixie Deans had all joined the club at knockdown prices and had fitted in perfectly. Stein had always been shrewd in his assessment of centre forwards; sadly, goal-scoring was now an area in which Celtic were deficient. In Europe, there was an early exit after a spineless performance against mediocre Austrians from Innsbruck after which Stein famously went to bed early – a direct contrast to his normal obsessive, insomniac behaviour. The calendar year of 1977 closed with nothing for anyone of a Celtic persuasion to be happy about.

Early in the New Year a crazy refereeing performance at Ibrox – from J. R. P. Gordon (Tayport) – compounded Stein's difficulties by gifting Rangers a scarcely deserved victory. Mr Gordon denied Celtic the most blatant penalty kick of all time and, while Celtic were still surrounding him in appeal, he allowed Rangers to take the goal kick without permission and run up the field unopposed to score.

It came as a relief when bad weather knocked out a few games but in the spring Celtic again experienced bad luck as they lost the League Cup final after extra time by 2–1 to Rangers again. Better fortune, and the presence of Kenny Dalglish, would have made a colossal difference and Rangers were allowed to go on and win the domestic treble without any real challenge from anybody apart from Billy McNeill's Aberdeen.

It was obvious that Stein had reached the end of the road at Parkhead and would have to be replaced. Billy McNeill, successful at Aberdeen, was clearly the man. McNeill returned to Celtic Park, along with John Clark, in the early summer of 1978. But what could be done with Jock Stein? He could not be sacked and he was offered the job as director of the Celtic Development Pools. Stein was originally happy in this role but disillusion set in quickly and he went to Leeds United as manager. He lasted for only forty days until the job as Scotland manager appeared. As a true Scottish patriot he was ideal, and his knowledge of the game remained unsurpassed. He held this position until his tragic death on the bench at Ninian Park, Cardiff in September 1985. Following the Argentinian fiasco of 1978 under Ally MacLeod, Jock Stein had restored some credibility to Scotland.

When he relinquished the manager's job at Celtic Park, he had apparently been offered a seat on the board. He would have been Celtic's first non-Catholic director, a move that would have been a further slap in the face to bigots everywhere. His move to Leeds and then to the Scotland job effectively prevented this from happening. Perhaps it was just as well that he did not take up Celtic's offer as Billy McNeill might have found it very difficult to work with his former boss looking over his shoulder. Indeed, there was the recent precedent of Manchester United, relegated from the top league in England largely because Matt Busby's two immediate successors (Wilf McGuiness and Dave Sexton) found Busby's continuing presence claustrophobic.

Stein's demise as manager at Celtic Park was sad, and entirely attributable to the transfer of Kenny Dalglish and the after-effects. Stein had been guilty of several fatal misjudgements: he had overestimated his ability to persuade Kenny to stay, and he had informed Liverpool that Dalglish was available. He might have insisted on an exchange deal with Liverpool for another talented player, plus cash. The major fault lay in not replacing Dalglish immediately as the supporters felt sickened and betrayed, leading to the bitter experience of that last season.

The long-term effects of the disastrous transfer were equally profound. Although Celtic did very well to reach the quarter-final of the European Cup in 1980, they did not again participate in European competition after Christmas until 2003. With a few spectacular but isolated exceptions, the team struggled in the 1980s; in the 1990s they sank almost without trace when a criminally unambitious board buried their collective heads in the sand in the face of Rangers' heavy spending. The steady decline in Celtic's fortunes – leading to that fateful day in March 1994 when Celtic almost went out of existence – had their roots in August 1977 when the club's best asset was sold spinelessly for money that was never reinvested in the team.

And yet there has been a recovery which proves Celtic have no need to feel second-rate. Any inferiority complex about clubs like Liverpool was finally brought to an end in March 2003. En route to their date in Seville, Celtic went to Anfield and won by two goals to nil. One goal that night was scored by an Englishman, the other by a Welshman and that fact, as well as the collective skill of the team, proved that Celtic were as big as Liverpool or even bigger as their attendance figures after 2000 indicated.

Dalglish himself had gone from strength to strength after going south, but it was a bittersweet emotion for those who had idolised him at Celtic Park. As Liverpool, with Dalglish the star man, kept winning trophies in England and in Europe, the player continued to be selected for Scotland, his 102 caps established as a record.

To end on a personal note, the writer recalls travelling between Moscow and Leningrad. On the train he met a Muscovite whose English was as rudimentary as the writer's Russian. Anxious to avoid being mistaken for a German or Englishman, he indicated 'Shotlandia' as his country. The man from Moscow beamed: 'Ah, Shotlandia! Boorns, Monstr, Dalglish!' 'Boorns' was a poet, 'Monstr' lives in Loch Ness – and the mention of the third, even after many years, caused distress.

Comments

The impassive, albeit classy, Dalglish had signed for Jock Stein in 1967, not for Celtic, and when he took his impassivity south for bigger prizes in 1977, it couldn't have been better timing for Liverpool but it couldn't have been worse for Celtic. It was like having a sour dessert after a banquet.

John Cairney

I was doing a summer course at St. Michael's College in the University of Toronto when I noticed a brief paragraph in the Toronto Globe & Mail, announcing the transfer of Kenny Dalglish to Liverpool for £400,000. I felt sick.

Tom Campbell

I could never understand the bitterness about Dalglish's move southward to Liverpool. He had been a brilliant player for Celtic, had performed conscientiously for seasons and decided to move on; he was perfectly entitled to do that. I don't think that he was popular with the Celtic fans in the way that Jimmy Johnstone was (and is). He was a bit like Johnny Haynes of Fulham in that he refused to turn a bad pass into a good one by making a heroic effort to get it – and that coloured the supporters' perception. Did Celtic, or Stein, use him as well as he could have? A player who can score thirty goals in a season should be employed as a striker, I think.

Bob Crampsey

I heard the news on a train coming up north from London. The guard told us in the tones of somebody announcing the end of the world that Dalglish had been transferred. It took me months to get over it. Apart from his own individual skill, just think of the effect he had on those around him: Joe Craig scored twenty-three goals in 1976/77 but only sixteen in 1977/78 while Ronnie Glavin netted twenty-six in 1976/77 and only eleven the following season. He was missed for years.

Gerry Dunbar

For me it was a thunderbolt; I was working in London at the time and there had been no mention in the newspapers about Dalglish's move – until it happened. I don't think Kenny owed Celtic anything; in fact, after seven years at Celtic Park he had been carrying the team for several seasons. Speaking of Kenny Dalglish, I used to work with his future wife Marina at the National Savings Bank in Cowglen. She was a lovely girl and Kenny had asked her out. In fact, it was the very day that he made his real competitive debut by scoring with a penalty kick against Rangers at Ibrox. He had arranged to meet her at Boots' Corner (where Renfield Street meets Argyle Street) but Marina's father, when he heard about the proposed rendezvous, was a bit miffed. He drove Marina to Boots' Corner, had Kenny pointed out to him, and very abruptly ordered the young man into the car.

Tony Griffin

This was my first vivid memory of betrayal by Celtic. I felt totally and utterly dejected. It was like a death in the family.

Craig McAughtrie

There seemed something clandestine about the whole affair, with Jock Stein apparently phoning Liverpool to tell them that Dalglish was available. It was a deal done privately, and I think Dalglish should have been put up for transfer openly with an auction for his services taking place.

Patrick Reilly

The transfer of Dalglish, although not unexpected, was a landmark in the modern history of Celtic. It underlined the fact that Celtic Football Club no longer saw itself as capable of competing at the highest level (namely, the European Cup), which participating in and aspiring to win the supporters had come to regard as their birthright.

I recall meeting one such supporter some ten years after the event who had never been to another Celtic match after Dalglish's departure. He was insistent that he never would return, so angry was he at what he saw as the board's betrayal: 'That mob would sell anything that moves at Celtic Park!' he spat out with such venom that I believe he would have kept his vow. He might not have been alone in his beliefs as that transaction in August 1977 shattered many illusions among the supporters.

Pat Woods

7

UNFORGIVEN

Gerry Dunbar

Simply appearing in the Celtic first team bestows on any player a modicum of fame. It might be of the fleeting or ephemeral variety; wasn't it Andy Warhol who said that everybody should get fifteen minutes of playing in the Hoops? But, during his Parkhead career, a footballer will become a well-known face, not least because of the nature of the media in the west of Scotland. If he is lucky, his exploits on the pitch will allow him a certain amount of longevity in the spotlight, endear him to the supporters and accord him a status akin to a minor deity. If he is very fortunate, he will transcend mortality and ascend into the pantheon of legends.

Alternatively, there are those who, for whatever reason, will find their particular chapter in the club's history cursed by a stroke of ill-fortune or shamed by some misdemeanour that will blight their entry in *The Alphabet of the Celts* forever and give them a rare insight into the reason why Coleridge's Ancient Mariner cancelled his subscription to *Albatross Watchers' Monthly*.

Few would argue that Maurice Johnston certainly staked his claim when, on Monday, 10 July 1989, he signed for Rangers and finally ended his turbulent affair with the club for which he had so frequently professed his undying love, an affair that, in the eyes of the

Celtic support, saw him take a road less-travelled: from hero to villain back to hero and then to the human incarnation of the contents of Beelzebub's dustbin.

Johnston's unrequited period lasted until 1984 when he was signed by Davie Hay. His Celtic-minded credentials were impeccable and his route to Parkhead had been a familiarly circuitous one. As a boy he had been sneaking into Celtic Park without his parents' permission and was once even the subject of a 'lost boy' announcement when he went to a European Cup tie against Kokkola with some friends and ended up on his own; for the record, nobody claimed him. A promising youngster, he was a regular in the Glasgow Catholic schools select and was offered professional terms with Partick Thistle in 1980 after impressing in a trial match against Celtic. Later the same night he was offered a similar trial with Celtic but having agreed to go to Firhill he turned it down; trials were to become a regular feature of his playing career. Peter Cormack gave him his break in the Thistle first team and he went on to score forty-seven goals in little more than two seasons before the Jags accepted an offer of £200,000 for him from Watford in November 1983. His seventeen goals in twenty games at Vicarage Road prompted Jock Stein to give him a Scotland call-up and he scored on his debut against Wales in a 2–1 victory after coming on as a half-time substitute. Under Graham Taylor, Watford reached the FA Cup final in 1984, losing 2–0 to Everton with Johnston leading the line. Celtic lost the Scottish Cup final to Aberdeen the same day and, as he put it in his autobiography: 'Honestly, I felt as disappointed for them as I did for us. I suppose it was round about then that I was reminded of where my heart really lay.'

He had heard a rumour that Celtic were willing to sign him if the price was right and, in August 1984, despite his success at Watford, he handed in a transfer request. It might also have helped that he had dropped a subtle hint when he attended a Glasgow derby in April, just a few weeks before the cup final. Interviewed live after the match by Radio Clyde's Paul Cooney he announced that he'd always wanted to play for Celtic and that he'd walk from Watford to Parkhead for Davie Hay. He got his wish in October. The news was broken to him on a midweek morning as the Watford players were gathering for a trip to Cardiff. He had been listening to Celtic songs through the headphones of his Walkman when he was called into Taylor's office and told he was being sold to Celtic for £400,000.

It was time for the love affair to be consummated, but the climax had more than a touch of burlesque about it. Davie Hay and lawyer Mel Goldberg had arranged to meet Johnston and his agent Frank Boyd in Langan's, an outrageously trendy London eaterie. The Celtic board were represented by director Jack McGinn, a man whose popular image on the Parkhead terracing was akin to a character in a Dickens novel, the one keeping Ebenezer Scrooge's wild spending in check. At some point during the meal – at which large amounts of lobster and champagne were consumed – a stripogram appeared, but the real entertainment came when the waiter proffered the bill. After Boyd had offered to pay, Jack magnanimously insisted that he would pick up the tab for this one. It was a historic moment; after all, £400,000 was a record transfer fee for Celtic, as well as a figure the accountant probably thought he'd never see on a club cheque, unless he'd eaten some dodgy Welsh rarebit before going to bed. Alas, Jack's spirit of largesse promptly went up like a flambé when he saw that the night's repast was going to set the assembled company back £480 and his solution to an embarrassing dilemma can only leave one wondering what on earth board meetings must have been like at the time. He offered to toss for it: heads or tails? Jack lost, then proposed best of three. He lost that as well.

For public consumption the reason given for Johnston's return north of the border was homesickness. Although this was partly true, he was actually turning his back on more money just to pull on the Hoops. He appeared on that Saturday's *Football Focus* where an incredulous Bob Wilson asked him why he was going back to Scotland. 'I just want to play for Celtic.' The formalities were duly completed on the Thursday evening when Johnston signed a two-and-a-half-year contract. He described it as, 'The best day of my life' and at the time swore he would never leave, picturing himself signing new deal after new deal.

The figures involved in this transfer soon were to pale into insignificance as football entered the boom period of the nineties. But, at the time, most of us were stunned that a Celtic board – in the vanguard of the fiscal prudence movement long before it became either a buzz word for Gordon Brown or an economic necessity for clubs at the mercy of their moneylenders – were willing to part with so much cash in a single deal.

Since taking over from Billy McNeill in the summer of 1983, Davie Hay had spent something in the region of £375,000 to acquire six players: full back Brian Whittaker from Partick Thistle (£50,000), striker Jim Melrose from Coventry City (£100,000), winger John Colquhoun (£60,000) from Stirling Albion, Allan McInally from Ayr United (£95,000) and Brian McClair from Motherwell (£70,000), yet another striker and the only one out of that particular list to have a genuinely successful career at Celtic. With Aberdeen and Dundee United enjoying an extraordinary spell of dominance, and Celtic exhibiting a worrying trend of losing crunch games, it was a frustrating time to be a supporter. The general feeling was that a lack of investment in the playing staff – despite having amassed quite a profit in transfer dealings during the previous few years – coupled with a willingness to replace genuine talent like Charlie Nicholas and Murdo MacLeod with journeymen pros was lowering the overall standard of the team's performances. This was reflected in the average attendance at league matches dropping, down by around 5,000 per home fixture. In truth, we looked well short of second best.

The Maurice Johnston transfer bucked the trend. It was a sign that the transcendentally optimistic among us took to mean that the fabled Biscuit Tin had finally been prised open and that the board were ready to meet the challenges that faced them head on, through a heady mix of imaginative speculation in the transfer market and an aggressively bold approach to investment in playing staff. To the sceptics, on the other hand, it was a desperate attempt to staunch the flow of punters who were finding alternative forms of masochism on a Saturday afternoon by blowing not only the aforesaid profits but also the recently acquired sponsorship money derived from a three-year deal with double-glazing company CR Smith.

Johnston went straight into the team for the league match against Hibernian at Celtic Park on 13 October 1984. At Davie Hay's suggestion he didn't warm-up on the pitch so that the first sight the Jungle would have of him was when he ran on in the Hoops. As he puts it himself: 'I'll never forget that ovation until I breathe my last. It was so emotional I just couldn't speak . . . the most exhilarating experience I have ever known. Put it this way, by comparison making love is like watching paint dry.' He didn't score in Celtic's 3–0 win that afternoon – even refusing the chance to take a penalty in case he missed and spoiled the occasion – but it wasn't long before he did open his account with a close-range header in a 3–1 victory at Tannadice a week later.

It wasn't long either before he was beginning to attract the kind of attention that suggested he was going to be fodder for the Glasgow tabloids as well as being a major irritant both to opposition defences and Celtic followers of a more traditional stripe in equal measure. What passes for the paparazzi in the west of Scotland, together with their attendant hackers of lurid gossip, had lost a rich vein of copy when Charlie Nicholas left Parkhead for Arsenal. It's true that the bold Charles was still good for the occasional headline but, at a remove of some distance, his London exploits were unlikely to shift as many red tops as a target on their own doorstep. With his dyed blond locks, earring, discreet white Porsche and louche affectation for champagne Johnston was easily the man to step into Charlie's sockless shoes. London had whetted Mo's appetite for the high life and he wasn't about to adapt to his new surroundings easily.

Towards the end of his first season with Celtic he had scored five goals in seven appearances in the Scottish Cup and had helped the club to the centenary final, due to be played at Hampden on 18 May 1985 against Dundee United. On the Wednesday before the match Johnston found himself standing in the dock of Glasgow District Court as stipendary magistrate Robert Hamilton passed up the chance to be awarded the freedom of the City of Discovery by fining the player £200, having found him guilty on a charge of resetting three stolen tracksuits worth £85. His co-accused, who had thirteen previous convictions, was jailed for sixty days. According to Sergeant William Donaldson, he had spotted them 'acting furtively' along with two others in a doorway adjacent to a sports shop up a lane in the city centre. They had been buying tracksuits liberated from the shop and were apprehended in mid deal. The actual offence had taken place while Johnston was a Thistle player but by the time the story broke it was Maurice Johnston of Celtic who was making the headlines. It didn't help that the players had to postpone their pre-cup final photo-shoot as a result of Johnston's appearance before the beaks.

On 17 March 1987 Johnston, this time in the company of his minder, was found guilty of assault on the premises of a popular Glasgow nightclub and fined £500 by Sheriff Archibald Bell QC. The incident had happened in November 1986. The police arrested him before dawn on 2 December and detained him at one of their guest houses – in Stuart Street – where he checked out the following afternoon at three. Following his court appearance Celtic suspended him for a week and he missed two league games (against Hamilton Accies and Clydebank) as well as Roy Aitken's testimonial against Manchester United.

Rumours that he was involved in recreational drug use – a common one was that he would customarily wear a long-sleeve jersey to hide needle marks on his arms – eventually prompted Celtic to admit him to hospital on the pretext of a check-up and he was found to be free of substance abuse. There was also a paternity suit that was ongoing throughout his first spell in Glasgow and a constant barrage of headlines about his very public social life that kept him on the front pages almost as much as on the sports pages.

Despite this, his contribution to the Celtic cause during his sojourn in the Hoops cannot be understated. He formed an incredible partnership with Brian McClair notwithstanding the fact that the two didn't speak to one another off the pitch (Chalky and Cheesy?) and in successive seasons between 1984 and 1987 they scored between them forty-two, forty-nine and seventy (!) goals. For a player of slight stature Johnston was possessed of considerable physical strength which, when allied to his considerable bravery, sharp reflexes and composure inside the penalty area, made him a natural finisher in the style of Denis Law. He had a prodigious leap that made him highly dangerous in the air and he could complement this natural ability as a striker with a sure touch on the ball, an eye for a telling pass and reserves of stamina and energy. He was a key player in the club's winning of the Scottish Cup in 1985 and the league on that unforgettable day at Love Street the following season. He later recalled the scenes after that particular match: 'Out on the pitch it was bedlam. I lost my boots, so I did my lap of honour in my black shiny walking shoes.' His record of 71 goals in 127 games (a strike rate of a goal every 1.7 games) stands comparison with some of the best forwards ever to have worn the famous hoops. Would that this was the end of his chapter in Celtic's history! As lovers we might have parted amicably and stayed good friends.

Johnston was to claim that police harassment, sectarian abuse and the constant glare of the media spotlight were contributory factors in his eventual departure from Celtic in 1987. Davie Hay even hinted that, 'There were people in the city of Glasgow who were setting out to wreck his career with Celtic. He thought he was the victim of a carefully orchestrated hate campaign. I tend to think he was right.'

It's impossible not to feel a degree of sympathy for someone who has sleazy tabloid reporters literally camped outside the front door of their house, of course, but I can't help thinking there was a degree of contributory negligence involved. The aforementioned biography – ghosted by Chick Young in 1988 and a particularly risible read, even by the appallingly low standards of this literary sub-genre – cites umpteen examples of victimisation. Yet there is not the slightest acknowledgement that perhaps a change of lifestyle or moderation of behaviour on the part of the player himself might have made some difference. Little more than a shameless attempt at self-justification posing as the confessions of a football 'character' – a Scottish euphemism for an immature, feckless individual incapable of foregoing a few nights of hedonistic indulgence for the sake of appearing to be too professional in his occupation – the book contains few passages where Johnston acknowledges that perhaps he could have done more to live up to the standards demanded by those paying his wages.

The parting of the ways, when it came, was inevitably messy. One newspaper story in 1986 read: 'Celtic superstar Mo Johnston is at the centre of a bizarre double agent mystery. Mo's former agent Frank Boyd is believed to be negotiating a new £200,000 deal to keep the striker at Parkhead. But that came as a shock to Mo's present agent the flamboyant Bill McMurdo.' The very mention of 'the flamboyant Bill McMurdo' is enough to send a shiver down the spine, even today. Not that 'the flamboyant Bill McMurdo' could ever be accused of acting against the best interests of Celtic. A quick read of his curriculum vitae would easily dispel any Celtic fan's feelings of unease at the thought of his being at the heart of any player's contract negotiations: 'Orangeman, freemason and fanatical Rangers supporter whose mansion at Uddingston, called Ibrox, is emblazoned with the red, white and blue of Unionism, with one room set aside as a shrine to Rangers. He was also a leading light and founder of the Scottish Unionist Party, which is violently opposed to the Anglo-Irish Agreement.' He was known to the Celtic fans simply as Agent Orange.

To be fair to him, McMurdo never let his political or religious principles get in the way of making a few quid and his clients all appear to have great respect for him, regardless of their persuasion. Club directors, by contrast, saw him in a different light and he was at one time or another banned from Fir Park, Tynecastle and Celtic Park, from where Jack McGinn wrote to inform him that he was *persona non grata*. In 1989 he attempted to sue Brian McClair over the proceeds from a sportswear sponsorship deal. After a two-day court case, presiding-Sheriff Andrew Lothian dismissed McMurdo's case with the words, 'I cannot accept Mr. McMurdo as a credible witness.'

Johnston later admitted that the newspaper story was, in its essence, true and that he had been stringing Boyd along while dealing with McMurdo. Boyd, as it happens, was still involved in the deal as a negotiator for Celtic. Call it a wild hunch but, once we realised who was involved, we resigned ourselves to losing the services of Maurice Johnston at the end of the 1986/87 season. There was a brief hope of a reconciliation when the board also dispensed with the services of Davie Hay – a week after giving him their blessing to spend £425,000 on Mick McCarthy and smash the club's wage structure into the bargain – and appointed Billy McNeill. But the new boss appeared in no mood to coax the player into staying when he was asked to comment: 'As far as I'm concerned Mo Johnston can sign for whoever he likes.'

Within a few days he did just that, and signed for Nantes. The love affair was over. Custody of the tracksuits was uncontested.

The departure of Johnston was bad enough, but big Billy had to contend with the loss of McInally, McClair and MacLeod as well. He succeeded to such an extent that Celtic won the double in the centenary year of 1987/88. While the board had backed the manager that particular season with money to spend on players, it was clear that this was a team that wasn't going to last. We waited to see what would happen during the summer of 1988 to strengthen the club from a position of success but the only new signing was Ian Andrews, a man who did goalkeeper impersonations, bought to cover for Pat Bonner when the latter succumbed to a back problem. After just nine games between the sticks, and following a mauling at Ibrox, Andrews was in turn replaced by Alan Rough. The spirit of 1987/88 soon evaporated in the wake of some poor league performances, the defence was registering itself as a state charity once again and the skids were put in place under another title challenge. Rangers were being moulded into an implacable foe under the Murray–Souness axis and they seemed determined to hammer as many nails as they could into Celtic's coffin in as short a time as possible.

Celtic had managed a more consistent run in the Scottish Cup and were due to meet Rangers in the 1989 final but the bad news was that Frank McAvennie had been sold for £1.25 million to West Ham and Andy Walker was suffering from an eye injury that would keep him out of the game. With such a shortage of striking power the prospect of finishing the season with a trophy looked like nothing more than wishful thinking. Until, that is, hope arrived from a most unlikely quarter. With the final looming on 20 May, we awoke bleary-eyed on the twelfth to the headline 'All One Big Happy Family Again'. Maurice Johnston was coming back.

It was scarcely believable. Not only were we about to re-sign a potent striker but also the board had allowed Billy McNeill to spend a new Scottish record fee of £1.2 million. In the understatement of the decade McNeill paid tribute to the new all-singing, all-spending board: 'I have not spent a million pounds before. It is something you could worry about but not in this case. Of course it's a lot of money but I had the easiest job in the world persuading the board that it was good value.' Billy had clearly won the best of three.

The player himself had appeared on national television to confirm that he was signing for Celtic and that he still had appalling taste in clothes as he sported a pullover resembling the aftermath of an explosion in Remnant Kings. Positively beaming, he declared in front of the cameras that he had rejected other offers to come back to play for his beloved Hoops. On a more intimate note, he revealed that his spell on the Continent had matured him – made a fine Camembert out of a Kraft cheese slice – and he wanted his daughter to grow up in Scotland and go to a Scottish school, something Johnston himself did on a rather infrequent, ad hoc basis.

As it transpired, Johnston had been making noises about coming back to Celtic while on international duty some months before. Roy Aitken made it clear to him that Billy McNeill was interested and told Johnston to phone McNeill. In his autobiography McNeill recalls this telephone conversation with Johnston: 'I warned him that I was no mood to be messed about, but he insisted that his intentions were honourable. I then asked Mo if his agent, Bill McMurdo, would be involved in any negotiations, but he again assured me that he would be handling that side of things himself.'

At this juncture the manager discussed the putative transfer with his board of directors and they then made overtures to Nantes that were received favourably. The clubs agreed the fee and the money was to be made available from the Frank McAvennie transfer. According to Billy McNeill, discussions went without a hitch and a deal was agreed quickly. The chairman, Jack McGinn, and director, Chris White, travelled to Nantes to finalise the transfer fee and lodge a deposit of £400,000. Johnston, meanwhile, signed a letter of agreement, outlining his personal terms, which he appeared delighted with. However, when he returned the rental car, he left his copy of the agreement lying on the front seat. Later it was returned to the club; so, Celtic not only had their own copy, they were also in possession of the player's documentation.

Celtic checked with representatives of FIFA who were in Scotland for the World Youth Cup finals and were assured that the document signed by Johnston complied with their regulations. It was watertight and binding. In view of this, they felt that it was propitious to go ahead with the press conference on 12 May to announce the return of the prodigal on a four-year contract.

In the *Glasgow Herald*, James Traynor summed up the thoughts of many who were baffled by Johnston's desire to return to the scene of so many of his personal problems: 'Few will be able to comprehend his decision to return to the goldfish bowl existence of top class football in the divided city of Glasgow, but it seems that everyone underestimated the persuasive powers of Billy McNeill.' It wasn't all we underestimated.

What we couldn't know was that things were far from watertight as far as Johnston signing a contract to play for Celtic was concerned. Indeed, like many a venture undertaken by the board at that time, one or two leaks had already begun to spring.

One of them was that Johnston's contract was not owned by the player, nor indeed by Nantes, but by a completely separate company, the representative of which was 'the flamboyant Bill McMurdo'. Aware of Celtic's interest in signing the player, but claiming no knowledge of a press conference arranged at Celtic Park, McMurdo sent his client to Paradise that day armed with a letter outlining the situation. It stated that he couldn't sign for Celtic until the club spoke to McMurdo. These days it doesn't seem unusual that the ownership of a player's contract could be held by a company, or a consortium of businessmen, but it appears to have been incomprehensible to Jack McGinn, who still maintains that Celtic would have been prohibited from dealing with an 'outside agency' on the basis that 'clubs deal with clubs'. Not content with leaving important documents lying around in hired cars, Maurice also neglected to show Bill McMurdo's letter to anybody inside Celtic Park. At which point the show degenerates into Grand Guignol. Although he was made aware that Johnston couldn't put his name to anything meaningful, Jack McGinn is reputed to have put his head round the door of one of the offices and said, 'Just kid on you've signed, we'll sort the situation out later.'

The fans travelled to Love Street the following afternoon for the last league fixture in better spirits than of late and with the distinct feeling that, although Johnston couldn't become a Celtic player until 1 July, it would be all right on the night. Johnston attended the match as well, travelling on the team bus, and was happy to sign autographs and wave to the fans as one returned from the wilderness.

Celtic won by a single goal, courtesy of Joe Miller. With the feel-good factor far from dissipated, a week later Celtic beat Rangers in the Scottish Cup final by one goal to nil, Joe Miller again netting the winner after latching on to a short pass-back.

It was some consolation for relinquishing the title in such abject fashion. As a measure of the balance of power between the respective sides, though, the swingometer had barely twitched back in the direction of the East End. And it was about to take another severe lurch towards Ibrox.

The first hint that all was not well with the Maurice Johnston transfer came on the Monday morning after the game at Love Street when the player failed to show up for a scheduled meeting with Billy McNeill and Jack McGinn. A week after the Parkhead press conference McMurdo was already being quoted in the papers as saying that there were contractual difficulties and that he was seeking legal advice over the deal. By the time the annual dinner of the Scottish Professional Footballers Association came around – two weeks after Celtic had done the deal with Nantes – Billy McNeill was becoming aware of rumours linking Johnston with a move to Rangers.

On 26 May, Johnston confirmed that there were problems about coming to Celtic. Some points in the contract bothered him, he said, but the trouble was all at the French end. However, two days' later the deal had collapsed.

According to Graeme Souness, the Rangers manager happened to meet McMurdo two days after Johnston's picture had appeared showing Maurice bedecked in his Celtic jersey. 'What are you doing letting Maurice Johnston sign for Celtic?' he said from under a perfectly trimmed moustache. Instead of informing Souness that it was what Johnston wanted and that he would be doing everything he possibly could to make sure his player got what he wanted, McMurdo informed Souness, from under a less than perfectly trimmed beard, that the player was still available. A long-standing admirer of the player, Souness put the idea to David Murray, got the go-ahead and arranged for further talks with McMurdo.

Although Johnston had been trying to avoid speaking to Billy McNeill, he was finally tracked down at a Scotland training camp. McNeill was clearly not happy at being mucked about: 'As soon as

I met Johnston my suspicions were confirmed. He was both evasive and, I think, a little embarrassed.' McNeill left Troon knowing that Celtic had a fight on their hands, but was encouraged by the fact that FIFA had assured the club the letter of agreement was binding. He flew out for a family holiday to the States convinced that the board would be able to put a stop to Johnston and McMurdo's plan to conclude a deal with our arch rivals.

We were all coming to terms with the fact that Johnston wouldn't be signing for Celtic after all. But it was also important that a weapon we were about to unleash on Rangers was not about to be turned round and used against us. The Celtic manager's avowed intention was to prevent what he termed 'any further monkey business'. He was given to understand that all Celtic had to do was pay Nantes the balance of the fee. Once they received the £800,000, which was still outstanding, Johnston would officially become a Celtic player. Whether we could have succeeded in getting Johnston to play was, of course, a different matter but, had Celtic followed the course McNeill implored the board to take, Johnston could not have signed for any other club without Celtic's blessing and, as far as McNeill was concerned, he would never have been allowed to become a Rangers player.

Talk about having your holiday spoilt! McNeill learned while he was away that the board had dropped all claims on Johnston and were now going to concentrate on signing players who actually wanted to play for the club. The way was now clear for Rangers to step in, although Johnston himself still insisted on denying rumours that he was on the verge of signing for Souness: 'Certainly I won't go to Rangers. They don't sign Catholics and, anyway, I don't want to go to Ibrox.'

The announcement that Maurice Johnston had signed for Rangers was delivered from the Blue Room at Ibrox amidst an atmosphere of undisguised smugness from those assembled round the table. Johnston – who sat throughout much of the meeting with his tongue literally embedded in his cheek – looked about as comfortable as a laboratory frog connected to the mains as he made his contribution to the afternoon's proceedings: 'I am absolutely thrilled', he said, sounding absolutely petrified. 'My admiration for the club is huge,' he added, which was something he'd kept to himself up until that point.

It kept everything else off the front pages. War, Famine, Death, AIDS, Pestilence, Recession, Depression: all paled into insignificance in west-central Scotland because Rangers Football Club had finally gone public on signing a player generally recognised as a Catholic.

I put it that way because Maurice was a Catholic only by the loosest possible definition. Transubstantiation, benediction, canon law: mention any of these to Maurice and his response would most probably be a vacant stare. Tommy Burns's autobiography has a chapter devoted to the importance of religion in his life. I've read every page of Johnston's 'book' more than once. (That's me paid for all my sins, incidentally.) Throughout his booze-fuelled odyssey in pursuit of blondes not one mention is made of his faith or the sacraments. There isn't a single reference to God in it. There's a chapter called 'Girls Just Want to Have Fun' about his sexual conquests, and loads of space given over to his debauchery, but very little on the mystery of faith. His reputation as a 'high-profile Roman Catholic' appears to have stemmed from the school he infrequently attended and an especially infamous League Cup final at Hampden. While playing for Celtic against Rangers, Johnston was red-carded for alleged head-butting an opponent and, as he left the pitch, he blessed himself.

Johnston wasn't even the first Catholic to sign for Rangers. There were even three in the space of three years once, albeit the years in question were 1888–91. In the twentieth century two names sprang less than readily to mind in Laurie Blyth and Don Kichenbrand, although the latter pretty much renounced his religion and kept it all a secret, ironically coming out of the Ibrox closet once again only in the wake of Johnston's press conference in the Blue Room.

Nevertheless, in the eyes of the Scottish public, Johnston was a Catholic, and Pandora's Box was now well and truly opened. It was safe at last to mention the C-word inside the Blue Room. It was all right now to acknowledge that Rangers had been practising sectarian discrimination as a signing policy, but it was all going to be different from now on.

The year before Glasgow was set to assume the mantle of

European City of Culture, it was going to be interesting to see how our citizens would take the news. The newspapers knew exactly where to get the most extreme reactions and posted their Kate Adies to various sectors of the front. Allan Laing for the *Glasgow Herald* was on the spot at the nearest Rangers social club to Ibrox. 'Everyone appeared to be speechless,' he wrote, 'One official said, "Nobody wants to talk about it."' The *Evening Times* had embedded Gordon Beattie in the Masonic Arms, a quaintly named hostelry in deepest Larkhall. His dispatches captured the devastation as the locals reeled in shock and awe:

> The signing of the ex-Celtic player has sent shock waves through the true-blue fans in Larkhall. Irate fans claim Rangers have turned their backs on their supporters. A member of the Larkhall Loyalists Supporters' Club has burned his scarf in protest over the signing. 'I felt sick when I heard about it; it's terrible. This is a kick in the teeth to Larkhall.'

The wife of the secretary of a Rangers Supporters' Club from East Kilbride declared that she had been suffering from insomnia as a result of disturbing religious visions involving Johnston: 'My blood is boiling. Is Mo Johnston going to run about Ibrox with his crucifix? I've thought about nothing else all night.' David Miller, general secretary of the Rangers Supporters' Association, was peddling an equally hard line, as the *Glasgow Herald* reported on 11 July 1989:

> I never thought in my wildest dreams that they would sign him. Why him above all? It's a sad day for Rangers. There will be a lot of people handing in their season tickets. I don't want to see a Roman Catholic at Ibrox. Rangers have always stood for one thing and the biggest majority of the support have been brought up with the idea of a true-blue Rangers team. I thought they would sign a Catholic eventually, perhaps in three or four years' time, but someone from the continent.

Perhaps Mr Miller thought Catholics from the Continent were a less-virulent strain than the home-grown variety. Tom Shields was able to fill his *Herald* diary with anecdotes from the Mermaid Bar. They included a remark from one Rangers supporter who seemed to be prone to a touch of hyperbole: 'Who does Souness think he is? God? He has ruined all our lives!'

A few days later the *Daily Record* claimed a world exclusive under the headline 'Death Threat to a Dog Named Mo'. The story breathlessly revealed that a wee woman in Dumbarton owned a mongrel dog, the eponymous 'Mo' of the headline, which had been the innocent victim of death threats from local neds, who had also threatened to break the poor creature's legs.

There was less of a tone of *fatwah* about the response of the Celtic fans but there was a backlash nonetheless. We had not just been jilted; we had been onto a promise only to be stood up at Boots' Corner. To many, Johnston was not a professional footballer offering his services to the highest bidder, but a Judas Escariot who had committed the ultimate act of betrayal. A Celtic diehard was even forced to name his newly born quads Eenie, Meenie, Minie and Pat.

Among 'the questions everybody is asking' in the *Sunday Mail's* Mo Johnston dossier was the one that quite a few people were curious about: 'Where will he live?' Johnston had actually stated once that he would sign for Rangers, but only if they paid him a million pounds and bought him Stirling Castle to live in. Archie McKay, the compiler of the newspaper's dossier, pointed out helpfully that Stirling Castle wasn't for sale, but he knew of a castle near Balquhidder that was. They even showed a picture of it. It looked like part of the Maginot Line. Another option was Graeme Souness's house near Edinburgh 'with its high walls topped with razor wire and security cameras.'

At least Salman Rushdie only had the Muslims after him.

These sound bites from the borderlands of reason might have sold a few papers, but the reality was that there was no massed revolutionary uprising. A crowd of around seventy was reported as having gathered outside the Ibrox front door and, despite being renowned for not having a predilection for surrender, they dispersed passively when invited to do so by the police. Rangers admitted thirty calls on the day of the signing demanding a refund of their season-ticket books. The callers were told refunds were not to be allowed under the circumstances, reminiscent of insurance claims refused on the grounds that the accident was 'an act of God' (or even Graeme Souness). The fact was that most of the Rangers supporters realised that their club had signed a good player and there were plenty waiting to take up the season tickets of those determined to throw theirs away. A negligible number of hardliners stayed away but they came back sooner or later. Where else was there for them to go?

Of the main characters involved in the drama, Billy McNeill is the one who emerged with most credit. The initial approaches to return to Scotland had been made by Johnston and the player was the one who had made the running. McNeill, like the rest of us, must have been convinced that somebody who was willing to appear on national television announcing his return to Celtic had every intention of actually doing it. The manager had been undeservedly embarrassed by Johnston's volte-face, despicable in the eyes of most objective observers.

The Celtic board emerged looking incompetent. They had refused to speak to Bill McMurdo on a point of principle and it backfired on them in spectacular fashion. Their misplaced idealism in releasing Johnston from his 'legally binding' obligations was perceived by many Celtic supporters as a weak and anachronistic response to the situation at a time when the world of the football movers and shakers was increasingly being dominated by a new breed of rapacious and single-minded club owners in the mould of Murray and Souness. The fact is that the non-payment of Johnston's tax liability was undoubtedly a red herring, but the board were never highly regarded in matters financial. It was easy to perceive penny-pinching at the root of it all, even though the truth is they were prepared to break the Scottish transfer record to buy Johnston in the first place.

Why they didn't – in Neville Chamberlain style – produce the piece of paper that Johnston had signed remains a mystery.

Graeme Souness and David Murray were given the journalistic equivalent of a standing ovation in the editorials and it would be churlish not to acknowledge that they had made a bold move. But as far as the cynics among us were concerned, they couldn't lose. They had already signed a black player and a Jewish player (and even the captain of England); so, it was clearly just a matter of time before they delivered a Catholic. Considering the circumstances,

Maurice Johnston is unlikely to have been the strategic objective. It all seems too spur-of-the-moment for that, but he became available and from their point of view it was a brilliant publicity coup as well as a chance to embarrass the Hoops. At a time when they were pursuing high-profile participation in European competitions, with one stroke they had fended off any potentially embarrassing interventions from the sport's governing bodies, allayed any suspicions that might have been held by potential sponsors and, crucially for us, delivered a kick to the nethers of Celtic which took the club years to recover from – a fact that perhaps did most to mollify some of the hardest of the Ibrox hard core.

The signing of Maurice Johnston made it clear to Rangers supporters that there were going to be more players who practised an erstwhile proscribed religion, and it was suggested at the time that the likes of Murray and Souness would no longer pander to a narrow-minded bigoted element among the Rangers support. Yet, among other incidences of *plus ca change* in more recent years, Rangers players like Jorg Albertz and Marco Negri were told not to bless themselves on the pitch. Perhaps had the Maurice Johnston affair been conducted differently, and for less-questionable motives, it might well have broadened the appeal of Rangers the way the appointment of Jock Stein as Celtic manager did for the Parkhead club back in the sixties.

Johnston may try to portray himself as being the self-possessed breaker down of ancient barriers of intolerance at Ibrox, but even at the time it was easy to see him as someone at the mercy of forces far beyond his comprehension that were manipulating him for reasons he could not understand. It is difficult to imagine what good he could possibly have foreseen coming of his actions – other than a healthy pay cheque – and he spent a little over two years at Rangers before finally admitting that he had bitten off more than he could chew.

He had been pretty quiet during Glasgow derbies, missing chances to such an extent that one sarcastic correspondent to *Not The View* urged the fanzine to lay off him as he was on a difficult fifth-column mission, but on 4 November 1989 he scored a late winner against his formerly beloved Celtic before wheeling away to celebrate in front of the Copland Road stand. In a gesture of magnanimous reconciliation, one Celtic fan attempted to present him with a half-eaten pie, although, given the distance and necessary trajectory, it was little surprise that Strathclyde's finest were to construe the incident as a breach of the peace. Far from keeping a low profile, Johnston found it virtually impossible to keep out of the tabloids, his misadventures including singing 'The Sash' at a Rangers supporters' function, and being sent home from a pre-season training camp with his face covered in cuts and bruises, the official explanation for which was that he had fallen on some bed springs.

He finally left for Everton in November 1991 and thereafter his career is a classic study in a player gradually fading away. He wound up in Kansas where, irony heaped on irony, he played his final game in the blue of Kansas City Wiz against the green-and-white hoops of Santos Laguna.

Was it a day that shook Celtic? It probably shook Rangers more, but it certainly did its bit to hasten the end of the old regime at Celtic Park. The day after the Ibrox press conference an intrepid, not to mention observant, reporter spotted the Union Jack flying at half mast over the main stand at Celtic Park. 'If the flag is flying at half mast it must have slipped down the pole,' said Tom Grant. It was, in fact, an ominous portent for Tom and his fellow board members.

At the end of January, following a 1–0 defeat at home to Motherwell, there was a demonstration in the car park outside Celtic Park. It wasn't planned or organised, but it was the first of its kind for a generation. Yet even as early as July 1989 the fans could see the writing on the wall. Sadly, the writing would have to be ten feet high, written in blood and signed by the manager of the Bank of Scotland, before anyone in the boardroom would take any notice.

Author's note
The quotations from Mo Johnston and Billy McNeill have been taken from their 'autobiographies': *The Maurice Johnston Story* by Mo Johnston and Chick Young, (Mainstream, 1986), and *Hail Cesar* by Billy McNeill and Jim Black, (Headline, 2004).

Comments

Mo Johnston was a showman with a football knack of getting goals. A media darling, he grabbed his moment in the sun, but it dazzled him and blinded him to the underlying verities he so lightly mocked.

John Cairney

Players move all the time, but few have been so reviled as poor old 'Mo', nicknamed 'Judas' by Celtic supporters who were not exactly joking. I'm reminded of Oscar Wilde's lines in 'The Ballad of Reading Gaol':

> Yet each man kills the thing he loves,
> By each let this be heard,
> Some do it with a bitter look,
> Some with a flattering word.
> The coward does it with a kiss,
> The brave man with a sword.

Tom Campbell

There was a supreme irony here. For decades Rangers had been lambasted by Celtic supporters for not signing 'Catholics' – and now that they had captured one the Celtic supporters were absolutely furious! I think Celtic's pride was hurt more than anything; he damaged them more in a psychological sense rather than a physical sense because he was never quite the same striker he had been before, excellent as he was.

Bob Crampsey

What can you say about him? For me, he was the lowest of the low – a real toerag. I think it was a personal thing; I mean, Alfie Conn, when he switched from Rangers to Celtic via Tottenham Hotspur, aroused feelings but never the same amount of hostility. I suppose

Alfie never went around flaunting a Rangers scarf a couple of weeks before joining Celtic.

Tony Griffin

What was it they were saying at the time? Something like 'Just for a few dollars more (or a suitcase full of cash?)' he left us.

Craig McAughtrie

I felt anger – but not just at Johnston. I was furious at the attitude of the Celtic directors in being outmanoeuvred so easily.

David Potter

I notice that the furore has not yet died down as there has been more controversy over Johnston's proposed appearance in a charity match, and his agent, Bill McMurdo, has volunteered the information that Johnston signed for Rangers against his advice. A strange personality, Mo Johnston. I remember that Danny McGrain commented that, on the morning of an Old Firm League Cup final, Johnston was the only 'Catholic' among the Celtic party who did not attend mass; of course, when Johnston was ordered off that day, he infuriated Rangers supporters by blessing himself as he left the pitch.

Patrick Reilly

The whole affair suggests more than an element of cack-handedness on Celtic's part. He never should have been paraded until he was signed, sealed and delivered.

Pat Woods

8

THE EXORCISM

Craig McAughtrie

On the ninth of May 1998 – the final day of the 1997/98 season – Celtic defeated St Johnstone, 2–0, at Celtic Park. Except for the date, that score-line would seem quite unremarkable. However, it was one of the most important results in Celtic's illustrious history, given that Celtic had exorcised a decade of frustration, anger, depression, despair, turmoil and agony.

The ninth of May 1998 was Judgement Day, and there was Deliverance.

The ninth of May 1998 was an exultant triumph, but it came excruciatingly and perilously close to being Armageddon.

The ninth of May 1998 was the day that the Celtic Family could celebrate again.

This, then, is the story of Celtic's journey on the one road to Paradise – an emotional roller-coaster thriller of a ride, with euphoric highs and gut-wrenching lows.

In order fully to understand and therefore appreciate the significance of Celtic's championship-winning triumph of season 1997/98, it is necessary to journey back in time; to 31 January 1965. This was the date that Celtic announced the appointment of Jock Stein as manager.

Over the next thirteen years, 'Mr Stein' would guide Celtic to the winning of twenty-five major trophies: ten league championships, eight Scottish Cups, six League Cups and, of course, the most memorable and historic triumph of the lot, the European Cup-final victory of 25 May 1967, when Celtic defeated Inter Milan, 2–1, in Lisbon to become the first British club (and still the only Scottish club) to win European football's most prestigious prize.

For a young Celtic fan like myself, born in the early 1960s, there was a genuinely held belief that the Hoops were all-conquering and that this Celtic glory would last forever. It was a great time to be a Tim!

Celtic's domestic dominance during this dramatic decade was made all the more remarkable by the fact that Rangers had a damned fine side throughout, and indeed the 1974/75 Celtic fans' joyous mantra from The Jungle – 'It's magic you know, it's gonna be ten-in-a-row' – went unfulfilled when Rangers finally ended the sequence.

However, mortality became evident to me when Jock Stein, returning from a summer holiday, was seriously injured in a car crash in the summer of 1975. Another transcending moment came in August 1977, when Celtic sold Kenny Dalglish to Liverpool. For a 15-year-old, the effects were devastating, as it took me at least two months to recover composure at school and perhaps longer for my stress-related acne to finally subside. It was the first and most salutary lesson that Celtic had the potential to be hazardous to my health, physically and mentally.

However, throughout a period of some five years under Billy McNeill's managership, there was always the perception amongst Celtic fans that our club was poised tantalisingly on the verge of something special, as there were so many fine players in Paradise. But, that Celtic defence . . . .

It was a poorly kept secret that Celtic's fifth manager was becoming frustrated by his directors after they refused to sanction a move for Aberdeen's Willie Miller, a player that McNeill viewed as the final piece in the Celtic jigsaw. Billy's frustrations would lead to his exit from Celtic in 1983 and, for me, there was a hiatus when I came to realise that there was a secret place within Celtic Park – the boardroom – where decisions were made that may or may not be in the best interests of Celtic or Celtic fans.

University, travel and active campaigning against Margaret

Thatcher had brought a new political awareness. I had become a Celtic cynic, soon to be labelled 'a malcontent'.

And then came the centenary season, 1987/88, when Billy McNeill returned to Paradise – via a supermarket car park – to rebuild a team that went on to become league champions and Scottish Cup winners. After arguably the most romantic, just and suitable con-clusion to a hundred years of Celtic history, the centenary side had all the basic ingredients to become another Celtic team with sustained success, but this being Celtic – a club with Catholic guilt written into its constitution – we began the process of self-destruction almost immediately. For the next five, soul-destroying years, Celtic and their fans were enveloped in blackness and despair, as we became all too familiar with names off the pitch and none too enthusiastic about events on it.

Cambuslang, White, Kelly, Grant, Cassidy, Gefinor, Dempsey, 'Back The Team – Sack The Board', Bhoycotts, Celts For Change and internal memos advocating the dismissal of Billy McNeill: it was a whirlwind as the 'custodians' of the family dynasties led our club, kicking and screaming belatedly, towards oblivion.

And God said, 'Let there be light!'

At the eleventh hour, a wee exile from Canada, a bunnet-wearing saviour formerly of Croy, Fergus McCann, stood on the steps of Paradise in March 1994 and 'The Rebels had won!' Having seized Celtic power in a bloodless (unfortunately) coup d'etat, Fergus McCann was the new authority at Celtic; and it was a fearsome authority that he ruled by. Belligerent, determined and argumenta-tive, and frequently hostile, 'The Bunnet' made promises, and began to deliver on each and every one of them.

Fergus promised the demolition of the antiquated Celtic Park (no longer compatible with post-Hillsborough realities), and a new Celtic stadium. Fergus delivered and the football cathedral that is the new Celtic Park was born, a monument to modernity.

Fergus promised a share issue and the chance for Celtic fans to buy into the dream. The 1994/95 issue was the biggest in the history of British football as 12,000 Celtic fans endorsed Fergus's vision by backing the financial revival of our club with our hard-earned cash – and all for a share certificate to treasure.

Fergus promised a restoration of 'playing football the Celtic way' by sacking 'Luigi' Macari, and Tommy Burns, the fans' favourite, was installed as our new manager. Before long, Tommy did indeed have Celtic playing football as our club should play the game, and over the next several seasons, Celtic fans would witness some quite breathtaking and spectacular football.

And, Fergus McCann had also promised that his Celtic would return to the ways of winning and trophies would arrive in Paradise. In May 1995, a prodigious leap and a powerful header by Celtic striker Pierre Van Hooijdonk had secured a 1–0 win over Airdrie and the Scottish Cup was won, our first trophy in six long, agonisingly painful years. From agony to ecstasy in a matter of months and from tears of sorrow to tears of joy, when Paul McStay held aloft the Scottish Cup at a sun-kissed Hampden Park.

Fergus promised that he would leave after his five-year tenure was over; and he did, in the spring of 1999. By then, the most apt epitaph of his tenure: 'We are glad he came, we are glad he fulfilled his promises, and we are glad he went!'

However, still there was Rangers, as our arch rivals continued to win championship after championship, dominating the domestic scene, though giving Celtic fans occasional moments of hilarity by their misadventures in Europe. Their sequence continued: six-in-a-row, seven-in-a-row, eight-in-a-row and then, finally, nine-in-a-row. A feat aided and abetted by the cheque book, and numerous incidents favouring them that had conspiracy theorists in meltdown. These included the inexplicable delay in the registration of Celtic striker Jorge Cadete, a saga that resulted in contagious paranoia amongst Celtic fans.

Try as he might, Tommy Burns could not get the better of Walter Smith's Rangers. Our proud record of nine-in-a-row was equalled, and Celtic fans mourned. Inevitably, with there being no sentiment either in business or in football, Tommy Burns paid the ultimate price, being sacked by Fergus McCann. But, the unthinkable was looming. What if Rangers surpassed our record? What if their nine became ten? What if the cherished legacy of Jock Stein should be in any way tarnished or diminished in significance? This could not be allowed to happen. There must not be a ten.

But how?

It would be fair to say that when Celtic announced the appointment of their new manager at a press conference on 3 July 1997, the media response was one of total bewilderment.

'Wim who?' was the almost universal greeting for the new man before the press pack scurried back to their employing kennels to do some research on the tubby, curly-mopped Dutchman, the 'product of a two-month-long exhaustive search by Celtic'. Their 'research' consisted mainly in poring over the public-relations blurb handed out by Celtic to the assembled scribes.

One or two journalists were deeply embarrassed having 'exclusively revealed' that the new Celtic manager would be Artur Jorge; other hacks betrayed their lack of knowledge of the global game, ignorant of football east of Leith and south of Berwick. However, in short order but in perfect time, the media went to press with their verdict: 'Wim Who?', 'The Second Worst Thing To Hit Hiroshima!' and 'It's Nigel From Eastenders!'

In fact, Jansen's curriculum vitae was impressive, experienced and varied, as a player and as a coach. He had won the European Cup with Feyenoord in 1970, ironically enough against Celtic; he had been capped sixty-five times for Holland during the era of Dutch total football; he had made two appearances in the World Cup final. And he is the only Celtic manager to feature in the movie *Trainspotting*, as he was the Dutch player making the futile attempt to halt Archie Gemmill as the diminutive Scot scored *that* goal in 1978!

As a coach, Jansen's apprenticeship had begun at Feyenoord where, in partnership with Wim Van Hanegem, he had steered the club to league and cup glory. And, he had coached abroad – with the J-League side, Hiroshima.

Celtic's financial saviour and high heid yin, Fergus McCann, had assembled his managerial team to champion the Celtic cause into this most crucial season. Jock Brown – lawyer, television commentator and pundit – became general manager; David Hay his assistant; Wim Jansen as head coach and Murdo Macleod his second-in-command. And it all seemed so perfect on paper. . . . It wuznae!

Wim Jansen would assess the strengths and deficiencies of his

Celtic squad in pre-season tours of Holland and Ireland. The emphasis would be on the word 'deficiencies'.

Celtic's current captain, Paul McStay, had been forced into premature retirement by a chronic ankle injury; Peter 'the pointer' Grant was nearing the end of his hunting days in the Hoops; Pierre van Hooijdonk, a player whose talents were matched only by a propensity for creating havoc, had been sold; Jorge Cadete, goal-scorer *extraordinaire*, had gone totally tonto, becoming a Howard Hughes-type recluse in his Never-Never-Land ranch on the outskirts of Lisbon, consoled by his pet canary and protected by his 'fearsome wife', his depressive illness to be miraculously cured only when he was sold on to Celta Vigo; Paolo Di Canio, one of the most exquisitely and gloriously talented players ever to don the Hoops, had a 'leetel problem'; otherwise known as 'money'.

In short, Wim Jansen had a team to build, and time was not on his side with competitive football fast approaching. In all, the new Celtic manager would make *nine* acquisitions for Celtic and, remarkably, he would successfully mould them into a cohesive unit, without the usual settling-in period. The Celtic Park revolving door witnessed an initial whirlwind of transfer activity. In came Darren Jackson from Hibs, Craig Burley from Chelsea, Stephane Mahe from Rennes, Jonathan Gould from Bradford City and Regi Blinker from Sheffield Wednesday. The Dutch winger, Blinker, had been 'traded' for the disgruntled and disruptive Di Canio who 'categorically had not been sold' for three million quid.

And then an event occurred that would transform our beloved club. Henrik Larsson became a Celtic player! I am prevented (lack of space, time and the necessary vocabulary) from waxing lyrical about the dreadlocked Swede's impact. Suffice to say, however, Jansen's familiarity with Larsson's contractual position at Feyenoord was a blessing as the purchase of the century was made. For a paltry six hundred grand, the striker – who would become known (inadequately) as 'The Magnificent Seven', 'The King Of Kings', 'The Messiah' or simply as 'Henke' – arrived in Paradise.

Amidst this wheeling and dealing, there was a sudden outbreak of competitive football, though it must be said it was the most inauspicious of starts domestically. Celtic began the championship race against Hibs at Easter Road. It was hardly inspiring, as Celtic succumbed 2–1 to the home side, with Henrik Larsson's now legendary first touch on his Celtic debut setting up Chic Charnley to score Hibs' winner. Worse was to come, however, as Celtic lost their second league fixture 2–1 to Dunfermline at Celtic Park.

Already Celtic were playing catch up with Rangers; they were six points behind the Ibrox side, with a double-header against St Johnstone to come for Jansen's team. The first encounter was on Coca Cola League Cup duty, with Celtic triumphing via a penalty kick in extra time. The Faithful were less than invigorated so far. However, the next two games would add belief to the hope that is always in our hearts. On 23 August we again travelled to the Fair City, where we were to witness a goal of such majesty we would appreciate that Someone was amongst us. Henrik Larsson gathered the ball in midfield before passing wide right to Simon Donnelly and the young Celt took one touch to control it before firing a cross into the St Johnstone penalty area. And there, arriving at pace, was 'The Magnificent Seven', diving headlong to bullet his header into the net. It was only Henke's second goal for Celtic (with 240 yet to come), but arguably it was one of the most sublime.

The next game to enthuse the Faithful was in the UEFA Cup, with Austrian side SC Tirol the visitors to Celtic Park. In a quite breathtaking and energising match, Celtic finally triumphed 6–3, meaning an improbable 7–5 aggregate win for the Bhoys.

Rangers beckoned next on the fixture list. However, a road-traffic accident in a Paris tunnel in the early hours of 31 August meant that the first Glasgow derby of the season was postponed. At the risk of being contentious, it must be said that the postponement suited Celtic much more than it did Rangers. We were still acclimatising as a team.

Consequently, the next competitive action was a League Cup encounter with Motherwell at Celtic Park, with the Faithful in buoyant mood following Rangers' exit from the competition to Dundee United the previous evening. Henrik Larsson's headed goal gave the Hoops the slenderest of victories before we played Motherwell again, at Fir Park, on league duty. Marc Rieper was the debut Bhoy in this league game, the Danish international defender joining from

Southampton as Wim Jansen's seventh signing. His no-nonsense reputation as a rock-solid defender was, however, not evident at Fir Park as Celtic's defensive sieve leaked two farcical goals. Thankfully, the team was capable of scoring goals aplenty, and a brace from Craig Burley and a third from Simon Donnelly provided Celtic with a boost for the challenge to come a few days later.

That challenge was Liverpool Football Club in the UEFA Cup. In the context of exorcising the curse of nine-in-a-row the UEFA Cup was an irrelevance but the double-header with the superstars of Liverpool proved a pivotal moment in the season. All the goals in this dynamic double-header were scored at Celtic Park during an enthralling encounter, with the on-pitch drama matched only by the passionate atmosphere in the stands. In an invigorating second-half display by Celtic, Jackie McNamara thundered home a glorious equaliser, before Liverpool keeper David James brought down Henrik Larsson in the penalty box for Simon Donnelly to step forward and crash his shot into the net off the underside of the crossbar. The drama did not end there, however, as in the final minutes, Liverpool's Steve McManaman raced the length of the field to score with what was probably the only on-target, left-foot shot of his career. At 2–2, Liverpool had the advantage with the second leg to come at Anfield.

Needless to say, however, thousands of Celtic fans travelled south for the return leg on 30 September. The Hoops were in optimistic mood following two league wins: over Aberdeen by 2–0 at Celtic Park, and Dundee United by 2–1 at Tannadice. Sadly, however, it was not to be, as an Anfield stalemate meant Liverpool progressed at our expense. Nevertheless, Celtic's valiant efforts on Merseyside – where Donnelly spurned two separate chances to score – were a source of pride, purpose and determination for the challenges ahead.

And during the month of October, that 'buzz' would propel Celtic to the League Cup final and – after the first quarter of the season – to the summit of the Scottish Premier Division, despite having given Rangers a six-point head start. On the final Saturday of October, Celtic went top – a dizzy and sensational feeling – after a 2–0 win against St Johnstone at Celtic Park. Goals by Henrik Larsson and Simon Donnelly meant Paradise was just that, as Rangers crashed

2–1 to Dundee United at Tannadice, courtesy of an Andy Goram howler and some shambolic defending.

The roller-coaster ride was now in full throttle.

Celtic Football Club could test the patience of a saint. November 1997 would be a month that tested our endurance; a thirty-day illustration of the club's history and a microcosm of a lifetime as a Celtic fan. It all began favourably enough, as Celtic won 2–0 at Dunfermline via a deflected shot from Blinker and a goal of delicious trickery from Larsson. Then, in the midweek, Paul Lambert signed for Celtic from Borussia Dortmund. Lambert was to become the keystone of Wim Jansen's Celtic and this piece of transfer business was as significant as the capture of the goal-scoring Larsson and the defensive pillar Rieper.

However, with a visit to Ibrox looming, behind the scenes there was controversy. Firstly, Davie Hay resigned from his position as Celtic's assistant general manager, with rumours that he and Jock Brown were not exactly bosom buddies. To compound this, Henrik Larsson and Tosh McKinlay were involved in a training-ground fracas; an alleged head butt and a black eye for Henrik and the tabloids had the required gruesome Celtic story as we travelled to the Death Star on league duty.

Suffice to say, it all went horribly wrong for Celtic. Marco Negri's flying elbow caused such damage to Alan Stubbs's face that he was unable to continue. Celtic's defence did not recover, even with the experienced Enrico Annoni as Stubbs's replacement. Goram twice denied Larsson with outstanding saves; Stephane Mahe was skinned by Brian Laudrup who set up Richard Gough to score the only goal, and Mahe was later red-carded. There would be no way back for Celtic.

It all seemed so horrifically familiar but at approximately 9.30 p.m. on Wednesday, 19 November, in the ninetieth minute of the next pulsating Celtic versus Rangers fixture, Alan Stubbs rose high into the air to meet a Jackie McNamara cross. The header flashed across Andy Goram and the ball bulged the back of the net. Celtic 1, Rangers 1. It felt like a victory, as for the entire game we'd been thwarted by Rangers' familiar tactics of defending, and hitting on the break; tactics that had seemingly worked for Walter Smith yet again after Negri, midway through the second half, had beaten Jonathan Gould all too easily at the near post. However, Rangers – reduced to ten men after Paul Gascoigne had flailed his arms at an opponent once too often for referee John Rowbotham's liking – had been forced deeper and deeper into defence until finally Celtic made the breakthrough. Mercifully for Celtic, justice had been done and Alan Stubbs and his Celtic teammates celebrated ecstatically having salvaged a point.

The Hoops then hammered the Arabs 4–0, thereby inflicting serious psychological damage to our Coca Cola League Cup-final opponents. This tournament was proof-positive that this Celtic side was capable of winning trophies. Having journeyed without conceding a goal to the final, which was played at Ibrox in front of a capacity crowd, Celtic were favourites to lift the trophy. We did not disappoint, as Celtic demolished Dundee United 3–0.

Celtic players, management, staff and fans celebrated wildly at the final whistle. However, as captain Tommy Boyd was presented with the League Cup trophy on the pitch, it must be said that Wim Jansen looked somewhat underwhelmed by the revelry around him. It might have been the most minor of the domestic honours but, as the tannoy blared out the Oasis song 'Roll With It', we were all determined to do just that. Roll with it all the way to the championship flag itself.

Winning the League Cup was a symbol of belief, belief that Jansen's Celtic could cross a finishing line as winners. However, could the Hoops cross the finishing line that mattered most?

History dictates that whichever of the Glasgow rivals wins the New Year clash goes on to win the league. Indeed, Celtic had last triumphed in this fixture in 1988, en route to a centenary season league-and-cup double. Since that marvellous year, Celtic had been in Purgatory, largely due to boardroom incompetence from which the club was only now beginning to recover.

Celtic's predicament going into this Glasgow derby of 2 January 1998 was stark: the Bhoys were four points adrift of pole-position Rangers, with Hearts also two points ahead of them. In short, Celtic needed a result. For a packed Celtic Park there was a familiarity about the way the match progressed. Celtic were dominant and a succession of goal-scoring opportunities were fashioned; but Rangers keeper Andy Goram repeatedly denied the Hoops, Harald Brattbakk his particular victim. And, all the while, Walter Smith's tried-and-trusted tactics of hitting on the break were a threat. When Brian Laudrup collapsed under a challenge from Alan Stubbs at the edge of the Celtic penalty box, our hearts missed a beat. Thankfully, referee Hugh Dallas was unimpressed by Laudrup's amateur dramatics. Yet, it served as a warning. With the score-line blank at half time, the tension had become unbearable, as the draw would more than suit Rangers' ambitions.

And thus it was more of the same in the second period: Celtic pressure, Rangers' defiance, no goals and, for Celtic, always the danger of the sucker punch. But then, in the sixty-sixth minute, God smiled on the righteous for a pleasant change. Jackie McNamara weaved his way forward, delivered the most precise of passes through the centre of the Rangers defence and Craig Burley was in on goal. The Celtic midfielder took aim and his low shot rocketed into the net, beating the exposed Andy Goram at his far post.

Bedlam in Paradise! The breakthrough had been made, and Celtic had made it!

Naturally enough, Rangers responded but there was a resilience and dogged determination about this Celtic, a mentality that had seemed almost alien in recent seasons. We defied them. A season-defining chain of events began when Henrik Larsson crossed towards the head of Stubbs, up with his forwards; Richard Gough piled over the top of the Celtic defender, holding him down – a penalty kick, surely? – but the ball broke to Lambert some thirty yards from goal.

The moment of destiny had arrived. Paul Lambert's strike was awesome, breathtakingly so, as the ball sped like a laser-guided missile spinning into the top corner of the net beyond the despairing Andy Goram.

Deliverance! Celtic 2, Rangers 0 as the Faithful celebrated wildly the goal, the moment and the result that was to prove pivotal. Feverish times lay ahead, but belief was building.

With Celtic now just one point behind our adversaries in second place, the New Year's resolution was to build on that position. Yet, we failed at the first hurdle, drawing 1–1 with Motherwell at Fir Park. Paul Lambert scored another thirty-yard scorcher, but Darren Jackson missed a penalty. And, needless to say, there was Celtic politics: Andreas Thom, Gordon Marshall and Tosh McKinlay all left Celtic Park for pastures new; details being published in the press about the full extent of the disagreements between the general manager, Jock Brown, and his departed assistant, Davie Hay. It seemed yet another indication of the Celtic self-destruct button.

A rescheduled midweek game against Dundee United at Tannadice resulted in a fortuitous win for Celtic. Trailing to a first-half goal by Olofsson, Simon Donnelly netted Celtic's late second-half equaliser, steering home his shot from an acute angle after Arabs' keeper Dykstra could only parry a Lambert strike. Jonathan Gould and the Celtic defence had resisted United's almost incessant pressure, and continued to do so, until, in the final minutes, Craig Burley's shot from the edge of the box was deflected – more than once, it appeared – into the net for Celtic's winner.

It would be true to say that February was the final month when everything went reasonably smoothly for the Hoops. From a packed fixture list, the results were encouraging, we played well, the ambience around the club was favourable and the team spirit well demonstrated.

The controversies, internal politics, internal strife and propensity for self-destruction would materialise once again soon enough. For the time being, however, there was 'playing football the Glasgow Celtic way'.

And we did!

A three-way tie at the top of the league, with Celtic, Hearts and Rangers separated only by goal difference. It was compulsive viewing, but not for the nervous. Something, therefore, would surely have to give in our next game at Tynecastle against Hearts on the Sunday. The reward for victory was pole position, as remarkably Rangers had only managed to draw with Dunfermline at Ibrox the day before.

The match was a thrilling affair, with Celtic giving their hosts a pummelling for large parts of the game, but the Hoops had only a Jackie McNamara goal late in the first period tangibly to demonstrate their superiority. There was, however, another factor in the equation: the referee, Bobby Tait. Celtic had opportunities aplenty to increase their single-strike advantage but missed chances and struck woodwork The referee rather generously allowed a full five minutes of injury time at the end of the game and Hearts, sensing Celtic's nervousness at having only a one-goal lead, charged forward in search of the equaliser, and duly got it in the final seconds through Jose Quitongo, whose acrobatic celebrations could have been enjoyable had Celtic not just been robbed blind.

Ever so slightly miffed, Celtic fans departed Tynecastle with the name 'Bobby Tait' being muttered in a most disrespectful way. We would have cause to do so again before the season had finished.

Suffice to say that the football purists have not demanded the next Hibernian–Celtic game be brought out on a commemorative DVD, though Celtic did leave Easter Road in a satisfied frame of mind. Three points were Paradise-bound, but Celtic's winning goal was a tad contentious. Alan Stubbs challenged Hibs keeper Bryan Gunn for a Jackie McNamara cross and clearly impeded the keeper. The ball fell kindly to Marc Rieper who thrashed his shot into the net for the solitary goal of the game. The Hibs fans were furious, but were then stunned into unbelieving silence at the final whistle as Celtic fans began cheering a late Jorg Albertz goal for Rangers at Ibrox. The German had equalised against Hearts, making the score 2–2. That result, coupled with Celtic's win, meant that the Hoops were top of the league as February ended.

Hoopiness!

If February was a month of ascension, then March was the month of contriving to self-annihilate our way to oblivion. Suddenly, Celtic seemed vulnerable and our own worst enemies were ourselves. It is of course the Celtic way. Tommy McLean, the Dundee United manager, who had been sent to the stand – or hamster cage – at Tannadice a week earlier during Celtic's 3–2 win in the Scottish Cup for abusing the officials once too often, exacted some revenge the next weekend at Celtic Park. To describe as 'tense' the atmosphere inside Celtic Park for the Arabs' visit would not do it justice. Rangers had lost the day before, 2–1 to Motherwell, and with Hearts drawing one apiece with Killie, Celtic had the opportunity to increase their lead at the top of the league.

It looked as though we had succeeded in doing just that when midway through the first half Simon Donnelly curled the sweetest of strikes into the net from the edge of the box. As the match progressed, with Celtic having failed to build on their advantage, the tension became too much; instead of urging caution the fans roared Celtic forward. Sadly, fans are not always the best tacticians and the adventurism was our undoing, as late in the game, Olofsson capitalised on a rare United forward foray and equalised.

Wim Jansen was raging post-match, as Celtic had thrown away two points through cavalier football against a side intent on sitting in and counter-attacking. Our folly was to blow the chance of a seven-point lead over Rangers and a four-point lead over Hearts.

Celtic's fortunate win at Pittodrie a week later was not, however, the story of the weekend. That arrived like a bombshell on Sunday, 22 March courtesy of Hugh Keevins and the *Sunday Mail*: Wim Jansen had a get-out clause in his contract. The existence of such a contractual clause is by no means unique, of course, but the inference of the story was that the Celtic manager was likely to activate the escape route and indeed might be doing so imminently.

The details contained within Keevins's 'exclusive' were of such intimacy that one could only assume that the 'source' was someone very close to Celtic Park's inner sanctum. Whoever he was, he appeared to knew precisely what was going on in the power struggle between Wim Jansen and Jock Brown. It was the grimmest of reading for Celtic fans, with the story registering force nine on Timdom's Richter scale, and the impact was added to when Jansen gave a television interview that more or less confirmed the authenticity of the revelations. Consequently, Jock Brown, attempting a public-relations' salvage exercise, failed abysmally to reassure Celtic fans.

Might Wim Jansen exit Paradise while Celtic were battling to preserve the legacy bequeathed by Jock Stein? Were we about to self-destruct yet again? It was with deeply troubled minds that the Faithful journeyed to Paradise for our final league fixture of March. Hearts were the visitors for what would hopefully be a reaffirmation that all was well at Celtic.

Sadly, it did not transpire that way. In a dour struggle, chances were very few and very far between and the game ended promptly on the stroke of ninety minutes as Celtic pressed frantically for the decisive goal. In the post-match aftermath, Celtic fans had another bone of contention to preoccupy them: Bobby Tait, again! Tait had not allowed for any injury time at the end of the goal-less game, with Celtic laying siege to Hearts, yet Stephane Mahe had been injured earlier and the match stopped for a considerable time to allow for treatment and then for him to be stretchered-off. Thoughts returned to the same referee's generous allocation of injury time at Tynecastle, when it was Hearts that were pressurising Celtic for an equalising goal.

The Conspiracy Theorists went into terminal meltdown when it was revealed weeks later that Tait, due to retire at the end of the season, had requested his final match in charge as a referee be at Ibrox, the home of his alleged favourites.

Although Celtic entered April in pole position at the top of the league, the mood amongst the Faithful had changed to one of angst. Anger, bewilderment, fear and frustration mingled in a hellish brew. There were justifiable concerns that Celtic were on the very edge of an abyss.

That mood did not change after our first fixture of the month. The occasion was the Scottish Cup semi-final at officially 'neutral' Celtic Park, and Rangers were our adversaries. Celtic fans might have been forgiven for hallucinating Tommy Burns and Billy Stark in the Celtic dugout as we re-enacted, within the ninety minutes, most of our encounters with Rangers from the preceding decade. Celtic dominated, pressed relentlessly for the decisive first goal, found Goram to be in inspired form and discovered the Rangers defence to be as resilient and well organised as ever. It was a frustrating match that changed dramatically for the worse when Alan Stubbs was injured and had to leave the field in the second half.

Directly from a valid claim for a Celtic penalty kick, Jorg Albertz raced up the field, squared to Ally McCoist and the striker scored the game's first goal. Harbouring a justifiable sense of injustice, Celtic chased the equaliser, only to be caught on the breakaway yet again, with Albertz scoring their second. Although Craig Burley scored a late consolation goal, Celtic heids were in the gas oven.

In desperate need of a morale boost, Celtic journeyed to Rugby Park on Wednesday, 8 April, and recorded a result against Kilmarnock that was crucial. Celtic battled through a fiercely contested first half for a 1–1 scoreline and the match-winning goal arrived in the fifty-fifth minute as a consequence of a delightful exchange of passes culminating in one from Jackson to Simon Donnelly. The young Celt was in on goal and, with Gordon Marshall advancing to meet him, he delicately chipped the ball into the net. The goal was a masterpiece of creation and execution, and justifiably amongst the very best of the season. Celtic celebrations were euphoric through-out the small Ayrshire stadium, which had been heavily infiltrated.

After thirty-one games, Celtic had a three-point advantage over Rangers, and guess who was next in the fixture list? The Temple of Doom beckoned and Celtic's objectives were simple enough: we must not lose. But, sadly, we did just that. Again Celtic found Goram providing a goalkeeping master-class, defying headers from Stubbs and Rieper and several attempts from Henrik Larsson, who troubled the Rangers rearguard throughout. However, the only goal of the first half came as a result of an unstoppable shot from another Swede, Rangers' Jonas Thern. Inevitably, with Celtic's increasing desperation, came the abandoning of defensive duties and Jorg Albertz raced upfield to deliver the knockout blow.

The result meant that both clubs were on sixty-six points with four games remaining for each, though Rangers were in front on goal dif-ference by one goal. Hearts, meanwhile, had faded from the picture. The bookies, seldom wrong, installed Rangers as favourites for the title, while Timdom's anxiety multiplied. Celtic cynics observed balefully that the Scottish media had again been active on the prop-aganda front. There was an appalling attempt to stitch up Harald Brattbakk who, at a Bhoys Against Bigotry meeting, was duped into giving a quote that finishing second in the league would be an acceptable result for Celtic. The Celtic players were livid and refused to talk to the press and the Fourth Estate reacted in predictable fash-ion: indignation and hyperbole about freedom of speech, freedom of the press and their fundamental rights to publish whatever crap they saw fit.

However, what was being less well-documented was Rangers'

growing discomfort with the pressure pot of the championship race. Several Rangers players had complained about the injustices of refereeing decisions, most notably Richard Gough, and about how Celtic were getting the rub of the green, an irony not lost on the Faithful.

The emotional roller-coaster was back on full throttle on 18 April as Celtic welcomed Motherwell to Celtic Park and the Bhoys did not disappoint, giving Motherwell a mauling and comfortably winning the game 4–1. The focus was now on Rangers at Pittodrie the next day and Aberdeen did the righteous thing, beating their guests 1–0, as Rangers' bottle crashed live on television.

Celtic's final game of April was against Hibs; on paper at least, a home banker. However, what had not been entered into the equation was the highly effective pre-match ranting of the Hibs manager, Alex McLeish, who had called for strong refereeing at Celtic Park. He had bemoaned the fact that Celtic and Rangers get all the decisions going from referees, a statement at least 50 per cent accurate. The natives inside Celtic Park were apoplectic with rage when the referee ignored two Celtic claims for penalties. Murdo MacLeod was sent to the stand for his reaction and even the calm Wim Jansen made barbed post-match comments in the wake of the 0–0 stalemate. Meanwhile, at the other end of the M8, Rangers trounced Hearts 3–0, finally extinguishing the Tynecastle club's challenge and moving to one point behind Celtic.

Two games to go. It was both exhilarating and terrifying.

At 4.45 p.m. – actually a bit later than that – on the afternoon of Saturday, 2 May, a new name entered Celtic folklore. It has not been afforded the same status as the likes of Albert Kidd, probably because of the next day's events; but suffice it to say Ally Mitchell deserved a Celtic medal. Late on at Ibrox it was a stalemate with Kilmarnock, chasing a UEFA Cup place, still making a game of it. But referee Bobby Tait had got his wish to officiate at Ibrox before retiring and would no doubt, we all suspected, award a soft penalty or something. Still goal-less . . . still . . . still . . . and still! Even after four minutes of injury time, Rangers were about to drop two crucial points! Hallelujah! Then, almost with the very last kick of the ball, Kilmarnock's Ally Mitchell appeared at Rangers' back post to meet a cross and thundered the ball into the net. 'Ally Mitchell!' screamed the radio commentator, and Timdom celebrated as Rangers crashed to a most unlikely defeat.

Celtic would travel to East End Park, Dunfermline, on Sunday, 3 May, needing three points to win the Scottish Premier Division. Three points that would seal Celtic's destiny, three points that would exorcise a decade of hurt, three points that would end Rangers' domestic domination and three points that would preserve the legacy of Jock Stein. Today, we would be crowned champions in Fife. Cheerio to ten-in-a-row!

After what was for many Celtic fans a sleepless night, the Faithful approached East End Park in their thousands. It was a sight to behold as the celebratory and colourful Celts, suitably attired for an occasion of such magnitude, walked up the Halbeath Road. The sun was shining brightly, the songs had started early and the mood was a Celtic carnival. Today was *the* day.

The Faithful crammed into every nook and cranny of the decrepit Fife stadium, roaring on the Hoops as they formed the Huddle. Immediately, Celtic were in the ascendancy: the defence was rock solid; the midfield dominant, with Burley and Lambert orchestrating the game, while in attack Larsson and Donnelly teased and tormented the Pars. And finally, it came; the goal that had worldwide Timdom celebrating wildly. In the thirty-fifth minute, Henrik Larsson, probing the Dunfermline rearguard, released a precision pass into the path of Simon Donnelly. The youngster was in on Westwater's goal and struck his shot into the net at the far post past the veteran keeper.

Bedlam! Ecstasy! Euphoria!

Sensing blood, Celtic went hunting for more goals and were rampant in the second-half, determined to score the killer second goal that would deliver the championship. Westwater saved brilliantly several times, the woodwork too saved the Pars and Larsson raced into the penalty box, the goal beckoned, but as Henrik prepared to pull the trigger with Westwater exposed, Craig Ireland pulled the striker back by the arm. Penalty! Penalty? No! The furious Celtic protests were waved away by referee John Underhill. It was a travesty and one that might have cost Celtic the ultimate prize.

The mood was changing. Celebration had morphed into anxiety.

The singing stopped and the praying and clock-watching began. Celtic began to look panicky. Jansen seemed troubled, very troubled. Ten minutes to go. In the eighty-first minute, Dunfermline made a substitution. Gerry Britton was replaced by a tall, gangly lad called Craig Faulconbridge, who galloped onto the pitch. A loan signing from Coventry City, this loon of a lad was about to mess with our heads.

In the eighty-third minute, John Underhill awarded Dunfermline a free kick near the centre circle. The Pars were about to launch an aerial bombardment. No problem to Celtic. Not with Rieper and Stubbs there. But nerves were getting the better of their normally sound judgement. The Celtic defence, rather than being on the edge of the penalty box, began to fall back deeper and deeper into Jonathan Gould's territory. Wim Jansen, spotting the basic error, gesticulated maniacally, hurling instructions from trackside.

Too late. The missile was launched. The ball dropped to Faulconbridge, whose leap towered over everyone. The header was not strong. Instead, it looped upwards. 'Over the bar,' I thought initially. 'Roof of the net at worst,' I thought again. 'Gould will catch,' I trusted. 'Crossbar,' I prayed and hoped.

'Fuck!'

The header hung in the air then plummeted like a stone in under the crossbar. Dunfermline, scarcely in the match, had equalised and Celtic hearts were torn apart. Seven minutes! Only seven minutes away from the realisation of all our dreams.

The Celtic Family wept.

As the week progressed, the despair of East End Park was gradually replaced with the realisation that Celtic were still masters of their own destiny. We had a final shot at glory. Going into the last weekend of the 1997/98 league campaign, Celtic were two points ahead of Rangers who would travel to Tannadice on Saturday, 9 May to play Dundee United, while Celtic would entertain St Johnstone at Celtic Park. Celtic's task was simple enough: we had to equal or better Rangers' result. If Celtic won, we would be champions, we would end the nine-year curse of Rangers and we would forever preserve our own nine-league-titles-in-a-row, rendering Rangers' achievement irrelevant. What's all the fuss? Celtic did it first!

Make no mistake; this was the objective. The Celtic teams of Jock Stein must *not* be bested by an era of Rangers mediocrity – in European terms – and we could not allow them eternal bragging rights. That would have been a torment beyond imagination. Such is the way of tribalism.

The build-up to the weekend's hostilities was painful to follow as a press agenda became obvious: Rangers' chance for history-making was the overwhelming editorial preference, with tabloids hinting at Celtic waning and Rangers resurgent. Ally Mitchell's moment had already vanished. Indeed, there were rumours – more than rumours – of the vast spectacular planned for Ibrox and the returning Rangers heroes flown by helicopter back to Mordor when (and not if) they triumphed.

It remained a traumatic week for Celtic fans everywhere, even though theoretically Celtic should beat St Johnstone. Well, we should beat them, shouldn't we? Shouldn't we? The Doomsday Scenario was looming as all too real a possibility. The Doomsday Scenario? We lose and Rangers win; and they would be champions by one point. We draw and Rangers win, even by a solitary goal, and the points tally would be equal, meaning they would be champions on goals scored. The Doomsday Scenario? Too gruesome to contemplate, though contemplate it we certainly did.

There was, therefore, neither bullishness nor wild expectation nor arrogant certainty as the Faithful flocked to the spiritual home on the afternoon of Saturday, 9 May. There was cautious optimism amongst a Celtic Family, where there is always togetherness and empathy. But there was no certainty. We had suffered too much pain over the last decade.

Wim Jansen's team selection was not a surprise. In a 4–4–2 formation, the Celtic line-up read: Gould; Annoni, Rieper, Stubbs and Boyd; McNamara, Burley, Lambert and O'Donnell; Larsson and Donnelly. The subs were Wieghorst, Blinker and Brattbakk. They, too, would have a part to play in the drama yet to unfold, one of them more than the others. The Celtic team took to the field to rapturous acclaim. Similarly, the Huddle was greeted by a cacophony of noise. It must have inspired even the most nervous of players. Perhaps, then, the emotional rendition of 'You'll Never Walk Alone', immediately before kick-off, was our reaffirmation of that belief in Celtic. A crescendo of passionate noise, it undoubtedly had an impact on the Celtic players chosen to represent us on the day in as moving a moment as ever witnessed in the new cathedral for football that Celtic Park had become.

Referee Kenny Clark whistled and the stage was set for Deliverance, or to Doomsday and the continuance of the Curse. In our wildest dreams and most far-fetched fantasies, we could not have imagined the second minute of the game. Henrik Larsson collected the ball wide on Celtic's left, close to the touchline about thirty-five yards from goal; he wove his way inside, dodging St Johnstone defenders until, some twenty-five yards out, he unleashed his shot. The ball left Henke's right boot laser-guided. It soared, it curled, it dipped and then it crashed into the top right-hand-corner of the net, past Alan Main's futile acrobatics.

Larsson's goal released an explosion of joy, the wildest of celebrations, as Celtic Park exploded in what can only be described as a volcanic eruption of happiness. It was bedlam inside Paradise.

As the euphoria settled to mere hysteria, there gradually came the realisation that, though we had the all-important breakthrough, there was yet some way to go. Certainly, we had the impetus and Larsson's goal had removed the potential for early frustration and nerves, but there could yet be a twist to the plot. East End Park had taught us much about the fat lady or, in that particular instance, the skinny striker.

Therefore, as news began to filter through to Celtic Park that Rangers had also taken the lead over Dundee United at Tannadice, our vulnerability became all-too-apparent. We needed a second goal. Craig Burley, Phil O'Donnell and Simon Donnelly all came close to delivering, but suddenly our precarious position was exposed when St Johnstone striker George O'Boyle had a gilt-edged opportunity to equalize; mercifully, he headed over the crossbar.

Half time seemed like an oasis, a period to calm frayed and shattered nerves. The second period burst forth, and again Celtic were pressing for that decisive second goal. We urged our warriors forward and, in the fifty-sixth minute, we rose to acclaim what we believed was that moment but Simon Donnelly's shot from nine yards was somehow saved by Alan Main.

Simultaneously with Main's heroics, the news arrived that Rangers were now 2–0 ahead. The tension became unbearable as the Doomsday Scenario started to rear its very ugly head again. We were so damned close, tantalisingly so, but we were also on the very edge of the abyss, deep within which lurked the Curse.

In the sixtieth minute, an exhausted Simon Donnelly was removed from the field. The frequently maligned Harald Brattbakk entered the fray, and as one might say, 'Cometh the hour, cometh the man!' Brattbakk, upon whom there had been such expectation since his December arrival, was on the verge of writing his name large in Celtic's history. The frail-looking Norwegian had been brought to Celtic Park as part of our search for goals. When he shone, he had been glorious, but he had not been consistently so; consequently, he had flitted in and out of the starting eleven. However, Harald Brattbakk was about to give Celtic *the* goal: arguably the most important goal since Andy Walker's at Ibrox in 1988 or Frank McAvennie's last-minute Scottish Cup final winner in the same year, or even Stevie Chalmers's strike to win the European Cup in Lisbon. And for that fact alone, we should be eternally grateful to Harald Brattbakk.

Tommy Boyd played a captain's part in the moment. He won the ball deep in Celtic territory on the right flank. Racing up the touchline, Boyd then passed the ball forward to Jackie McNamara, already in full flight down the right wing. Jackie looked up and crossed the ball first time into the path of Harald Brattbakk, who had arrived at the penalty spot in a sprint. Harald, without a second's hesitation, exquisitely side-footed the ball into the right corner of the net. A precision finish from the coolest man in Paradise!

Deliverance!

What followed remains a blur of raw, unleashed emotion and celebration. Ten years of agony and frustration evaporated, and around Celtic Park there were scenes of spectacular revelry. It was chaos. Wonderful, glorious, unrestrained chaos! Indeed, a friend of mine – who works for the BBC – tells me that the cameraman perched in the north stand was instructed by his producer to focus his camera properly, and to stop with the shoogly pictures. 'I can't!' he screamed back. 'The whole bloody place is shoogly!'

The Celtic carnival continued. The songs were belted out. There were tears. There was dancing and, appropriately enough, much derision hurled Ibrox way. There would be no curse of ten-in-a-row! The prize was ours! We were champions!

Arguably, there will never be a Celtic moment quite like that again. The memories remain vivid. And, when Celtic took to a hastily erected podium, centre stage, to receive the Scottish Premier Division trophy, I freely admit that I sat down and wept. Ten years of pain and suffering had gone and the sensation was one of ecstasy, and also overwhelming relief. It was just too much for me, personally.

* * *

Two days later, on Monday, 11 May 1998, at a press conference in the Jose Arveladze stadium, where Celtic were preparing to play Sporting Lisbon in a friendly fixture as a contractual agreement from Jorge Cadete's transfer to Celtic, Wim Jansen resigned.

It had been inevitable. The very public fall-out between the Celtic manager and his general manager, Jock Brown, had sealed that fate. Unforgivably, Jansen's departure from Celtic was not given the prominence it deserved. The Faithful were too busy partying and Celtic Football Club was too busy rewriting history and Wim Jansen's part in it to afford the little Dutchman his deserved status.

What should be recorded, however, is that a successful manager is *the* most important employee of any football club. Eventually Celtic came to appreciate that fact, though it took until the summer of 2000 to do so. Then, and only then, did Celtic start to recover from the loss of Wim Jansen.

Comments

The Wim Jansen 'saving' season was proof of the efficacy of prayer and it illustrated that Celtic always come out on the side of angels on the really big occasions, especially when the odds are stacked against them: the Coronation Cup, the St Mungo Cup – and even 'Quizball'.

John Cairney

The tension was unbelievable. Supporters sat down quietly beside their neighbours, nodded grimly, shook hands even. And Henrik scored after only ninety seconds. We were all on our feet in a flash; somebody a couple of rows behind threw his cup of Coca Cola in the air – I don't think he even knew he had done so – and drenched about twenty of us. We didn't care! Not one bit!

Tom Campbell

Harald Brattbakk was probably the worst top-flight striker ever seen in Scotland, and yet he scored that vital second goal, and took it beautifully too. What was it about Harald? He played some-times like a man having trouble with his bifocals; something seemed to go wrong between his looking up to see the goal and then looking down to see the ball.

Celtic, despite Larsson's early goal, looked extremely nervous – just as they had the week before at Dunfermline.

Bob Crampsey

You could have cut the atmosphere that day at Celtic Park with a cricket stump, it was that tense. I remember how delighted I was for Harald Brattbakk when he scored that decisive second goal after all the unfair criticism he had endured. After that, the party could start!

Gerry Dunbar

I was working that day in Aberdeen, and unable to get close to a radio even. But I managed to slip away for a moment and was able to hear that Henrik Larsson hud scored in just two minutes. Only eighty-eight to go! I was kept posted by a friendly security man and it was agony – with Celtic leading by only one goal – and Rangers two goals up at Tannadice! Eventually, I got into the car and turned on the radio, just in time to hear Chick Young's voice announce: 'It looks as if the league championship is going to . . .' and I could hardly breathe until he said 'Celtic Park'. I drove home in a happy glow; and on the way home I saw one car, weaving erratically towards me, sunroof up and the driver's fist punching the air in jubilation!

Tony Grifffin

Relief! Sheer, bloody relief!

David Potter

The game at East End Park the previous week (when Celtic gave up a late equaliser) made the St Johnstone match all the more nerve-wracking. Unbelievable tension in the ground – and for the days preceding the match. Even after Larsson's early goal it was a most nervous occasion.

Patrick Reilly

9

SUPER CALEY GO BALLISTIC . . .

Tom Shields

It was the best of times, it was the worst of times, it was the age of wisdom, it was the age of foolishness, it was the epoch of belief, it was the epoch of incredulity, it was the season of Light, it was the season of Darkness, it was the spring of hope, it was the winter of despair, we had everything before us, we had nothing before us, we were all going direct to heaven, we were all doing direct the other way – in short, the period was so far like the present period, that some of its noisiest authorities insisted on its being received, for good or for evil, in the superlative degree of comparison only.
(Charles Dickens, A Tale of Two Cities)

The night Super Caley went ballistic was among the worst of times in Celtic's history. But events at Celtic Park on the night of 8 February 2000 led eventually to some of the best of times for the club. Inverness Caledonian Thistle's dispatch of Celtic in the third round of the Scottish Cup was a memorable moment. Equally unforgettable was the headline in the *Scottish Sun* the next day.

While Celtic's highly-paid players toiled and showed little inspiration at Celtic Park, the sports staff at *The Sun* office in

Kinning Park were in better form. Paul Hickson, chief sports sub-editor, interviewed later in *Guardian Media*, said:

> The headline came long before the final whistle. Caley were 2–1 up. It had looked like a straightforward evening. We expected Celtic to win, but it soon became obvious something big was happening. Celtic losing to a team nobody had heard of or could even spell, that was the story. The Scottish sports editor, Steve Wolstonencroft, mentioned the 1960s headline used when Liverpool striker Ian Callaghan once scored three goals against QPR. It went something like: 'Super Calli Scores a Hat Trick, QPR Atrocious'. I didn't know it. I hit back with 'Super Caley Go Ballistic, Celtic Are Atrocious'.

The headline, as much as Celtic's exit from the cup, was the talk of the steamie, or the water-cooler moment as an urgent and spontaneous workplace talking-point is apparently now known. The neat twist on the song from the film *Mary Poppins* might have rubbed salt in the wounds of Celtic fans who were not feeling entirely 'supercalifragilisticexpialidocious' the next morning. Other followers of the Hoops, who take a less apocalyptic view of football, accepted the headline with a wry smile in the same decent and stoic manner they had stayed to the end and applauded the Inverness players in the stadium the night before. This sportsmanship was mirrored by the gesture of the Celtic Park catering staff, who put a few cases of beer on the Inverness Caley team bus to sustain celebrations on the road north.

Rangers supporters, already delighted with their team's ten-point lead in the league over their rivals, and revelling in David Murray's announcement of a £22 million buying spree to further strengthen the team, had an extra spring in their step that day. The legions of non-Old Firm fans quite simply hadn't laughed so much since Berwick Rangers put Glasgow Rangers out of the Scottish Cup in 1967.

The teams that night:

Celtic: Gould, Boyd, Mahe, Tebily, Riseth, Healy, Blinker, Moravcik, Viduka, Burchill, Berkovic. Substitutes: Kerr, Petta, Wright.

Inverness Caledonian Thistle: Calder, Teasdale, Golabek,

Mann, Hastings, Sheerin, Tokely, McCulloch, Wilson, Christie, Wyness. Substitutes: Byers, Bavidge, Glancy.

Inverness Caley won 3–1. Barry Wilson put Inverness ahead in sixteen minutes when he headed home a cross from Sheerin as the Celtic defence slept. Mark Burchill equalised within a minute, his goal resulting from a fortunate rebound from a defender after he tried to pass to Viduka. The Inverness lead was restored in twenty-four minutes when a Bobby Mann header was going nowhere in particular until a deflection from Lubomir Moravcik's boot put the ball in the net. Victory was sealed as early as the fifty-seventh minute when Celtic conceded a cheap penalty, Regi Blinker impeding Wilson from behind, with Sheerin gratefully converting.

These bare facts go nowhere near explaining the full story. Ian Paul of *The Herald* said in his match report:

> If the scoreline seems incredible to those who were not present, it was no less stunning for those of us who were on site, but not just because of Caley's fine, indeed, wonderful show, but also because of the depth of mediocrity to which Celtic sank. Let there be no doubt, Inverness deserved their victory as their frequent attacks were far more potent than those of the multi-million pound Celtic side.

Steve Paterson, the Inverness Caley manager (who must in more recent troubled times have taken some solace in memories of that night at Parkhead), said: 'I felt Celtic's weakness was that, when moves broke down, they had no direction or leadership in the middle.'

As the early drama in the match unfolded, the Celtic support seemed unaware of the full horror that was to unfold. Tom Campbell, long-time student of Celtic, recalls: 'Inverness led by 2–1 at half time and I remember huddling in the concrete stairwell with a pie and Bovril listening to two mature supporters. I remember agreeing with one of them when he said: "Well, with them in front, it should make it more entertaining in the second half."'

I was at the game and expected, as you do, that Celtic would prevail even when they went behind. But in that second half, the team was possessed of an aimlessness and lack of heart. Even before the visitors' third goal, the suspicion had begun to form that Inverness had the beating of Celtic. This feeling of unease had been exacerbated by an inauspicious and – at that moment on the terraces – inexplicable substitution at half time of Ian Wright for Mark Viduka. The circumstances of Viduka's failure to reappear for the second half, as they were later revealed, proved to be testament to the sickly condition of Celtic Football Club, which was more deep-seated malady than malaise. Viduka was involved in a heated debate in the dressing room with assistant coach Eric Black, evidence that the Celtic management were far from in full control of their playing staff. Team spirit was a commodity in short supply.

The contrast could not be greater with their opponents that night. Inverness Caledonian Thistle had been formed only five years before but had quickly worked their way up to the first division of the Scottish Football League. As coach Steve Paterson pointed out, nine of his players had come out of the Highland League and proved themselves at the higher level. They were a tidy team who played hard for each other. But they were essentially journeymen, as epitomised by goalkeeper Jim Calder, a bricklayer by day, who had considered dropping down a grade to play for Strathspey Juniors. He was persuaded to hang on a bit longer and thus enjoyed his moment of fame with a clutch of fine saves at Celtic Park.

In the pre-match publicity much had been made of the fact that when it came to atavistic allegiances, a number of the Inverness players were Celtic-minded, as the saying goes. Paul Sheerin, who set up Inverness's first goal and scored the clinching penalty, was quoted in this respect, as was Charlie Christie, who had been a Celtic player. But there was not a shred of doubt about the commitment of all the Inverness squad to the red, white and blue jersey in stark contrast to the lack of immediacy, verging on ambivalence, exhibited by some of the highly-paid Celtic team.

Now, there is a strong Highland flavour to this tale and I must admit the temptation to get into Brahman Seer mode by suggesting that there were portents of a terrible visitation (*Ochone, ochone*) upon Celtic. But the omens were scarcely propitious when the original fixture had been postponed ten days previously when high winds blew chunks of metal off the Lisbon Lions stand at Celtic Park. It is never nice when bits fall off your club's shiny new stadium. It is even worse when the damage prompts the reoccurrence of a rumour – vouchsafed as true by surveyors, architects and other building experts unnamed but probably not Celtic-minded – that the cost-conscious Fergus McCann had built the new Celtic Park on the cheap, using inferior-quality steel. Such folklore and urban myth is the stock-in-trade of those obsessed members of the Old Firm divide who examine in a permanent ambience of attrition the rival's pro-bity, stability, profitability, durability and any other kind of ability. The net result on either side is usually risibility.

On the night of the rematch it was not the stadium but the Celtic team which fell apart. There had been ample evidence of frailty in league performances as Celtic slipped behind Rangers. Before the cup encounter with Inverness, Celtic had taken only two points from their previous three league games. In all three matches they had been leading at one stage.

In the most recent match Celtic had lost 3–2 to Hearts at home, surrendering a two-goal lead in embarrassing circumstances. Matters were made worse by Eyal Berkovic, Celtic's Israeli midfielder, appearing in the public prints to concede the league title to Rangers with sixteen games still to be played. Berkovic was further quoted as saying that Rangers deserved to win the championship more than Celtic. This is not what the fans, who were financing Berkovic's £25,000 weekly wage, necessarily wanted to hear.

Celtic had been unconvincing in the previous league match at Kilmarnock, which ended 1–1 with most of the headlines devoted to Ian Wright and Jim Lauchlan continuing an on-field feud up the tunnel. Despite being taken to the referee's room for a ticking-off from referee Kenny Clark, Wright became involved in a fracas with fourth official Willie Young. The scant respect shown to coach John Barnes by Regi Blinker after he was substituted was another indi-cation of the chaos and discontent that was engulfing the Celtic squad. Barnes, never the disciplinarian, merely said: 'His reaction just shows he cares. Regi wasn't playing any worse than anyone else, I just wanted to change things.'

Ironically, not long before his cataclysmic career-ending collision with Inverness Caley, the inexperienced Celtic coach had been named

Scottish Premier League manager of the month in December 1999. A
1–0 victory over Dundee in the League Cup had been followed by
SPL wins against Hibs, Aberdeen and Dundee United by the more
than respectable margins, respectively, of 4–0, 6–0 and 4–1. It was
John Barnes's little moment in the sun, even if it was a December
sun. The month, the year and the millennium ended with a fixture
against Rangers at Celtic Park. In an evenly contested match, the
points were shared at 1–1 but it was Rangers who headed off for
the winter break with a four-point advantage and a game in hand.

The deficiencies at Celtic Park were not entirely due to the
naivety or inexperience of the rookie coach. The deep-seated problems were at a higher level. It was Kenny Dalglish, director of football operations, who appointed his old Liverpool colleague as coach
even though Barnes himself said he did not think he was ready to
take on the daunting task at Celtic as his first step into football
management. Dalglish insisted and Barnes, a clever player and a
clever man whose self-confidence can sometimes be seen as arrogance, accepted the job.

There was a disturbingly similar template to Dalglish's own
appointment. He was hired by Allan MacDonald, Celtic's new chief
executive who had replaced Fergus McCann as the man who called
the shots on the day-to-day decisions on how the club was run.
MacDonald had come from British Aerospace with a big reputation
for his ability in big business. However, MacDonald's recruitment of
Dalglish, his idol and golfing partner, seemed more the action of
a supporter playing fantasy football manager than a cold and
calculating executive. MacDonald christened the Dalglish–Barnes
partnership 'the Dream Team', forgetting that such an epithet
usually has to be earned: like Johann Cruyff and Ronald Koeman
winning the European Cup for Barcelona in 1992; like Michael
Jordan and the USA basketball team who took the gold medal at
the Olympics in the same city that same year.

Unlike many Celtic fans, MacDonald obviously did not see
Dalglish as something of a burned-out case, a man with no apparent
football aspirations left, but while the fire had gone out, the financial motivation remained. The prophetic words of a Newcastle fan
came to pass. Commiserating with Celtic fans on the appointment

of Dalglish, the Geordie said: 'He will leave you with a squad containing some expensive and dodgy players. The heart will have gone out of the team.'

The departing Fergus McCann, who had come to learn a thing or two about football managerial personnel during his five years in Paradise, was reputed to have said he might consider hiring Kenny Dalglish as director of golf. Theoretically above MacDonald in the new Celtic pecking order was Frank O'Callaghan who had succeeded McCann in his other role as club chairman. O'Callaghan had been headhunted for the job. He was seen as a safe pair of hands, a former financial director of the Stakis hotel group and then chairman of MacDonald Hotels, a thriving property-based enterprise. O'Callaghan held, or had held, non-executive directorships with various large Scottish companies and was thus seen as qualified to represent Celtic plc at the big business table.

Other parts of Callaghan's curriculum vitae seem less critical for the job of chairman of Celtic in the modern era. He was vice-chairman of St Aloysius College, the Jesuit-run Glasgow school he had attended. His sport of choice as a young man was rugby and he had been active in running the Aloysian former pupils' fifteen. The game plan was that O'Callaghan would have a much lower-profile role than previous Celtic chairmen and this certainly came to pass.

It was to be a new era and goodness knows the supporters were ready for a new era. The 1990s had been the leanest of years. In the first half of the decade, the club had disintegrated under the old regime. The Tommy Burns years brought hope, a lot of good attacking football and one Scottish Cup in 1995 with a 1–0 victory over Airdrie. It was scant consolation as Rangers powered towards their nine league flags in a row and threatened to surpass the Celtic record. There was one season of respite as Wim Jansen led the team to a glorious, if slightly nervously achieved, league title in 1997/98. But chaos returned. Jansen had left after one year and so did his successor Josef Venglos after an interesting season in which he left no legacy of trophies unless you count Lubomir Moravcik.

Enter the dream team. Readers should at this point brace themselves for a painfully obvious but unavoidable extended metaphor.

As the 1999/2000 campaign progressed, the dream rapidly became a disturbed sleeping pattern before evolving into a fully fledged nightmare that night against Inverness Caley.

There was some bizarre behaviour from the men at the top. Chief executive MacDonald revealed to an avid Sunday press that Celtic had employed a behavioural psychologist to study referee Hugh Dallas's performance in the Old Firm game the previous May. That was when Rangers won the league, Dallas was hit by a coin and then had his windows broken. You can expect this kind of lunatic behaviour from fans. You don't expect chief executives to go hire psychologists to investigate referees.

Kenny Dalglish came up with the equally bright idea of holding pre-match media conferences at such press-hostile venues as Baird's Bar, the Hoops-mad pub in the Gallowgate, and at the social club of the Celtic Supporters' Association, a venue from which sports writer Hugh Keevins was excluded by an over-enthusiastic official.

On the playing front, it appeared that the coach was being left alone to make his own mistakes. There was mystification, some resentment, public debate, but mostly confusion on the part of players regarding the Barnesian 4–2–2–2 formation. There were high-scoring victories under Barnes, but mostly against Aberdeen who, in those days, were struggling at the bottom of the league. Crucially, there were two defeats against Motherwell in the space of a month and losses at Tannadice and Ibrox.

Matters were going awry but there was no sense of any urgency from the dream team. After losing 3–2 to Motherwell on 28 November, Barnes told the press: 'All things being equal we could have taken something from the game. I thought we did okay apart from the three goals.' It was eerily reminiscent of Liam Brady, another top-class player thrown straight into management at Parkhead, who had incurred much wrath from the fans by being philosophical in defeat when Airdrie put Celtic out of the League Cup in 1991.

The gloom over Paradise was intensified by the absence of Henrik Larsson after his horrendous leg-break at Lyon on 4 November. His replacement, Ian Wright ex-Arsenal, should have been a ray of sunshine with his goal-scoring ability and his cheeky-chappie ways. Alas, this new chapter in Wright's football career appeared to be eclipsed by his considerable showbiz commitments. He was definitely up for a lark on the park when things were going well but when the chips were down, your average season-ticket holder wasn't seeing much return on the £20,000 a week they were paying for Mr Wright.

On the signing front, the failure to deliver from richly-rewarded players such as Berkovic and Wright was eclipsed by the collective madness that resulted in Celtic's purchase of Rafael Scheidt. Somehow Celtic had managed to spend £5 million on that rare commodity, a Brazilian who cannot play football. MacDonald, Dalglish, Barnes and company thought they were buying an international-class defender. They were sold a pup. These things can happen, but the risk is substantially reduced if someone from the club actually goes to watch the player in action before lashing out on big transfer fees and wage deals.

On a personal note, I had lost faith in the extended dream team early in that season. In an article in *The Herald* on 8 November, I wrote, admittedly after a depressing four days in which Celtic went out of Europe, lost Henrik for the rest of the season and were defeated 4–2 by Rangers:

> As John Barnes might say, it was just a blip. We are not talking here about Celtic's defeats by Lyon and Rangers. It appears that the 5–1 victory over Kilmarnock was the blip in a decidedly downward spiral for the Parkhead club. Book now for the end-of-season dance at the Jock-Stein-Birling-In-His-Grave Lounge.
>
> Mingling, as we do, with the ordinary Celtic fan, we hear words which are quite clear. The new regime will not do. If Barnes is a football prophet, he is too far ahead of his time. His system, whatever it is, does not work. Good players have become bad. Moderate players have become worse. Celtic now has a defence that is not even capable of constructing a wall to defend a free kick. Barnes has not only lost the dressing room, he has lost the entire stadium.
>
> The simple remedy of throwing the manager to the wolves is not available at this moment to Celtic. Allan MacDonald, the chief executive, begat Kenny Dalglish as director of football who begat Barnes as first-team coach. If one goes, they all have to go. For they operate as a triumvirate. But it is a triumvirate without leadership.

Power without responsibility. Big wages without accountability. The Celtic chairman is, I believe, a chap called Frank O'Callaghan. Perhaps we might hear from him this week. It is time for him to show some leadership. Celtic is not just a plc, it is a football club and a way of life for the 60,000 fans without whom there is nothing.

As usual, the Celtic board didn't listen to me. It is a constant source of amazement and sadness to me that Celtic have not had the wisdom to give me a job as a consultant, a green blazer and a seat near the directors' box. The club did actually employ me that season as a columnist in the *Celtic View*, with a remit to supply some humour in between the Pravda-esque editorials. It was not the hardest job in the world writing about your team and being a fan who actually received money each month from Celtic.

There were a few downsides to writing the column. The plan was to call it 'Tim Shields Diary' but the powers that were did not fancy the 'Tim' reference and, bizarrely, it ended up being named 'Timothy Shields' Diary'. Plus, any occasional attempts at a side-ways dig at the dream team or between-the-lines references to the madness that was going on at Parkhead were rigorously censored. Standing tall on my journalistic integrity – or maybe getting out before I was thrown out – I resigned at the end of the season. This was just before a bloke called Martin O'Neill arrived. Closing 'Timothy Shields' Diary' in the *Celtic View* was not my best career move.

One of my tasks as a chronicler of amusing Celtic moments was to attend in February 2000 the Tommy Burns Supper, a legendarily enjoyable event organised by the Celtic-minded students of Edinburgh and Heriot-Watt universities. Guest of honour was John Barnes who was affable and made a witty, off-the-cuff speech. The student organisers, as was their wont with the non-Scottish, con-fronted Barnes with a piece of poetry in broad Scots. Barnes said it was like a conversation between Kenny Dalglish and Paul Lambert.

Barnes spent nearly five hours in the genial company that night, impressed and possibly slightly bemused by the intensity of the Celtic fans at play. This was a week before the Inverness Caley cup game and, with hindsight, the manager might have been better occupied watching videos of the upcoming opponents.

Suspicions that Celtic did not treat the cup-tie against Caley with due respect might be confirmed by the fact that the director of football operations was not present. Dalglish was in Spain taking in a youth tournament at La Manga, presumably trying to spot stars of the future. Unfortunately, La Manga is better known for its golf courses than it is as a football venue and there was much comment on Dalglish's devotion to golf clubs over his devotion to a football club.

Barnes paid the price for his inexperience when he was sacked two days after the Caley match. His assistant Eric Black was offered a different post at Celtic Park but chose honourably to fall upon his sword. Terry McDermott, the ex-Liverpool player, also departed from a backroom job which appeared to be that of social convener, an excess and indulgence entirely typical of the dream team. The other jester, Ian Wright, was off within a week to join Burnley.

The ship had sunk but MacDonald and Dalglish clung to the wreckage. Dalglish took over the running of the team. There were brave expressions of unity and resolve, yet again, to restore the fortunes of Celtic Football Club. But the *dramatis personae* were gradually to exit stage left. O'Callaghan, a thoroughly decent man who was not suited to the arduous and unremittingly fraught task of being Celtic chairman, left in May to be replaced by the much more pro-active Brian Quinn.

There was to be a significant arrival in June 2000. Dermot Desmond, Celtic's biggest shareholder and the man who effectively pulls the strings, was faced with the dilemma of how to restore order and progress at the club. The Irish entrepreneur was also, famously, confronted by an emotional fan outside Celtic Park during the time of uncertainty while a new manager was being sought. The supporter approached Desmond as he left the stadium and pleaded: 'Gonnae stoap the sufferin?'

It may have been the financial angst rather than the supporters' suffering that prompted Desmond's swift and unequivocal appointment of Martin O'Neill as manager. It proved to be an excellent bit of business and a new era was, indeed, ushered in at Celtic Park.

O'Neill joined in June. Dalglish departed at the end of the month, unwillingly and in ungracious circumstances with a dispute over compensation, from a post as director of football operations which had ceased to exist. Dalglish eventually received a £600,000 out-of-court settlement.

MacDonald had apparently also intimated to the board in that summer his intention to leave once the new ship Celtic was on an even keel. When he left, MacDonald was a sadder and wiser man. He told Thomas Jordan of the *Evening Times*:

> I would have always felt bringing in Kenny, and whatever backroom staff he wanted, was something we needed to do because he was such a Celtic man who had enjoyed success in the most competitive league in the world. With hindsight, I wish I had never done it. I wasn't alone at the time in thinking the Dream Team was the right choice, but I do take the responsibility. Once I realised it wasn't working, I quickly corrected it.

Of Dalglish's absence on that night of the Caley match, MacDonald said:

> I told Kenny I felt uneasy about him going to La Manga in Spain to watch a tournament. He was very confident and I was perhaps over-anxious in these matters.
>
> That was really the first time Kenny had not been in the dressing-room and trouble blew up. The next day, he wasn't on the first plane back from La Manga, as he had promised. That was the defining moment for me. Here was a crisis at the club I loved and those responsible for the football management side hadn't a grasp of it.

Author's note:
I was going to apologise for inserting myself perhaps inappropriately into this tale but then I thought, if I don't insert myself into Celtic's history, no-one else will.

Comments

The last time the Highlanders came to Glasgow it was with Bonnie Prince Charlie, and they made their camp on Glasgow Green near Shawfield. I wish Caledonian Thistle had done the same and played Clyde instead of us. But then Clyde would probably have beaten them.

John Cairney

February 8 was a raw, miserable night with a chill in the air as Celtic stumbled against Caley; six months later in brilliant sunshine Celtic beat Rangers 6–2. As the poet said in Ecclesiastes:

A time to weep, and a time to laugh;
A time to mourn, and a time to dance.

Tom Campbell

A surprise, yes – but there had been some trail-flares before in the Scottish Cup involving Highland clubs. I remember Celtic struggling against Elgin City; they were a goal down quite near the end, I believe. Buckie Thistle beat a strong Queen's Park side in the mid-1950s and Fraserburgh beat the Dundee side that went on to win the league championship the next season. The Highlands seemed to produce useful cup sides – much more so than other regions such as the Borders or the south-west of Scotland.

Bob Crampsey

That was one of the few games I missed that season; but I had an excuse. As I was putting on my coat to leave for the match, my wife announced that she was definitely going into labour; so, we headed for the maternity hospital to be delivered of a daughter. That was the good news. The bad part was listening with disbelief on a portable radio to what was happening at Celtic Park. In the next issue of Not the View, *I remember one contributor noting that if Jock Stein had been Celtic manager that night, a certain Mark Viduka – apparently upset at half time by criticism – would have got no further than 'I'm not . . .' before feeling the Big Man's wrath.*

Gerry Dunbar

Thank God the match on the Saturday was postponed! Suppose it had been played at Celtic Park before a really big crowd and in reasonable conditions. We probably would have won . . . and at the end of the season Henrik Larsson would have returned; just think John Barnes might still be our manager! God works in mysterious ways.

Craig McAughtrie

Well, as they say, history repeats itself. Just like at Arthurlie, more than a hundred years ago, Celtic were knocked out by rank out-siders. And it meant changes at Parkhead; out went Barnes and Dalglish, and in came Martin O'Neill!

David Potter

Rudyard Kipling wrote of the British reverses at the start of the Boer War:

> We have had no end of a lesson;
> It will do us no end of good.

When you consider what transpired as a consequence of that sur-prising result, Celtic came out of the affair rather well.

Patrick Reilly

The worst result in terms of worldwide publicity in Celtic's history! That headline! The Arthurlie cup tie a hundred years earlier could be covered up as a local affair and gradually forgotten, but the whole world knew about this one.

Pat Woods

10

THE TWILIGHT OF THE GODS

Pat Woods

It was all so very different then, back on that sunny afternoon at Fir Park in May 1966 when Celtic, with a 1–0 victory courtesy of Bobby Lennox's goal 'in the last minute of the last game of the season' clinched their first league title in twelve years, and the first of the historic nine-in-a-row under Jock Stein. There would be a curious if not exact parallel with the situation that faced Celtic at the same venue twenty-nine years later, again on the last day of the league season. In the earlier case a 4–0 victory for Motherwell would have handed the title on goal average to Rangers, who had already completed their league programme; in 2005 a draw for the reigning champions at Fir Park would mean the championship for Rangers if Celtic's greatest rivals – who had a four-goal, goal-difference advantage over the Parkhead club – won at Easter Road on an afternoon when both matches were being transmitted live simultaneously by satellite-television company Setanta. That electronic saturation was in total contrast to 1966 when live coverage of Scottish domestic football was unthinkable.

Another difference was the fact that nobody – and I mean nobody – expected Celtic to slip up in 1966. Indeed after Celtic had won their penultimate league match of the season against

Dunfermline Athletic at Celtic Park on the Wednesday, Rangers vice-chairman John Wilson had sent a telegram of congratulations to the champions-elect. Its first sentence read: 'The chase is over.' But the sense of joyous anticipation that had marked the finale at Motherwell in 1966, prompting many of the Celtic fans shoehorned into Fir Park to celebrate the triumph by dancing on the roof of the enclosure, was not being replicated by the fans who wended their way there on Sunday, 22 May 2005. Any outward manifestation of confidence had a distinct undertone of apprehension.

Still fresh in the collective memory was a similar last-day scenario two years earlier, which had ended in numbing 'failure' for Celtic, culminating in a barren season; a scurvy reward for the players' efforts in one of the most memorable seasons in the club's history. Defeat in the UEFA Cup final in midweek, pipped to the title by Rangers on goal difference a few days later. It couldn't happen again, or could it?

The reasons for the supporters' unease were not hard to find. Motherwell, where Celtic had once suffered the club's record defeat (an 8–0 humiliation in April 1937 a few days after winning the Scottish Cup) was a venue that had held unhappy memories for the visitors in green-and-white in recent decades. There was an early-round defeat in January 1976 in the Scottish Cup, when Kenny Dalglish was Celtic's captain and Celtic had been two goals up after thirty-nine minutes; a bizarre interlude in April 1977 when two Andy Lynch own goals contributed to a 3–0 defeat four days before Celtic clinched the title at Easter Road; another early Scottish Cup exit in 1994 with ex-Celt Tommy Coyne scoring the only goal, and five weeks before Fergus McCann's takeover heralded the modern Celtic era. And, finally, an early-season league reverse in September 2002 that proved a contributory factor in Celtic being brought down at the final hurdle in the aforementioned trophyless season.

Cockier Celtic fans could dismiss those setbacks as history, though the latter episode should have provided food for thought. Uppermost in the minds of the more nervous was the decidedly unconvincing form that their favourites had exhibited during the lead-up to this date with destiny.

Everyone knew that, minus the talismanic Henrik Larsson, the

2004/05 season would be a difficult one for Celtic as the man himself reminded his legions of admirers when his new club, Barcelona, visited Celtic Park for the first group match in the Champions League in mid September. His goal after coming on as a substitute was like a dagger to the heart.

Being drawn against the Spanish giants and AC Milan in the same group was like the Celtic players having their legs cut off before they could even take the field. But it is too easily forgotten that during their first three group matches (against Barcelona at home, and away to AC Milan and Shakhtar Donetsk) Celtic had at one (all too brief) stage been in the ascendancy before succumbing to defeat; the loss of three goals on each occasion inflicting damage to the players' self-belief that can only be guessed at.

But one can surely point to that night of 29 September 2004 in the San Siro (when Celtic seemed set to take away their first-ever away point in the Champions League) as *the* body blow when two goals were conceded virtually in injury time. That was the point when Celtic's season began to unravel. Those costly late goals hinted at uncharacteristic lapses of concentration in defence; unfortunately, those lapses were to accumulate in alarming fashion over the next two months. They served to put Celtic out of contention in the Champions League, contributed to elimination from the League Cup and rendered their prospects of retaining the championship severely undermined. The Ukrainian champions Shakhtar Donetsk punished the visitors for their uncertainty at the back after Celtic had squandered two reasonably good opportunities to take the lead, but the Scottish champions' fallibility was highlighted even more dramatically only four days later at struggling Livingston in a way that, even allowing for the after-effects of a gruelling European assignment, should have had the alarm bells ringing. An evident malaise set in after Celtic sprinted to a four-goal lead with barely half an hour gone. But then two goals were conceded in such a slipshod manner that a side which should have been dead and buried came back to a 4–2 deficit shortly after the interval and scented the prospect of a draw.

Nevertheless, those who reassured themselves that this was but a temporary blimp in Celtic's procession to another championship could point to the league table, which at that point indicated the champions would go into their next league fixture on 27 October 2004 against Aberdeen at Celtic Park in a comfortable position:

	P	W	D	L	For-Agst	G-D	Pts
Celtic	10	9	1	0	28 7	+21	28
Rangers	10	6	3	1	16 3	+13	21
Aberdeen	10	5	4	1	11 5	+6	19

A dispassionate observer may have concluded that Rangers and Aberdeen were jousting for the runners-up spot as Celtic strolled to their second title in a row. Indeed, for all the later official denials, Rangers manager Alex McLeish surely would not have kept his job had an unknown side from the island of Madeira (CS Maritimo) won their UEFA Cup tie a few weeks earlier instead of bowing out from the competition after a penalty shoot-out at Ibrox.

Celtic's failings kept him in the Ibrox hot seat. The lethargy and lassitude that had manifested itself at Livingston resurfaced against Aberdeen that Wednesday night as Celtic conceded two sloppy goals in the first six minutes then fought back to parity before going down by three goals to two. The Dons' winning goal – again as a consequence of failings in defence – came at the very end of injury time. A pattern was emerging that was to become a template for Celtic's season, namely the loss of late goals. Prso's eighty-fifth minute equaliser in the quarter-final of the League Cup at Ibrox two weeks later set Rangers on the path to an extra-time victory, the first of two defeats at the hands of the old rivals within a period of eleven days. The second defeat brought Rangers to within one point of Celtic at the top of the league table after a tousy encounter again at Ibrox, where the sendings-off of Thompson and Sutton left Celtic with no hope of retrieving the situation. Those lapses in discipline only aggravated an increasingly worrisome injury situation that highlighted the squad's lack of strength in depth. Midfielder Alan Thompson had been forced to miss the match in Donetsk while defenders Stephen McManus and Stanislav Varga, and striker Henri Camara, had to be withdrawn during the Livingston match, and all this at a time when forwards John Hartson and Chris Sutton plus midfielders Neil Lennon and Paul Lambert were also nursing niggling injuries.

The Celtic players and management team could not afford to feel sorry for themselves while the challenges of the rest of the season loomed. In any case there were many who were already suggesting that the chickens were coming home to roost in the wake of Celtic's failure to invest properly post-Seville. The critics, not least among their own fans, would point to the transfer policy at that time. In season 2003/04 only Michael Gray – a 30-year-old full back on loan from Sunderland who made only ten appearances (six of them as a substitute) during his brief stint at Parkhead – and the young midfielder Stephen Pearson, a £350,000 purchase from Motherwell, were acquired. This was hardly adequate to bolster an ageing squad, although it was topped up early in season 2004/05 by the recruitment from Wolverhampton Wanderers of Henri Camara – on a loan deal that cost £1.5 million for the year – and the Brazilian midfielder Juninho, signed on a free from Middlesbrough. Neither Camara nor Juninho made the expected impact and both would depart before the end of the season, voicing criticism of their experience at Celtic Park under Martin O'Neill.

And so there was nothing else for it but to soldier on with a squad further handicapped by long-term injuries to two promising youngsters: John Kennedy, a central defender, and forward Shaun Maloney. As autumn turned into winter, fans were becoming accustomed to (and eventually disenchanted by) 'nervy' football on Celtic's part as opponents sensed a certain vulnerability, particularly at what had come to be seen in the O'Neill years as 'Fortress Parkhead'. Supporters now sat on the edge of their seats as Celtic failed to put away many teams who only recently were seen off with ease. Indeed, on many occasions, visiting sides were humiliated by the 'power game' and 'long-ball set-piece football' that had, even at the height of its effectiveness, caused many observers rather unfairly to characterise Celtic under Martin O'Neill as 'Leicester City plus Larsson'.

Nevertheless, despite their travails, Celtic managed to keep their attention firmly focused on the main prize despite two home defeats that, at the time, appeared to have inflicted terminal damage on their title aspirations. Rangers seemed to be back in the driving seat when they beat Celtic 2–0 on 20 February 2005, and again when Celtic lost by the same score to Hearts in early April. However, by this time, the title race had developed into a game of pass the parcel, with neither Old Firm challenger capable of taking a firm grip on the championship by capitalising on the setbacks to their opponents. This state of affairs persisted until 24 April 2005 when Celtic's 2–1 victory at Ibrox gave them a seemingly unassailable five-point lead with only four matches left for both halves of the Old Firm. Everyone, not only the Celtic support at large, but also the media, Rangers fans and a number of players at Ibrox assumed that the title was in the bag for Celtic. Rangers' failings had contributed to Celtic's confidence. Remarkably, the Ibrox men had dropped seven of the nine points available from their three league fixtures; they had even lost to Dundee United, a side that did not make it into the top six when the late-season split kicked-in after thirty-three fixtures, and a side that would only avoid relegation on the last day of the league programme.

Surely Celtic could not possibly blow it? However, almost completely overlooked amid the euphoria of the Ibrox victory was an event that was to have a decisive influence on the destination of the championship. Craig Bellamy – a pacey forward who had almost single-handedly transformed a jaded-looking Celtic since his arrival from Newcastle United on a loan deal during the January transfer window following a bust-up with his manager, ex-Ranger Graeme Souness – had been taken off injured in the forty-eighth minute at Ibrox. The injury happened at a time when the Celtic fans were still singing his praises after a typically intelligent goal that had seen him outwit a Rangers defender before curling the ball into the net beyond the keeper.

The hamstring injury meant that he would miss the next two fixtures. The first of these was at home and Celtic lost 3–1 to a youthful, effervescent Hibs side that could count itself unfortunate to have lost the earlier league fixture at Parkhead after comprehensively outplaying a home side whose defence had struggled (as so often in the past couple of years) to cope with quick-moving, quick-passing opponents. Rangers – who would not drop any more points after that loss to Celtic – took immediate advantage, beating Aberdeen at Pittodrie and moved ominously to within two points of Celtic. Bellamy returned for the clash on 15 May with Hearts at Tynecastle to help his adopted club to a narrow and nervous 2–1 victory, which set up the last-day decider on 22 May.

Celtic remained favourites to retain their title, not least because Motherwell, an injury-hit side, had been shipping goals. The Fir Park men had lost twelve of them, no less, in three recent encounters with Rangers, five of them coming in a League Cup-final rout that had left their veteran goalkeeper, ex-Celt Gordon Marshall, deeply embarrassed by his performance.

However, two statements made only two days before 'Super Sunday' suggested to me that Celtic, aware that they could only lose the title now, were the team feeling the greater pressure. Alan Thompson admitted to *The Herald* that Celtic players were feeling the intensity of the pre-match build-up: 'We sat down this morning wishing that the game was taking place tomorrow [the Saturday] but we will just have to wait a bit longer.' (21 May 2005)

Unaccountably, with probably his most bizarre utterance at any Celtic press conference, Martin O'Neill, who had always offered a straight bat to suggestions that he might head back south, suddenly said: 'These five years have been pretty decent and there's as good a chance of me being here [next season] than not.' Without being prompted, he then volunteered the following: 'But, if you are asking if I will be leaving to go to another football club, then the answer would be "No".' (*Scottish Daily Express*, 21 May 2005). It left the intrigued members of the media free to speculate about the manager's future, a question that was answered on the day of the match by a revelation in the *News of the World* that, indeed, O'Neill would leave at the end of the season to devote more time to the welfare of his wife Geraldine, whose serious illness had been revealed a year earlier; it was a situation that must have imposed considerable strain on the manager since the diagnosis.

The two title contenders entered a nerve-tingling last lap with the table reading as follows:

	P	W	D	L	For-Agst	G-D	Pts
Celtic	37	30	2	5	84 33	+51	92
Rangers	37	28	6	3	77 22	+55	90

However, even before the kick-off at Fir Park, Tom Lucas, Motherwell's sports psychologist, claimed to have detected signs of exhaustion among the Celtic team and was particularly encouraged by the visitors' warm-up: 'It was sloppy and they did not look physically or mentally equipped.' (*The Herald*, 24 May 2005). It was not the first time Lucas had incurred the wrath of Martin O'Neill. In the wake of Celtic's defeat at the hands of Rangers (the 2–0 reverse at Celtic Park in February 2005) he was quoted in a tabloid newspaper as having described Celtic goalkeeper Rab Douglas – clearly at fault for the opening goal – as having been 'a bag of nerves' since arriving at Parkhead in October 2000. 'Tom Lucas?' an allegedly puzzled O'Neill had responded. 'If he is our top sports psychologist, we are all in a bit of trouble in this country.' (*Daily Mail*, 10 March 2005)

That episode had been all but forgotten as Craig Bellamy – apparently determined to ram the words of such critics down their throats – provided an immediate declaration of intent at Fir Park, winning a corner inside the opening twenty seconds after a forceful run down the left wing. Then, a few minutes later, he rounded off a move involving Chris Sutton and John Hartson by evading Craigan and delivering a ball into the box that just eluded the inrushing Sutton.

Such was the early menace of Bellamy that Motherwell were fortunate not to be down to ten men after only ten minutes. He was hauled down by Kinniburgh as he threatened to run-in on goal but referee Hugh Dallas – officiating at his last match as a grade-one referee – waved play on despite the flag-waving of his assistant referee who was situated only a few yards from the incident. However, that decision seemed destined to count for little when, in the thirtieth minute, the pressure that Celtic had been steadily exerting since kick-off paid off with the all-important (and nerve-settling) opener. Alan Thompson, taking advantage of hesitation on the right-hand side of the Motherwell defence, headed for the byline before sending in a low cross destined for Bellamy at the back post. The Motherwell keeper Gordon Marshall could only parry the cut-back, which was more like a cross-shot to some observers. Chris Sutton reacted quicker than anybody else in the box, and lunged in to prod home a vital goal from around eight yards out.

That breakthrough – much to the relief of Celtic-minded people at the game and also to those listening or watching all over the world – had come after only six minutes. It followed football's equivalent of a storm warning when Motherwell's Australian forward Scott McDonald – a Celtic fan from a predominantly Celtic-supporting fam-ily – had squandered a scoring opportunity during a rare Motherwell counter-attack. He found himself one-on-one with Celtic's towering, if somewhat erratic defender Bobo Balde, and opted to shoot instead of squaring it to one of two teammates in a better position to score.

Despite this scare, Celtic were able successfully to negotiate a tense first half and to head for the sanctuary of the dressing room still very much in pole position for the championship. This was because at Easter Road the game was still goal-less, despite an astonishing miss: Rangers' Nacho Novo had failed to exploit a tenth-minute misjudge-ment by Hibernian goalkeeper Simon Brown, leaving the Spaniard with an open goal. But his shot – albeit from a tight angle – failed to enter the empty net, rebounded off a post and into the keeper's arms.

After the interval, Celtic and their fans were anxious to extinguish Rangers' hopes as quickly as possible. But they almost came unstuck within minutes of the restart when both Douglas and Varga failed to cope with Paterson's inswinging corner kick and Didier Agathe's face took the full force of Craigan's net-bound header. Kinniburgh then attempted to prod the ball home but a goal-line clearance was completed when Jackie McNamara, Celtic's captain, blocked his follow-up.

Normal service was quickly resumed by Celtic's pounding of the Motherwell goal, but four spurned opportunities inside the space of eight minutes proved fatal to Celtic's title quest. In the fifty-fourth minute John Hartson, who ended the season as top scorer in the league, headed Thompson's cross over the bar from only six yards out. Two minutes later the industrious Petrov sprung Motherwell's offside trap with a superbly weighted pass that set Bellamy free on the left for a clear run on goal, but the Welshman's side-foot finish was saved by Gordon Marshall. The big keeper was proving a formidable barrier to his former teammates, as he had done in 2003 at Rugby Park in similar circumstances on the last day of that season. Within the next five minutes Marshall denied Sutton – when the Englishman was clean through on goal – and then Hartson, who hit a volley straight at him after Bellamy nodded the ball into his path from McNamara's cross.

On the hour, Rangers suddenly turned the screw on a visibly anxious Celtic side, whose supporters' mounting concern was being caught graphically in television close-ups. Thomas Buffel's defence-splitting pass had set up Nacho Novo for a cross-shot that deflected off a Hibernian defender and into the net. As a frustrated Celtic strained to score the second goal that would secure the title, there was evidence of fractiousness creeping into their play; Didier Agathe, for example, was berated by no fewer than four teammates for a misplaced pass.

As the match entered the last twenty minutes, an increasingly ragged Celtic – demoralised and exhausted by their failure to turn territorial superiority into goals – sat-in deeper, apparently having decided to see out time. It was a risky strategy, if indeed that was the intention. Then a tired-looking John Hartson was replaced in the seventy-fifth minute by the fresh legs of young Craig Beattie, the only substitute used by Celtic on the day. Celtic supporters held their collective breath twelve minutes from time when Douglas flapped at another Paterson corner and Petrov hooked the ball to safety, as the always-dangerous Scott McDonald loitered with intent. It was but a stay of execution. The anxiety of the visitors was palpable: Celtic's midfielder Neil Lennon asked the referee how much time was left, and was concerned when told that five minutes plus injury time remained.

It is too tempting to suggest that there was an inevitability about Motherwell's eighty-eighth minute equalizer; that it was a product of the uncertainty, if not near-paralysis, that had gripped Celtic's defence as the team struggled to the finishing line. After Varga had failed to head the ball sufficiently clear of the danger zone,

Foran's mishit, bouncing shot was controlled by Scott McDonald on his chest. The young Australian swivelled and hooked the ball high over Douglas into the net.

It was all over, as every Celtic fan in the world knew. Neil Lennon articulated the feelings of the Celtic players: 'I had a sinking feeling at the pit of my stomach. It was total disbelief.'

Salt was rubbed into Celtic's wounds in the final minute when a Motherwell breakaway culminated in McDonald – inevitably McDonald – cutting in from the right to hit an angled shot that hit Varga's outstretched leg and looped over Douglas into the net.

It was a scarcely deserved win for Motherwell with two very late, and somewhat fortuitous, goals. The first came about after a sclaffed shot and the second was the product of a deflection. The home side had not won this match; Celtic had tossed it away, and on such a vital occasion.

Green-and-white despair at Fir Park; delirium at Easter Road where the last twenty minutes had been a case of 'After you, Claude,' as both Rangers and Hibernian settled happily enough for the visitors' 1–0 win. Rangers had taken the three points they set out for, and were content to preserve the one-goal lead as they had no need to improve their goal-difference advantage over Celtic. Tony Mowbray – the Hibs manager and ironically an ex-Celt* – rationalised his side's failure to attack more aggressively by pointing out that a heavy defeat might have cost his club a coveted UEFA spot: their closest rivals Aberdeen were two goals up against Hearts at half time and were threatening to snatch the European spot away with further goals. So intent was he on this strategy that Ian Murray – Hibs captain and on the way to Ibrox in the close season – later admitted to the *Sunday Mail* of 10 July that he had joined in an attack with ten minutes left, only to hear his manager on the touchline 'screaming at him to get back into defence'.

The miraculous nature of Rangers' deliverance was underlined

---

* Mowbray, as Celtic's captain, has been credited with the introduction of Celtic's famous 'huddle', introduced to promote solidarity and raise morale. He had done well in his first season at Easter Road in charge and interestingly it was stated in an article in the *Sunday Herald*, on 26 May 2005, that he was approached by Celtic to see if he would be interested in succeeding Martin O'Neill.

by the following observations in Rob Robertson's match report in *The Herald*: 'At the end, Rangers supporters invaded the playing surface, many visibly shocked that their team had sneaked the league title at the death from Celtic.' (23 May 2005) The *Scottish Sun's* coverage that same day included the confession from a 'clearly shell-shocked and somewhat disbelieving' Rangers manager Alex McLeish that he had 'actually prepared something of a speech if he hadn't won the championship'.

Given the pressure of the Old Firm rivalry, recriminations were inevitable on the losing side. These were exemplified by the emotional wreckage in O'Brien's, a Celtic bar in Glasgow's Saltmarket; a distraught fan was seen to mouth 'a bunch of fucking bottlers' vehemently as the television screen showed Celtic players trudging off the pitch. One of those players, Stanislav Varga, later revealed that he went straight home that Sunday evening and made sure he was incommunicado by turning off the telephone receiver. He barely slept that night, replaying over and over in his mind the events of that afternoon. He claimed that all of his teammates agreed with him: they regarded it as the most traumatic, and worst, day of their careers; it eclipsed even the crushing disappointment of Seville two years' earlier.

As for Martin O'Neill, he had composed himself sufficiently after the match to state that: 'The championship is over thirty-eight games. We didn't do it today and Rangers deserve to win the championship because they have finished at the top of the league.' Two weeks' later, after handing over to his successor Gordon Strachan, he was in more reflective mood, as reported in *The Scotsman*. He told the newspaper's chief football writer, Glenn Gibbons: 'I know most people think that losing the league title was caused by age and infirmity in the team, but I don't agree. I think the problem was almost entirely psychological. I think it was a question of the erosion of the will that takes you through these demanding programmes year in, year out.'

The squad of players wasn't big enough to win honours he asserted, a situation exacerbated by Celtic's financial position: 'When we were involved in the demands of the Champions' League, several players were peripheral, not really contributing, and the group who could do the business wasn't really big enough. If you had the money, you could have a bigger core of top-quality players and that was something that I felt over the past year, that the same group was being asked to go to the well every day.' (6 June 2005) Perhaps, physical and mental fatigue had contributed equally to the decline.

It was reported that Celtic offered the champagne kept on ice in their Fir Park dressing room to Motherwell, who accepted the magnums and 'celebrated wildly'. The aforementioned Tom Lucas admitted that this was 'a nice gesture that was appreciated given the circumstances' but added the barbed comment: 'We celebrated a great season but we never handed the title to anyone; Celtic lost it.' (*The Herald*: 24 May 2005)

A headline in *The Herald* – 'Ten Months, 38 Matches and Three Crazy Minutes' – was a good attempt to sum up the turbulence of a remarkable final day. But it could not possibly capture the anguish of Celtic supporters, for whom the mental scars of a nightmarish experience will take a long time to heal.

* * *

Motherwell: Marshall, Corrigan, Craigan, Fitzpatrick (Clarkson 88), Kinniburgh, Fagan, Kerr, Paterson, Foran, Hamilton (Britton 85) McDonald. Subs not used: Corr, Higgins, Keogh, Connolly, Smith.

Celtic: Douglas, Agathe, Balde, Varga, McNamara, Petrov, Lennon, Sutton, Thompson, Hartson (Beattie 75), Bellamy. Subs not used: Marshall, Valgaeren, Lambert, Maloney, Laursen, McGeady.

Referee: Hugh Dallas

Attendance: 12,944

Yellow cards: Foran (Motherwell): 2 minutes, for 'unsporting behaviour' in jostling with Bobo Balde. Craigan (Motherwell): 43 minutes, for 'unsporting behaviour' in fouling Craig Bellamy. Bellamy (Celtic): 44 minutes, for entering the field of play without permission after receiving treatment for an injury.

And the consequences?

Celtic were left only with the flat beer of a Scottish Cup final against previously relegation-threatened Dundee United six days later. A mood of anti-climax and deflation was palpable when Celtic fans turned up at Hampden Park, more out of a sense of obligation than genuine anticipation of an allegedly showpiece event.

Consolation prize it may have been, but there was a trophy to be won and Alan Thompson duly obliged with a deflected free kick early on. It was the only goal of a tedious affair that seemed to underline the obvious: that the last rites were being witnessed of a team that had, to all intents and purposes, died the previous Sunday. A lingering death, as an obituary might put it. Yes, there were cheers and tears at full time for Martin O'Neill who would not be staying on to start the rebuilding process.

It was the end of an era at Celtic Park: the manager Martin O'Neill resigned to take care of his seriously ill wife, Geraldine; his assistants John Robertson and Steve Walford also tendered their resignations shortly afterwards. They were the men who had helped Celtic to silverware in Scotland: three championships, three Scottish Cups and two League Cups within a five-year period; they were the men who had helped restore respectability for Celtic in European campaigns, and who had astonished the football world with an unforgettable campaign that culminated in the UEFA Cup final in 2003. They were quickly gone, however, with the heartfelt thanks of all Celtic supporters; but with the strange feeling that perhaps they had stayed too long.

Several players were said to have played their last games for the club. The feeling was that a clear-out was inevitable and welcome. The goalkeepers Rab Douglas and Magnus Hedman, despite their considerable experience, had never entirely satisfied the support with their consistency; their mistakes on the most vital of occasions had cost the club dear; they too left. Defenders Ulrik Laursen, Stephan Henchoz and Joos Valgaeren had not made themselves indispensable and were released, while the inconsistent and occasionally rash Bobo Balde was rumoured to be on the verge of signing for a European side. Fringe players such as Jamie Smith, Momo Sylla and David Fernandez were made available for transfer but a considerable effort was made to retain Craig Bellamy, in vain as it transpired. A surprising loss was the sudden departure of captain Jackie McNamara to Wolverhampton Wanderers.

Questions were also asked of the wisdom of retaining older players such as John Hartson, Neil Lennon, Alan Thompson and even Chris Sutton, all of whom were on the downward slope of their careers.

It was a genuine crisis at Celtic Park and for once the tabloids were correct in stressing this with their blaring headlines.

And how did the new era begin at Celtic Park?

Astonishingly – in view of the club's history of crisis-management – the transition was relatively seamless. Martin O'Neill had conveyed his intentions to his directors some months previously and had tendered advice on the question of his successor, who turned out to be Gordon Strachan. The announcement was made quickly and without any time for the tabloid rumour-mill to swing into operation. Strachan was the former Dundee, Aberdeen, Manchester United, Leeds United and Scotland player; he had also managed Coventry City and Southampton before taking a sabbatical from the game.

The new manager started to look for replacements for the departed players with a sensible emphasis on bolstering his defence; he started with the purchase of an impressive new goalkeeper in Artur Boruc from Legia Warsaw, a man challenging for a place in the Polish national side. Three new defenders were acquired: Adam Virgo from Brighton for £1.5 million, 'Mo' Camara, a free transfer from Burnley, and Paul Telfer, a veteran from Southampton. Two other defenders from China were being considered, and a Japanese midfielder Shunsuke Nakamura, playing in Italy's Serie A, signed in July. Maciej Zurawski, a Polish internationalist striker from Wisla Krakow was picked up for the expenditure of £2.5 million and Arsenal's Jeremie Aliadiere was obtained on a loan deal.

Every new player represents a gamble on the manager's part. It remains to be seen if these newcomers will be able to fit in at Celtic Park, help the club to retain its eminence within Scottish football and make an impact in Europe.

Almost certainly there will be a change in Celtic's playing style. Under Martin O'Neill, Celtic were essentially a long-ball team with a built-in advantage at set-pieces; they were a powerful side with a fierce will to win. That determination, when combined with considerable expertise at the basics, made them a difficult outfit to beat. Latterly, however, it was not enough for some supporters, who long for Celtic teams playing in an attractive and entertaining manner with flair and colour.

The future promises to be different from the recent past, though the initial signs were not encouraging, with a lingering aftershock from that Motherwell debacle evident in the first competitive match of season 2005/06, when Celtic, horrendously slipshod in defence, went down to their record defeat (5–0) in European competition at the hands of unknown side Artmedia Bratislava in the first away leg of a qualifying round in the Champions League. That embarrassment was nearly wiped out when Celtic restored some pride with a 4–0 victory in a return leg at Celtic Park, watched by a remarkable 50,000-plus crowd.

Where else would such a multitude have turned up in the hope of seeing a miracle, particularly since that exit from Europe had come only a few days after Celtic, on their return from Slovakia, had let slip a 3–1 half-time lead before having to settle for a last gap 4–4 draw in their opening league fixture – at Motherwell. Of course!

Comments

I couldn't bring myself to pick up a newspaper – or at least the sports pages – for a week after the debacle at Fir Park. How could Celtic lose to a Motherwell side that was simply playing out its fixtures? The support was totally stunned at the events of the closing minutes of the season, stunned in incomprehension.

Patrick Reilly

One of the most distressing days I have experienced as a match-going Celtic supporter since 1958! It ranks up there like the defeats in Scottish Cup-final replays to Dunfermline Athletic in 1961 and to Rangers in 1963. It was even more numbing than the losses to Feyenoord in the European Cup final of 1970 and to Porto in the UEFA Cup final of 2003. At least those were to sides of real class.

David Potter

The signs of decline had been there for some time. It must have been devastating for the supporters to limp along until three minutes from the end of the season.

Bob Crampsey

I watched the match with the Ottawa Celtic Supporters Club on the Sunday morning. They sat in growing apprehension as the second half unfolded and Celtic lay back in defence; nobody was too surprised when the strategy misfired, but the anguish was real and heartfelt.

Tom Campbell

Even after almost 120 years of football, with its inevitable ups and downs, a single defeat for Celtic can cost heartache and despair. The pain, the sorrow, the horror of it all at the closing minutes of the season at Fir Park.

John Cairney

We blew it!

Craig McAughtrie

BIOGRAPHIES

JOHN CAIRNEY

Best known as 'the man who played Robert Burns', John Cairney has had a distinguished career as an actor for more than fifty years including performances on the stage, on film and on television where he gained lasting fame as *That Man Craig*.

In recent years he has turned his talent more and more to painting and writing. His literary output includes two volumes of autobiography, works on Robert Burns, Robert Louis Stevenson and Charles Rennie Mackintosh as well as a forthcoming biography of Celtic legend Jimmy McGrory.

Despite being a resident of New Zealand, where he lives with his wife Alannah O'Sullivan the actress-writer, John remains fiercely Scottish – as a glance at his titles might suggest. Another lifetime Celtic supporter, he has kept in close touch with the goings-on at Celtic Park on and off the field with a fanatical interest.

TOM CAMPBELL

Born in Glasgow, Tom still recalls with horror that his first Old Firm game ended in an 8–1 win for Rangers in 1943 – but takes some cold comfort in the fact that, as a wartime fixture, it was an 'unofficial' match.

Tom emigrated to Canada in 1956 and, after two years as a minor civil servant in Ottawa, decided to take up teaching. He started off as an elementary teacher, and was promoted to principal of St Paul's, Alliston just north of Toronto. After marriage in 1964, he moved to Ottawa as a secondary-school teacher, and ended up as department head of English at Glebe Collegiate, the city's largest school. After retiring in 1989, Tom returned to Scotland where he now lives in Edinburgh with his partner Pauline.

He is the author (or co-author) of several books on Celtic's history including the highly-regarded *The Glory and the Dream* (with Pat Woods). He is an occasional columnist with *Keep the Faith*, and a frequent contributor to *The Celt*.

BOB CRAMPSEY

Educator, journalist, broadcaster, novelist, dramatist, biographer, football-cricket-golf historian: Bob Cramsey has done it all, and even found time to be 'Brain of Britain' in 1965 and to write an engaging autobiography called *The Young Civilian* about the wartime years in Scotland.

Bob was born in Mount Florida, and still lives in the neighbourhood within walking distance of Hampden Park. Fittingly, he has been a Queen's Park supporter since childhood, and his brother played in goal for 'the Amateurs'. Married since 1958 to Veronica (Ronnie) a practising doctor and now with four grown-up daughters, Bob embarked on a teaching career after his National Service with the RAF. He started off in Forfar Academy but soon found himself back in Glasgow at Holyrood and St Aloysius College where he taught history. In 1974 he was appointed headmaster at St Ambrose in Coatbridge where he remained until his 'retirement' in 1986. Retirement was scarcely the word as he has kept busy with writing, broadcasting and after-dinner speaking engagements.

In 2000 he was most deservedly honoured by Stirling University with an honorary doctorate for his services to sport and literature in Scotland.

GERRY DUNBAR

Born in 1960 in Glasgow, Gerry comes from a Celtic-minded family and points out that his son is named Thomas, and that if his second child had been another boy he would have been christened Michael (Tom and Michael Dunbar were early Celtic stalwarts). In another link with Celtic, Gerry attended St Roch's, both primary and secondary, in the Garngad – the birthplace of Jimmy McGrory – before attending Glasgow University where he studied English Literature.

After graduation Gerry worked briefly as a civil servant before embarking on a career as a teacher; he still teaches, in St Andrew's, Carntyne where probably not too many of his pupils are aware that he is the co-founder and editor of *Not the View*, the longest-running Celtic fanzine. This fanzine arose out of the despair of Gerry and several other Celtic supporters at the way the club was drifting at the time (1988). It proved an immediate success and, unlike other short-lived imitations, it has shown remarkable staying power as well as genuine literary merit.

Gerry is married to Bernadette, and they have two children, a boy and a girl aged 5 and 6.

TONY GRIFFIN

Born in Glasgow in March, 1953 and brought up in Pollokshields, Tony was educated at St Aloysius (where he was taught briefly by Bob Crampsey). He later worked as a civil servant with the National Savings Bank in Cowglen for four years before moving to London with Texaco. In 1980, Tony was transferred to Aberdeen, and in 1986 he joined Total Oil, also based in Aberdeen. Apart from a two-year secondment to Paris in the mid-1990s, he has been based in Aberdeenshire since 1980.

Tony is married to Sarah, an Australian, and they have three grown-up daughters and are kept busy with Flynn, an energetic black Labrador. Tony took an Open University degree in humanities in the 1980s and is the co-author of *A Season in the Sun*, an account of Celtic's 1966/67 season. He has also written several articles on aspects of Celtic for various publications including *The Celt*.

CRAIG BURNS MCAUGHTRIE

Born in 1962 Craig spent his formative years in Bishopbriggs, before entering Glasgow University in 1979. After graduation in 1984, he moved to Fife where he was a veterinary surgeon for some seventeen years.

He changed careers to better utilise his passion for Celtic by writing for a variety of publications, both on the internet and in print; he also published anonymously some interesting and highly original work on the club's recent history. He was then a five-year veteran of what he now describes as 'the murky world of Celtic fanzines', having written tirades for most of them at various times. He ventured into a risky online enterprise, a website known as *Keep The Faith* (www.keep-the-faith.net), devoted to Celtic matters. Thanks to hard work by everybody connected with it, this electronic fanzine has proved highly popular as well as being both entertaining and instructive. Its expansion into a major football website keeps Craig 'incredibly busy, night and day'.

Craig continues to live in Fife with his soulmate, Lesley, and their son, Liam, described as the image of his father including his reddish hair and an abiding interest in Celtic.

DAVID POTTER

Raised in Forfar, educated at St Andrews and living in Kirkcaldy, David Potter taught Spanish and Classics at Glenrothes High School until his recent retirement. Married to Rosemary, he is the father of two daughters and one son – and has recently become a proud grandfather.

David is a man of many interests: an elder in the Church of Scotland, producer, director and performer of plays (including the authorship of one based on the death of John Thomson), umpire in the Scottish National Cricket League, hill walker and prolific Celtic historian.

As well as being a frequent contributor to *The Celtic View*, the match-day programme, *The Celt* (a fanzine for those wth an interest in the club's history) and *Keep the Faith* (a highly popular Celtic website), David has found time to write several books about Celtic and its personalities including biographies of Willie Maley, Bobby Murdoch, Jimmy Quinn, Patsy Gallacher and the imminent life of Jimmy Delaney. In addition, David has written *The Encyclopaedia of Scottish Cricket*. Indeed, a Renaissance man.

PATRICK REILLY

A Glasgow man, educated at St Patrick's, Anderston, St Mungo's Academy and the University of Glasgow and later at Pembroke College, University of Oxford, Patrick was Professor of English Literature at the University of Glasgow and subsequently head of the department. Since his retirement in 1997 he is Professor Emeritus at the University.

Patrick, whose Ph.D at Oxford centred on Jonathan Swift, has written several books of literary criticism as well as work in journalism and broadcasting. A lifetime Celtic supporter, he recalls his first Celtic match as being a wartime league fixture against Albion Rovers for whom a young Jock Stein was making his debut as a trialist.

TOM SHIELDS

Born in 1948 in Househillwood, a leafy subdivision of the Pollok region of Glasgow, Tom still hopes to be elevated to the House of Lords as the Earl of Pollokshields. He was educated at St Robert's primary and Lourdes secondary (no miracle) and in between was experimented upon for four years at Bellarmine comprehensive school by Glasgow Corporation education department.

He began an engineering degree at Strathclyde University in 1966 and graduated in Spanish in 1998, apparently the longest time ever recorded at this institution to finish a degree. Shields worked as a journalist for the *Sunday Post* and the *Glasgow Herald* and, as we write, is still getting a wage as a freelance columnist and sports diarist with the *Sunday Herald*. The University of Strathclyde saw fit in 2003 to confer the honorary degree of doctor of the university upon Shields for his work as writer of the *Glasgow Herald's* diary column. A year later the university conferred the same degree on Henrik Larsson for scoring loads of goals and being a role model.

Shields has followed Celtic since 1955 but has also attended matches at Ibrox (very briefly and only to be sociable with his Rangers-supporting friends) and at Cathkin and Douglas Park, and retains a genuine affection for Third Lanark and Hamilton Accies.

Shields had a brief career as a columnist for the *Celtic View*, also known as *Pravda*, but resigned due to an inability to follow the party line.

PAT WOODS

A prolific contributor to various Celtic publications including *The Celt* and *The Celtic View*, Pat is the author of *Celtic FC, Facts and Figures (1888–1981)* published by the Celtic Supporters' Association.

However, he is better known as the co-author of several well-regarded books about aspects of Celtic: *One Afternoon in Lisbon* (with Kevin McCarra) and *The Glory and the Dream*, *Rhapsody in Green* and *Dreams and Songs to Sing* (all with Tom Campbell).

His encyclopaedic knowledge of Celtic, both past and present, has been called upon by such other football writers as Archie Macpherson, Bill Murray and Gerry McNee who have all acknowledged his unparalleled work as a researcher.

Pat was born in Bangor, North Wales in 1946 but was educated in Glasgow at St Mungo's Academy and worked in the Glasgow public-library system for many years until his recent retirement. He lives in Glasgow with his wife Rosalind.